FILMMAKE
editee
ANTHON

D1562247

1. *James Whale*, by James Curtis. 1982
2. *Cinema Stylists*, by John Belton. 1983
3. *Harry Langdon*, by William Schelly. 1982
4. *William A. Wellman*, by Frank Thompson. 1983
5. *Stanley Donen*, by Joseph Casper. 1983
6. *Brian De Palma*, by Michael Bliss. 1983
7. *J. Stuart Blackton*, by Marian Blackton Trimble. 1985
8. *Martin Scorsese and Michael Cimino*, by Michael Bliss. 1985
9. *Franklin J. Schaffner*, by Erwin Kim. 1985
10. *D. W. Griffith and the Biograph Company*, by Cooper C. Graham et al. 1985
11. *Some Day We'll Laugh: An Autobiography*, by Esther Ralston. 1985
12. *The Memoirs of Alice Guy Blaché*, 2nd ed., translated by Roberta and Simone Blaché. 1996
13. *Leni Riefenstahl and Olympia*, by Cooper C. Graham. 1986
14. *Robert Florey*, by Brian Taves. 1987
15. *Henry King's America*, by Walter Coppedge. 1986
16. *Aldous Huxley and Film*, by Virginia M. Clark. 1987
17. *Five American Cinematographers*, by Scott Eyman. 1987
18. *Cinematographers on the Art and Craft of Cinematography*, by Anna Kate Sterling. 1987
19. *Stars of the Silents*, by Edward Wagenknecht. 1987
20. *Twentieth Century-Fox*, by Aubrey Solomon. 1988
21. *Highlights and Shadows: The Memoirs of a Hollywood Cameraman*, by Charles G. Clarke. 1989
22. *I Went That-a-Way: The Memoirs of a Western Film Director*, by Harry L. Fraser; edited by Wheeler Winston Dixon and Audrey Brown Fraser. 1990
23. *Order in the Universe: The Films of John Carpenter*, by Robert C. Cumbow. 1990 (*out of print; see No. 70*)
24. *The Films of Freddie Francis*, by Wheeler Winston Dixon. 1991
25. *Hollywood Be Thy Name*, by William Bakewell. 1991
26. *The Charm of Evil: The Life and Films of Terence Fisher*, by Wheeler Winston Dixon. 1991

27. *Lionheart in Hollywood: The Autobiography of Henry Wilcoxon*, with Katherine Orrison. 1991
28. *William Desmond Taylor: A Dossier*, by Bruce Long. 1991
29. *The Films of Leni Riefenstahl*, 2nd ed., by David B. Hinton. 1991
30. *Hollywood Holyland: The Filming and Scoring of "The Greatest Story Ever Told,"* by Ken Darby. 1992
31. *The Films of Reginald LeBorg: Interviews, Essays, and Filmography*, by Wheeler Winston Dixon. 1992
32. *Memoirs of a Professional Cad*, by George Sanders, with Tony Thomas. 1992
33. *The Holocaust in French Film*, by André Pierre Colombat. 1993
34. *Robert Goldstein and "The Spirit of '76,"* edited and compiled by Anthony Slide. 1993
35. *Those Were the Days, My Friend: My Life in Hollywood with David O. Selznick and Others*, by Paul Macnamara. 1993
36. *The Creative Producer*, by David Lewis, edited by James Curtis. 1993
37. *Reinventing Reality: The Art and Life of Rouben Mamoulian*, by Mark Spergel. 1993
38. *Malcolm St. Clair: His Films, 1915–1948*, by Ruth Anne Dwyer. 1997
39. *Beyond Hollywood's Grasp: American Filmmakers Abroad, 1914–1945*, by Harry Waldman. 1994
40. *A Steady Digression to a Fixed Point*, by Rose Hobart. 1994
41. *Radical Juxtaposition: The Films of Yvonne Rainer*, by Shelley Green. 1994
42. *Company of Heroes: My Life as an Actor in the John Ford Stock Company*, by Harry Carey Jr. 1994
43. *Strangers in Hollywood: A History of Scandinavian Actors in American Films from 1910 to World War II*, by Hans J. Wollstein. 1994
44. *Charlie Chaplin: Intimate Close-Ups*, by Georgia Hale, edited with an introduction and notes by Heather Kiernan. 1995
45. *The Word Made Flesh: Catholicism and Conflict in the Films of Martin Scorsese*, by Michael Bliss. 1995
46. *W. S. Van Dyke's Journal: White Shadows in the South Seas (1927–1928) and Other Van Dyke on Van Dyke*, edited and annotated by Rudy Behlmer. 1996
47. *Music from the House of Hammer: Music in the Hammer Horror Films, 1950–1980*, by Randall D. Larson. 1996
48. *Directing: Learn from the Masters*, by Tay Garnett. 1996

49. *Featured Player: An Oral Autobiography of Mae Clarke*, edited with an introduction by James Curtis. 1996
50. *A Great Lady: A Life of the Screenwriter Sonya Levien*, by Larry Ceplair. 1996
51. *A History of Horrors: The Rise and Fall of the House of Hammer*, by Denis Meikle. 1996
52. *The Films of Michael Powell and the Archers*, by Scott Salwolke. 1997
53. *From Oz to E.T.: Wally Worsley's Half-Century in Hollywood—A Memoir in Collaboration with Sue Dwiggins Worsley*, edited by Charles Ziarko. 1997
54. *Thorold Dickinson and the British Cinema*, by Jeffrey Richards. 1997
55. *The Films of Oliver Stone*, edited by Don Kunz. 1997
56. *Before, In, and After Hollywood: The Autobiography of Joseph E. Henabery*, edited by Anthony Slide. 1997
57. *Ravished Armenia and the Story of Aurora Mardiganian*, compiled by Anthony Slide. 1997
58. *Smile When the Raindrops Fall*, by Brian Anthony and Andy Edmonds. 1998
59. *Joseph H. Lewis: Overview, Interview, and Filmography*, by Francis M. Nevins. 1998
60. *September Song: An Intimate Biography of Walter Huston*, by John Weld. 1998
61. *Wife of the Life of the Party*, by Lita Grey Chaplin and Jeffrey Vance. 1998
62. *Down But Not Quite Out in Hollow-weird: A Documentary in Letters of Eric Knight*, by Geoff Gehman. 1998
63. *On Actors and Acting: Essays by Alexander Knox*, edited by Anthony Slide. 1998
64. *Back Lot: Growing Up with the Movies*, by Maurice Rapf. 1999
65. *Mr. Bernds Goes to Hollywood: My Early Life and Career in Sound Recording at Columbia with Frank Capra and Others*, by Edward Bernds. 1999
66. *Hugo Friedhofer: The Best Years of His Life: A Hollywood Master of Music for the Movies*, edited by Linda Danly. 1999
67. *Actors on Red Alert: Career Interviews with Five Actors and Actresses Affected by the Blacklist*, by Anthony Slide. 1999
68. *My Only Great Passion: The Life and Films of Carl Th. Dreyer*, by Jean Drum and Dale D. Drum. 1999

69. *Ready When You Are, Mr. Coppola, Mr. Spielberg, Mr. Crowe*, by Jerry Ziesmer. 1999

70. *Order in the Universe: The Films of John Carpenter*, 2nd ed., by Robert C. Cumbow. 2000

71. *Making Music with Charlie Chaplin*, by Eric James. 2000

72. *An Open Window: The Cinema of Víctor Erice*, edited by Linda C. Ehrlich. 2000

73. *Satyajit Ray: In Search of the Modern*, by Suranjan Ganguly. 2000

74. *Voices from the Set: The* Film Heritage *Interviews*, edited by Tony Macklin and Nick Pici. 2000

75. *Paul Landres: A Director's Stories*, by Francis M. Nevins. 2000

76. *No Film in My Camera*, by Bill Gibson. 2000

77. *Saved from Oblivion: An Autobiography*, by Bernard Vorhaus. 2000

78. *Wolf Man's Maker: Memoir of a Hollywood Writer*, by Curt Siodmak. 2001

79. *An Actor, and a Rare One: Peter Cushing as Sherlock Holmes*, by Tony Earnshaw. 2001

80. *Picture Perfect*, by Herbert L. Strock. 2000

81. *Peter Greenaway's Postmodern/Poststructuralist Cinema*, edited by Paula Willoquet-Maricondi and Mary Alemany Galway. 2001

82. *Member of the Crew*, by Winfrid Kay Thackrey. 2001

83. *Barefoot on Barbed Wire*, by Jimmy Starr. 2001

84. *Henry Hathaway: A Directors Guild of America Oral History*, edited and annotated by Rudy Behlmer. 2001

85. *The Divine Comic: The Cinema of Roberto Benigni*, by Carlo Celli. 2001

86. *With or Without a Song: A Memoir*, by Edward Eliscu. 2001

87. *Stuart Erwin: The Invisible Actor*, by Judy Cornes. 2001

88. *Some Cutting Remarks: Seventy Years a Film Editor*, by Ralph E. Winters. 2001

89. *Confessions of a Hollywood Director*, by Richard L. Bare. 2001

90. *Peckinpah's Women: A Reappraisal of the Portrayal of Women in the Period Westerns of Sam Peckinpah*, by Bill Mesce Jr. 2001

91. *Budd Schulberg: A Bio-Bibliography*, by Nicholas Beck. 2001

92. *Between the Bullets: The Spiritual Cinema of John Woo*, by Michael Bliss. 2002

93. *The Hollywood I Knew: 1916–1988*, by Herbert Coleman. 2002

94. *The Films of Steven Spielberg*, edited by Charles L. P. Silet. 2002

95. *Hitchcock and the Making of Marnie*, by Tony Lee Moral. 2002

96. *White Horse, Black Hat: A Quarter Century on Hollywood's Poverty Row*, by C. Jack Lewis. 2002

97. *Worms in the Winecup: A Memoir*, by John Bright. 2002

98. *Straight from the Horse's Mouth: Ronald Neame, An Autobiography*, by Ronald Neame. 2003

99. *Reach for the Top: The Turbulent Life of Laurence Harvey*, by Anne Sinai. 2003

100. *Jackie Coogan: The World's Boy King: A Biography of Hollywood's Legendary Child Star*, by Diana Serra Cary. 2003

101. *Rungs on a Ladder: Hammer Films Seen through a Soft Gauze*, by Christopher Neame. 2003

102. *The Classically American Comedy of Larry Gelbart*, by Jay Malarcher. 2003

103. *Perpetually Cool: The Many Lives of Anna May Wong (1905–1961)*, by Anthony B. Chan. 2003

104. *Irene Dunne: The First Lady of Hollywood*, by Wes D. Gehring. 2003

105. *Scorsese Up Close: A Study of the Films*, by Ben Nyce. 2004

106. *Hitchcock and Poe: The Legacy of Delight and Terror*, by Dennis R. Perry. 2003

107. *Life Is Beautiful, but Not for Jews: Another View of the Film by Benigni*, by Kobi Niv, translated by Jonathan Beyrak Lev. 2003

108. *Young Man in Movieland*, by Jan Read. 2004

109. *A Cast of Shadows*, by Ronnie Maasz. 2004

110. *Body and Soul: The Cinematic Vision of Robert Aldrich*, by Tony Williams. 2004

111. *Showdown at High Noon: Witch-Hunts, Critics, and the End of the Western*, by Jeremy Byman. 2004

112. *A Take on British TV Drama: Stories from the Golden Years*, by Christopher Neame. 2004

113. *George Arliss: The Man Who Played God*, by Robert M. Fells. 2004

114. *And the Stars Spoke Back: A Dialogue Coach Remembers Hollywood Players of the Sixties in Paris*, by Frawley Becker. 2004

115. *Hollywood in Wide Angle*, by Jack Rothman. 2004

116. *William Beaudine: From Silents to Television*, by Wendy L. Marshall. 2004

117. *Leo McCarey: From Marx to McCarthy*, by Wes D. Gehring. 2004

Script in hand, I've just made Audrey Hepburn laugh during a rehearsal for *How to Steal a Million*, outside the Hotel Ritz in Paris, 1965. Peter O'Toole, left, looks on and giggles.

And the Stars Spoke Back

A Dialogue Coach Remembers
Hollywood Players of the Sixties in Paris

Frawley Becker

Filmmakers Series, No. 114

THE SCARECROW PRESS, INC.
Lanham, Maryland • Toronto • Oxford
2004

i 0810851571

SCARECROW PRESS, INC.

Published in the United States of America
by Scarecrow Press, Inc.
A wholly owned subsidiary of
The Rowman & Littlefield Publishing Group, Inc.
4501 Forbes Boulevard, Suite 200, Lanham, Maryland 20706
www.scarecrowpress.com

PO Box 317
Oxford
OX2 9RU, UK

British Library Cataloguing in Publication Information Available

Library of Congress Cataloging-in-Publication Data

Becker, Frawley, 1929–
  And the stars spoke back : a dialogue coach remembers Hollywood players of
the sixties in Paris / Frawley Becker.
    p. cm. — (Filmmakers series ; no. 114)
  Includes index.
  ISBN 0-8108-5157-1 (pbk. : alk. paper)
  1. Becker, Frawley, 1929– . 2. Dialogue coaches—United States—Biography.
3. Motion picture actors and actresses—United States—Anecdotes. I. Title.
II. Series.
PN1998.3.B427A3 2004
791.4302'8—dc22   2004008283

Printed in the United States of America

♾ ™ The paper used in this publication meets the minimum requirements of
American National Standard for Information Sciences—Permanence of Paper
for Printed Library Materials, ANSI/NISO Z39.48-1992.

For my muses,
Gina Gennaro and Marina Gromoff

Contents

	Acknowledgments	xiii
Chapter 1	Connecting the Dots	1
Chapter 2	Speak the Speech Trippingly	11
Chapter 3	Two Directors, Both Alike in Dignity	26
Chapter 4	The First Lady	39
Chapter 5	Peter the Great	64
Chapter 6	I, Jupiter; I, Rex (with a nod to Cole Porter)	86
Chapter 7	*La Révolution Française*—Once More with Feeling	104
Chapter 8	Strolling Players	116
Chapter 9	Paid Holiday	132
Chapter 10	The Bad Boys of France	141
Chapter 11	The Friends Thou Hast	157
Chapter 12	Pure Imagination	171

Chapter 13   For Richer, for Poorer, in Sickness and
             in Health   187

Chapter 14   You Can Take the Boy Out of France,
             But . . .   202

Chapter 15   At Long Last Literature   213

             Index   233

             About the Author   241

~

Acknowledgments

Quote from *The Iceman Cometh* by Eugene O'Neill is from *The Iceman Cometh*, Random House, New York, 1946.

Quote from *The Lion in Winter* by James Goldman, permission granted by Raoulfilm Inc.

Quote by Dylan Thomas, from *Under Milk Wood*, copyright © 1952 by Dylan Thomas. Reprinted by permission of New Directions Publishing Corp. and by David Higham Associates, for J. M. Dent & Sons, Ltd., London, 1975.

Photograph of Lawrence Weingarten and Katharine Hepburn at the 46th Annual Academy Awards courtesy of the Motion Picture Academy of Arts and Sciences, © Academy of Motion Picture Arts and Sciences.

Anonymous Enraged. Interdit de Interdire, les murs de mai 68, Paris, L'Esprit Frappeur, 1998.

Gomez, Michel. *Mai 68, au jour le jour*, Paris, L'Esprit Frappeur, 1998

The Library, Royal Academy of Dramatic Art, Bristol, England, 2001.

Osborne, Robert. *65 Years of the Oscar, The Official History of the Academy Awards*, New York, London, Paris, Abbeville Press, 1994.

Violet, Bernard. *Les Mystères Delon*, Paris, Flammarion, 2000.

Note: With the exception of the Academy Award photograph and those photographs where indicated to the contrary, all photographs are from the author's personal collection.

CHAPTER ONE

~

Connecting the Dots

"What does a dialogue coach do?" I asked.

I was sitting in a suite in the Hôtel La Trémoille just off the Champs-Élysées. Across from me was film director Robert Parrish, who was soon to begin shooting a movie for 20th Century Fox, *Up from the Beach*, in Cherbourg, France. Parrish had just offered me a job, one that would turn out to be the first in a long string of films, first in France as a dialogue coach and later in Hollywood as a location manager. A string of films that would lead me to what the tabloids in their inimitable manner refer to as hobnobbing with the rich and famous. It would lead me to shopping with Audrey Hepburn, nightclubbing with Peter O'Toole, going to the racetrack with Omar Sharif, dancing with Shirley MacLaine, getting high with Kevin Bacon, witnessing a domestic spat with Rex Harrison, and scurrying Warren Beatty through reporters in Tahiti. What-does-a-dialogue-coach-do was a question that would start a new career for me, launch me into forty years of film work, and thrust me up with the stars, although then, back in 1964 in Paris, I hadn't the foggiest notion of what a dialogue coach was.

"Well," said Parrish, "a dialogue coach rehearses the actors, gets them prepared before they reach the camera." He pulled his chair up closer to me. He was a tall man nearing fifty and had the bushiest salt-and-pepper eyebrows I'd ever seen. Beneath them were two intense blue eyes with a look that I would learn later was one of gentleness and compassion. He had received an Oscar for film editing in 1947 for *Body and Soul* and a nomination in 1949 for *All the King's Men*. While the editing award went to *The Champion* that year, *All the King's Men* copped the best picture Oscar and two acting Oscars as well. A few years later, after I worked with Oliver Reed, I realized that a good editor can make an actor look glorious, even if he isn't. Parrish was never considered a great director, but he'd been a protégé of John Ford, and he would have hundreds of riveting Hollywood stories to tell over dinners—in fact, he was the first real *raconteur* I met (Henry Miller would be the second).

"I'm doing this movie with Cliff Robertson and Red Buttons," Parrish continued. "You could run lines with them, but mostly it's because I have a bunch of French actors who make up the supporting cast." He went on to say he needed someone to get them to be able to perform comfortably in English, get them to the point where they weren't thinking about their lines. He hoped, too, that they'd speak clearly enough that he wouldn't have to dub them later.

"Why me?" I asked Parrish.

"We have coaches in Hollywood, of course. But we're on unknown ground here in Europe. I mentioned it to Darryl and he said, 'If you can find a good coach in Paris, hire him.'" Darryl was Darryl F. Zanuck, the legendary producer who had single-handedly saved 20th Century Fox from financial ruin in 1962 by putting almost every major male star in Hollywood in an epic about the allied invasion of Normandy, *The Longest Day*. It made money all over the world. The premiere in Paris had Edith Piaf singing *La Marseillaise* from an illuminated Eiffel Tower platform, with fireworks going off behind her. This outlandish showmanship was a toss-up between kitsch and vulgarity.

"I read an article about you in one of the London papers," Parrish continued. "About the theater you were running here in Paris, and the Albee plays you produced. And the glitterati who attended opening night. It read like a Who's Who of Paris society." He smiled, and I swear if there were ever any truth to the expression that someone's eyes twinkled, his did at that moment. "I figured, if you could handle that crowd, you could handle movie stars. Besides, I need someone who speaks French, and you do, and I need someone who's worked with actors, and you have." He told me the production manager would set the salary, but that it would probably be about a hundred dollars a week, all expenses paid. For a quiet kid from Philadelphia about to foray into the movie world in 1964, I thought it was terrific.

Actually, I wasn't that much of a kid. I just looked like a kid. Thirty-four looking twenty. And a thin, sophomoric voice that hadn't molted, to boot. An aura of youth that I would have to fight for many years, since people sometimes wouldn't take me seriously at first. In 1969 I grew a trim Renaissance beard and mustache to look older; I have them to this day.

What brings you to take a leap in life, to jump into the unknown? Some people can't, even with opportunity ripening under their noses. I've always believed that any given moment of your life is really a sum total of all the other moments that go before, so you're more prepared for that chance than you think. Then there's derring-do. Simple guts. For some reason, I always had that. Taking a flying tackle from directly behind the kid running with the football when I was fourteen, mindless of the dirt and cleats kicking up into my face.

A dozen flashbacks were invading me now, sum-totaling up to this moment where Bob Parrish was about to place me smack inside the film business. Back I went in my mind, hopscotching from the box I was standing in to my early years, the years that had led me here. First, there had been my interest in drawing, designing the high school class pin and doing caricatures of my teachers for the year book. Then there had been a bachelor's degree in psychology from the University of Pennsylvania a few years later. Psychology had been the midway point between medicine, which my father had wanted for me, and the arts, for which I had a natural bent. Then two years in the army in the Medical Corps during the Korean War, followed by two years of civilian work as a large department store display man in Philadelphia, and then, with funds and dreams gathered like sheep wool, a one-way ticket in 1955 on the *Île-de-France* to Southampton and Le Havre and then the train to Paris. A one-way ticket. Like I said, guts.

Paris. Like so many Americans of that period, I fell in love with the city. She became my instant mistress. Beautiful. Mysterious. Demanding. Calling me from every street corner, every intimate café, every plaza roundabout, every bridge lamp making aureoles of light in the dark, every Robert Doisneau photograph come to life. I would walk for hours, day or night, to discover my mistress's hidden secrets, but as with all good mistresses there were always more secrets than discoveries, and though I would remain with her for a constant seventeen years, to this day there are unknown parts of her I rejoice in discovering on my occasional trip back to renew the affair.

It was just ten years after World War II had ended. Cocteau was there, in his flowing black cape at the Café Les Deux Magots. With Marais. The painter Foujita, too. And Hemmingway the itinerant visitor. I was led into Edith Piaf's apartment on Boulevard Lannes by her discreetly gay secretary. I had coffee in another apartment on Boulevard Péreire with the mother of a dead American ballerina whose on-point statue had been placed at the entrance of the Père-Lachaise cemetery and is still there. I saw the newspaper headlines the day saxophonist Charlie Parker died: *"L'oiseau est mort!"* Boris Vian was reading his poems in the *caves* of the Left Bank, and Juliette Gréco was singing in them. On the Right Bank, Patachou was balladeering in the *boîtes* of Montmartre. Ionesco's *The Bald-headed Soprano* and Genet's *The Maids* were all the talk. I accidentally discovered Sylvia Beach's Shakespeare and Company, the delightful Left Bank bookstore where you could loll for hours on large sofas and read. It was a time when there was no toilet paper in the café rest rooms, just ripped squares of newspaper hanging there, and Americans carried a Paris copy of the *New York Herald Tribune* all day as backup. It was three-room apartments with no bath or shower and a Turkish cabinet for three families on the hall landing. (What's a Turkish cabinet? A hole in the ground in a small, square space. No seat, just two cement or metal ovals where you put your feet when you squatted, and a chain nearby that inundated everything with water.) And it was constant workers' strikes leaving you without gas, electricity, buses, or—most incredibly—firemen. It was public baths on Sunday. It was crowded metro cars in a miasma of garlic and sweat, with people pressed in so tightly against you that if a hand moved you were groped. It was three-course meals for eighty cents, wine included, less at student facilities. It was a time when concierges lorded over your life as well as the building you lived in. Monsieur Delpierre cohabited with Mademoiselle Bonnet in an apartment decades, even centuries, before puritanical America would do that. The golden age of French cinema was still going strong with realistic performances by Jean Gabin, Michèle Morgan, Gérard Philipe, and Michel Simon, while America was making Doris Day–Rock Hudson froth. It was a time when the boulevards were dotted with *pissotières*, when Coca-Cola was deemed deleterious to your health and was banned, when milk was boiled every morning at home or steamed in the cafés to make café au lait, because, irony of ironies, pasteurization was not in general use, despite Louis Pasteur's great discovery. It was a time when the central marketplace, les Halles, was bustling with vigor in the middle of the night as merchants built walls of carrots and leeks and wreaths of watercress. It was the benevolent sisters flitting down flights of steps in front of Sacré-Coeur like birds, their enormous white-winged headgear flapping in the air. It was pushcarts and stands of every edible item known to man in the markets of rue Mouffetard and rue Lepic. It was, indeed, the chestnut trees in blossom, but what the songs didn't tell you was that when the blossoms were full of rain water, they fell all about you as you promenaded through the streets, forming both a carpet to walk on and a shawl on your shoulders. It was pale, wispy linden blossoms, too, and acacia trees. Tulips in April, lilies of the valley offered on May 1st, Workers' Day, for good luck, and roses in June in the Bagatelle gardens. It was nineteenth-century slate roofs and wrought-iron balconies, a tone poem in gray stone, in gray streets, in gray skies.

It was the only place to be if you were a romantic young man in 1955 who didn't want to go into medicine.

The nine years that separated my first April in Paris from my meeting with Bob Parrish had been devoted largely to theater work. In my first year in Europe, I left beloved Paris for a short time to study set and costume design at the Ruskin School of Fine Arts in Oxford, England. I was the only one in the class interested in theater design. All the other students were doing oils and endless sketches of statues in the Ashmolean Museum. I designed and executed costumes for the various colleges—Magdalen, Merton, Jesus, and others. Because it was Oxford, the emphasis was on the classics: *The Changling, Mandragola, Noah, Troilus and Cressida*. I pored over the stunning Victorian color plates of Racinet's *L'Histoire du Costume* at the Bodleian Library, which became my second home. Then I went back to my digs above the tea shop at Iffley Lock and designed. Later, Percy Horton, the drawing master, would come to performances of the plays and grade me on the costumes he saw, since I had no time for oils and statues.

When I moved back to Paris, my first job was as a night porter in a hotel near Place de la Madeleine. It was a combination tourist hotel and what the French call a *hôtel de passe*, so the streetwalkers were constantly bringing in their johns just as some middle-class family from Germany was checking in. Then came a job as a bank teller in an American Express office on an American military base at Saint-Germain-en-Laye, just outside Paris. When my bank duties were over at six o'clock, I would rehearse plays with Studio 128, a theater company I'd organized on the base, which would later be performed at the camp movie theater or at the eighteenth-century Théâtre Montansier in nearby Versailles: *Born Yesterday*, *Summer and Smoke*, and *The Women*, among others. The Théâtre Montansier, a small gem, had been Marie Antoinette's personal theater, and we used to hoist the flats painted at the military base up through the back loading platform that overlooked the gardens of the palace. Delighted with these productions and the fact that I was providing recreation for G.I.s who wanted to act as well as for the thousands who attended, two generals eventually called Washington, and a position was created whereby I could work as a civilian for the Department of the Army directing shows. Until then, I'd been employed as a "French national" at the bank. And so, earning dollars again and enjoying PX privileges, I directed and produced plays for the next three years.

As my career shifted into the professional arena (that is, getting paid for my theater work), I phoned my parents back in the States. "I thought you wanted to design," responded my father, "not direct or produce." The implication was all too obvious. I had changed from pre-med to a psychology major, then to a department store display man, then back to school to design, and now *this*. Obviously I wasn't *settled*. And I was living abroad, something no one else he knew did.

I thanked the French influence around me as I immediately turned my back on guilt, as all good Frenchmen do. "It's all connected, father," I replied, unflappable. "The arts are all connected. You move sideways."

I don't think he got that, or ever would. He just saw it as another job change. He was very singular in purpose, my father. One decided very early in life what one wanted to do, then one pursued it and did it. As he had done decades earlier with life insurance, as my brother had done with surgery.

In 1959, I formed what I believe was the first African-American theater company within the military, "The Harequin Guild." This was six years before Martin Luther King Jr. led his march from Selma to Montgomery, so it was still more correct to say "first Negro theater company." I think I might have been influenced by seeing Josephine Baker in the revue *Paris Mes Amours* at the Olympia Theatre that year, and wondering why the military theater companies were always white. But putting together an all-Negro company was no easy task. The group of budding actors wanted to do Lorraine Hansberry's *A Raisin in the Sun*, an up-to-date piece about a black family in Chicago moving into a white neighborhood, but I convinced them not to go for the obvious immediately. What about Shakespeare's *The Taming of the Shrew*, I asked? If we're going to break stereotype, let's break it! And the rush was on. We all quaked a bit on opening night, not because it was Shakespeare in full Elizabethan costume, but because many of the generals and their wives who had bought tickets, had kept asking, "This is the musical version, right?" It was, after all, only a few short years since the movie *Carmen Jones*, and isn't that what Negroes did, sing and dance? On opening night, the top brass sat there in the audience, shoulders adorned with stars and birds, mouths agape at the mellifluous speech flowing from the actors. *The Taming of the Shrew* was a mind-blowing and howling success. *Then* we did *A Raisin in the Sun*.

In 1961, I left that job and formed an organization in Paris the goal of which was to produce professional plays in English in the City of Light. An English company led by Edward Sterling had preceded me, performing between the two world wars. But no one had seized the torch since. My major cohorts in this affair were two extraordinary *femmes du monde*, Colette de Jouvenel, daughter of the great French writer Colette, and la Comtesse Paola de Rohan-Chabot, a noblewoman whose husband's line preceded the French Revolution by more than a hundred years. Such dates of lineage have great importance in French society; later titles are looked at with just a touch of disdain, the way old money looks at new money here. These two ladies were refined, witty, and worldly, traveled with literary and artistic people, and wore mostly woolen skirts and matching cashmere cardigans. Their hair was always coiffed perfectly at any hour of the day or night, and they wore little makeup and simple jewelry. The joke circulated Paris that the difference between a French lady and an American lady was that the French lady would look at herself in the mirror before going out in the evening and remove an accessory, while the American lady would look at herself and add one. They were elegance personified, Colette and Paola, the last cry in chic. With them, I had drinks or dined with Françoise Sagan, Jean Marais, Marguerite Duras, Arnold Wesker, Janet Flanner, Liz Smith, and Princess Lee Raziwill, Jackie Kennedy's sister. I was the young American who spoke fluent French, who had an idea to produce professional English-speaking plays there in Paris, and wasn't that terribly *amusant*? Though I never asked for it or sought it, I soon found myself in a new role: *le chéri des salons*. The darling of the drawing rooms. But while these women were all charm, they were also all amateur. They knew their world well, but play production was another thing. It seemed to take me forever to get them focused on the real purpose of our organization. We were forever dining late. Then, while I went to bed, they visited the *boîtes* in fashion, danced all night, supped at the central market place early in the morning, and rose early afternoon the next day. I could never see Colette before 4:00 P.M., when she was having breakfast in her apartment on rue de Beaujolais, the apartment her mother once inhabited. I would try to get Colette de Jouvenel focused on business problems, obtain her signature on a few necessary letters, and then dash to the post office before it closed at 7:00 P.M. Had I been working with theater professionals, the entire affair of the English-speaking theater might have culminated in six months; as it was, it took two long and painful years to get the theater going. But two years that were full of the charm, wit, beauty, elegance, and eloquence for which the French, or at least the Parisians, are justifiably known; it was the endless effervescence of champagne.

Eventually, in June 1963, we opened Paris Playhouse with two Edward Albee's one-act plays: *The Zoo Story* and *The Death of Bessie Smith*. David Wheeler directed the first play, I the second. I'd met with Albee and his agent, Jack Hutto, over breakfast in New York, and Francophiles that they both were, they gave me a real break on royalty payments. We flew in professional New York actors—Olive Deering of the Actors Studio and writer-actor James Leo Herlihy for the lead roles, with Gary Collins, Jody Carter, and Richard Shepard doing major support. Smaller roles were cast from the American colony of expatriate actors in Paris. The deluxe velour-covered program contained no less than seven letters of dedication from literary titans Jean Cocteau, André Maurois, Joseph Kessel, James Jones, Françoise Sagan, Armand Salacrou, and Edward Albee himself. When the plays finally opened at the Théâtre Charles-de-Rochefort in a blazing gala, Paola surprised us all with truckloads of Moët Chandon that mysteriously appeared. She accomplished this through her sister, Francesca, who was married to Frédéric Chandon de Briailles, heir to the great champagne dynasty. At intermission, corks popped and flew and the coruscating champagne poured out as if the generous heavens had opened up to do so. Thanks to Colette and Paola, the affair attracted *le tout-Paris*, which is the French equivalent of New York's "four hundred." The British ambassador attended, as did the Maharanee of Baroda and several Rothschilds. So did Princess Grace of Monaco, with her father-in-law, Prince Pierre. Assorted international nobility and American and French actors were peppered through the audience, all of it comprising what Bob Parrish had termed, with that twinkle in his eye, the *glitterati* of Paris. The magazine *Paris Match* did a two-page color spread on the event that closed the 1963 Paris social season. There were reviews in every major Paris newspaper, and in the States the *New York Times* and *The Village Voice* ran articles. And the theater was launched without one American cent; it had all been financed by the French.

Paola introduced me to Princess Grace almost immediately after her arrival in the lobby. In true French style, I leaned forward when she extended her ungloved right hand and gave it the courtly *baise-main* royalty perforce required. I had learned that you don't really kiss the hand, you barely dry-brush it with the lips, sometimes not making contact at all. She was charming and beautiful. We talked of American theater and English theater, and I quickly told her the history of Edward Sterling, the Englishman who had run a professional English-speaking company in Paris during the summer months, between the two great wars.

"But since World War II, no one has attempted it again."

"Until now," she said.

"Yes. And I think there's some sort of homage to his legacy. This is the same theater that he used."

"Where in the States are you from?" she asked.

I smiled. "Philadelphia. Like you."

"Where in Philadelphia?"

"West Oaklane," I replied. While I knew this middle-class area at the west end of the city was respectable, it was a far cry from the blue-blood wealth of the Main Line, where the Kelly family dwelled.

We talked of other casual things, and I was careful not to mention the fact that I had helped her brother, Jack Kelly Jr., a brilliant sculling athlete like their father, but less than a brilliant student in a psychology class at the University of Pennsylvania. We had taken the same class, and it fell to me to cram the poor lad's handsome head with a hundred vital facts the night before he took a final exam. He passed, *grâce à moi*. I was told later by Paola that the fact that I *didn't* mention this episode to the princess was proof that I had truly become a French diplomat.

Princess Grace thought it was very exciting to have a professional English-speaking theater in Paris. I told her we had other plays in mind that could follow. "I love Pinter's '*The Birthday Party*,'" I said.

"If I can be of any help, please let me know," Princess Grace offered graciously. I thanked her, and then the buzzer sounded, announcing that the show was about to begin. She offered her hand again, and again I brought my lips within a hair's breadth of her fingers. She joined Prince Rainier's father and the two of them made their way into the theater auditorium.

Some of the press covering the event that night reached London and Bob Parrish's living room. And so there I was, almost a year after the Albee plays, in Parrish's suite at the Hôtel La Trémoille, being offered my first job in the movies. I accepted it eagerly. And if my father would berate me for yet another career move—and he did—it seemed to me that the arts wherein I had been dabbling for eight years were, after all, related. And that everything I had done until that point, and ever since, was connected.

CHAPTER TWO

~

Speak the Speech Trippingly

Up from the Beach was being filmed in Cherbourg at the tip of a peninsula called Cotentin. The real name of the area was La Manche, the French word for coat sleeve and for the English Channel since it resembled a sleeve. The old national road from Paris to Cherbourg takes you through Bayeux, where I stopped to see the extraordinary, fragile tapestry attributed to Queen Mathilde in the eleventh century. The Bayeux tapestry is crewel work, a form of embroidery, and is strung out like an unraveled roll of gauze extending around the walls of the room.

Farther on, I entered Sainte-Mère-Église, the famous village largely liberated by American paratroopers during the WWII Normandy invasion. Still farther on were apple orchards, cow pastures, ponds of watercress. The region abounded in pont l'évêque, livarot, and camembert cheeses, hard cider, fresh seafood, cream sauces, apple tarts, and calvados brandy. During the filming, one of the local farmers would deliver homemade calvados, redolent with the smell and taste of apples, to the production trailer. The farmer would giggle when he received his payment, for he was making an illegal sale. But since nearly everyone in the region harvested apples, nearly everyone stilled homemade calvados. The gendarmes attached to the film even purchased a few bottles themselves. Calvados was strong and delicious. The one I bought was in its first year, off-white in color. It darkens through keep-ing, and a calvados that has aged fifteen years or so has the color and strength of cognac.

Based on George Barr's novel *Epitaph for an Enemy*, the story of *Up from the Beach* was really quite good. A few American soldiers, led by a sergeant (Cliff Robertson), liberate some French villagers holed up as hostages in a barn during the Allied invasion. Since the nearby village is in German hands, the G.I.s march the villagers to the sea to put them on boats for England. But the boats are packed with wounded soldiers, and the British beach master has no instructions to evacuate civilians. The sergeant is ordered to march them back, being told that the village is now liberated. But when they arrive, the village is again in German hands and the sergeant is once more ordered to take the villagers back to the coast. And so they all continue to trek back and forth through the film, from village to coast, from coast to village. Along the way, they inherit a Nazi officer prisoner, the sergeant falls for a young French girl in the group of villagers, the girl's grandmother is strafed by a Ger-man Messerschmitt, and a lost American soldier (Red Buttons) is added to the group by a colonel (Slim Pickens), who doesn't know what else to do with him.

The cast was impressive. Besides Robertson and Buttons, Broderick Crawford and English actor James Robertson Justice played officers who, along with Pickens, kept the villagers moving. Young Austrian actor Oskar Werner, fresh out of *Jules and Jim*, had been cast as the Nazi officer; Françoise Rosay and well-known French actors of the Comédie-Française were in strong supporting roles; and Irina Demick was the young French girl, looking exactly as she had when she'd ap-peared in *The Longest Day* as a Resistance fighter. This last touch was upon the insistence of producer Darryl F. Zanuck, who was having a well-publicized affair with her at the time. "The public wants to know what happened to that girl with the bike in *The Longest Day*," he would say. "Well, this is her story after D-Day!"

Cliff Robertson was not amused. He thought the movie was the sergeant's story, and he told that to Bob Parrish. When Parrish in-formed Robertson that the reason they were all there in Cherbourg, every last one of them, was really because Zanuck wanted to see more of Demick on screen, Robertson grumbled and uttered the only clever line during his three months there: "Yeah, you should call this picture *Up from the Bitch.*"

And so the mismarriage began. Robertson was making the sergeant's story, Demick, tutored by DFZ, was making the French girl's story, and Parrish was making the villagers' story, which he felt was the heart of the film.

Disgruntled over concept, Cliff Robertson fought Irina Demick at every turn. She was not a worthy opponent, being basically a sweet, unmannered girl who had simply been pushed by the ego of a world-renowned producer, and who possessed no wiles against a star out of the Hollywood system. "I wish Darryl wouldn't try to make an actress out of me!" she cried the first day I came to rehearse with her in her trailer. "I'm not an actress! It's just Darryl who wants that for me! I wish he'd just give me the money instead, and leave me be!" It was a *cri du coeur* and absolutely defined their relationship.

Irina spoke some English and had a decent ear, so it was not too difficult to coach her. Françoise Rosay was an old veteran warhorse who had performed in many English films and even on the London stage. She was the widow of one of France's most respected film directors, Jacques Feyder, and her three sons were all in the film industry. Even some American film aficionados knew who she was. Her English was excellent, better than Robertson's. With his Actors Studio technique and an attempt to "toughen" up his sergeant, Cliff was slurring his speech more and more. At one point, in his trailer, I called his attention to it, and he bristled. "Is that how you expect me to say the words," he asked, "clipped and precise like that?" He was clearly poking fun at my educated tones.

"No, of course not," I replied. "But I think that's where you need to start as an actor before you become the sergeant who *doesn't* speak with clipped and precise diction." He stared at me, and I suddenly thought, "Who am I to tell him how to deliver his lines?" I realized in a flash this was not going to be an easy job, going to the heart of what an actor is supposed to possess already: diction, accent, intention, memory. Robertson held my look a long moment, during which time I saw myself on the road back to Paris. "Yeah, maybe," he grumbled and made his way to his makeup table, where he began to apply brown eyebrow liner onto the thinning spots of his hair line.

I immediately related the incident to Bob Parrish, in case he needed to deflect a complaint from Cliff. "That's what you're here for," he said simply. "You're just doing your job. If he brings it up to me, I'll back you up. But you do need to know something. You can be replaced. I can be replaced. Anyone on this crew can be replaced. But not Cliff Robertson. Because we've already shot three days of film on him." To his credit, Robertson never brought up the issue, and though I think he continued to look at me as some kind of educated dilettante pronouncing words too precisely, he was able to channel the information into the character he was playing. Though he was occasionally unpredictable and touchy, Cliff worked hard at his craft. There was, however, no question that he was concerned mostly with old number one. There was, for example, the incident when Parrish had moved the camera in for a close-up and crouched down next to him, to talk about the emotion of the moment. Cliff was lying on his stomach, M-1 rifle cocked near his head, looking over a dirt berm.

"Now, Cliff," said Parrish, "you know there may be some Germans over there, and you're thinking about the men with you and the villagers in the barn."

"Right," said Cliff. "You want me to look off in their direction?"

"Just for a second."

"Want to see that look?"

"Yes," said Parrish. And he moved to the camera, which was also low to the ground, and peered through the lens.

"Not getting too much white of the eye, are you, Bob?"

I was stunned. My background had been in theater, where you never heard an actor worrying about how much white of the eye you saw. I expected Robertson to be concerned only with the emotion of the moment, not with the way he looked. In truth, the close-up is always tricky, where pores become craters. Still for an actor who had been praised for his naturalistic work in *Picnic*, I wondered how much he was concerned with the scene.

Red Buttons was pleasant enough, but I never felt any real attachment to him. He had arrived with his wife and a slew of vitamin and mineral supplements. Back then, the French assistants thought he was crazy or a hypochondriac or both. Actually, he was twenty years ahead of the French, who not until the '80s would come to understand what dietary supplements were. Buttons always knew his lines and had no problem whatsoever rehearsing with me. I just never sensed any real fire in him; this, despite his best supporting actor Oscar in *Sayonara*. I even got to play a scene with him in a jeep. Bob Parrish wanted me to do the small role of a spit-and-polish lieutenant who arrives with Buttons and Slim Pickens in a jeep and chews out Roberston for not filling out a report. I asked Parrish why, with a number of American actors in Paris, he wanted to cast me. I'd never been in front of the camera before and I was a nonactor. He said I looked and spoke exactly how he wanted that character to, and would I do the part? I did, although the only two things I remember about that now was that I felt dwarfed and not terribly mannish next to Slim Pickens (who would?) and that Buttons simply sat next to me in the jeep, offering neither comfort nor suggestion to the neophyte actor.

About ten days after we started shooting, the alcoholics arrived: James Robertson Justice and Broderick Crawford. I'd had some experience back in the army medical corps with alcoholics. I knew they couldn't be trusted, and I knew they always made excuses.

"Oh, God, I'm sick today," moaned Crawford when I went into his trailer to rehearse with him. He looked exactly as I'd seen him on the screen: big, portly, a smashed face. "I think I must've had a bad oyster last night." St-Vaast-la-Hougue with its oyster beds was only a few miles away, and the restaurants of Cherbourg abounded in the freshest crustaceans, oysters, clams, and half a dozen different varieties of fish. The chances of Crawford's becoming ill on such fare was infinitesimal.

"Do you want me to tell Bob Parrish?" I asked.

"No, I'll tell him later. Right now, you can help me run the lines, make sure I know them. I don't trust my memory today." And we ran the scene. Many times. Of all the stars in that movie, he and Irina Demick were actually the easiest to work with and the most eager. I think Crawford saw me as some kind of support for him. And despite whatever drinking problem he had, he was warm, kind, and generous. Over and over, he invited me to visit him on the coast of Spain, where he had a house. "Next to Robert Ruark's house," he insisted on saying each time. Ruark had been one of America's best-known columnists and authors in the '50s and '60s, rivaled only by Walter Winchell.

I accompanied Crawford to the set late in the day. He had a scene inside a storage warehouse on the Normandy beach with Robertson. Most of the dialogue was Crawford's, and though he was letter-perfect in his trailer, he began to sweat and blow lines in rehearsal. I stood nearby, script in hand, and threw him lines as one would throw a life-saver to a drowning man. Parrish's keen eye sized up the situation immediately.

"We're not going to shoot the scene today, Brod," he said. I just want to rehearse it and check your makeup with the lights. We'll shoot it tomorrow."

"Sure, Bob. I'll probably feel better tomorrow. Must've eaten something really terrible last night."

The next day, of course, was just as bad. After I met with Crawford in his trailer, I went to find Parrish on the set.

"How is he?" he asked me.

"Same as yesterday," I replied.

"Come here. Let me show you something." And he took me to the spot where the camera was set from the rehearsal the night before. But now up against the wall of the warehouse there were several stacks of huge barrels. "If he's not steady on his feet, I'll lean him up against the barrels and that will support him. I want you right behind this first barrel. If he misses a line, throw it to him right away. You're not on camera, I'm framing right at the end of his body."

And that's how Oscar-winner Broderick Crawford got through his big scene that day, leaning against the barrels, with me whispering the words the moment I heard a pause that wasn't rehearsed. Later, Parrish would simply edit out my voice and mix in some other background ambient sounds—jeeps, distant conversation, ocean waves. They had to do quite a few takes, but mostly because the sweat was pouring down Crawford's face, and they frequently had to mop him up. But the scene played.

Years later in Hollywood, I ran across Broderick Crawford again. He was guest starring in a Columbia Pictures Television show. *Medical Story*, I think. I was doing research for several of the shows at the time: *Medical Story*, *Police Story*, *Joe Forrester*. It was said at that point that Crawford had completely dried out. I walked up to him on the set and said hello. He replied in kind, but the scowl told me he had no idea who I was.

"You don't remember me, do you?" I asked.

"I have to be honest. I don't."

"We worked together on *Up from the Beach*, a little over ten years ago. I was the dialogue coach."

"*Up from the Beach?* My God, I was so sick then!"

This time he meant "sick" in a totally different way. He meant that he had been drinking at the time. I admired his frankness, which, of course, was part of the program he was on. He laughed. "I don't remember doing a lot of that movie. You helped me get through it, didn't you?"

"Yes, several times."

He grabbed me and hugged me. "Thank you," he said simply. I was deeply moved. This great bear of a man, known for his tough roles, had reached out to me and, in so doing, admitted his own weakness. Then we talked a little of Bob and Kathie Parrish, who were then living in Sag Harbor, near the tip of Long Island, and Crawford told me how much he had liked Parrish and was grateful to him for not firing him from the movie.

"Bob wouldn't have fired you. That's not his style."

"No," he said. "He's a classy man."

"So are you," I replied. "How come you never play classy parts?"

"They pay me for being a slob." He smiled and gave me a wink, as if we were sharing some secret. Then the 2nd assistant director came up to him to say that they were ready for him at camera. He waved goodbye to me and moved on into the lights. I watched the rehearsal for a few moments. The old Willie Stark force was there, he was sure of his lines, and there was no sweat streaming down his face.

Oskar Werner arrived. I'd loved his performance in *Jules and Jim* and thought he was enormously talented. A production chauffeur had driven him up from Paris, and Bob Parrish had asked me to be the first to meet him. Parrish was shooting an action sequence without dialogue that morning, so I wasn't needed on the set. Werner was taken to his trailer, which had been parked near the catering tent. I entered and introduced myself. Werner knew who I was from his conversations with Parrish.

"Do you have a copy of the script?" he asked. "Bob Parrish's secretary sent me one, but I think it's an old one." I said I could lend him mine for a while and run down another at the production office. "Good," he said. "Give me about an hour or so to look it over, and I'll meet you at the caterer's and we'll rehearse. After lunch, I'm supposed to do a makeup test." He was soft-spoken, well-mannered, and very good looking, with a line of even white teeth that I learned later were probably false. He also had a sad, haunting quality to his blue eyes that I couldn't define and that absolutely riveted me to him.

An hour later, I rejoined him in the empty catering tent, ready to do a fast run-through of all his scenes. "We need to wait till I speak to Bob," Werner said. "This script isn't what I agreed to do." The Nazi officer was completely whitewashed, completely sympathetic. Werner went on to say that there was a tendency at that time to make the Nazis in movies more sensitive, and that that wasn't the way they were. "I discussed this point with Bob and with Darryl Zanuck when I accepted the movie and Zanuck promised they'd change the character, and I see they haven't changed anything!"

So we didn't rehearse. We sat in the tent and talked about Paris and the surge of quality English and Italian films that artistically were head-and-shoulders above the rest of the movie market then. After a while, the crew came in for lunch. Though the long tables never bore any official designations as to who sat where, most of the tables took on a specific character: the director and the actors usually sat together at one table, the assistant directors and script girl at another, the grips sat together, the electricians sat together, and so on through the various trades, although anyone at any time could sit anywhere. In a second, the grips moved in to the table where Werner and I were sitting. Werner immediately jumped up and started shaking hands with all the grips, introducing himself and addressing them in perfect French. The grips were all smiles, recognizing him instantly. (Who in France *hadn't* seen *Jules et Jim?*) Much later, when I went to Hollywood, I discovered that the land of liberty dictated strong class differences, all stemming from the number of zeroes you had on your paycheck, so the stars could talk only to directors and producers and the directors and producers talked only to God. Certainly with *Jerry Maguire*, which I worked on in 1996, I never saw any of the many credited producers, except Cameron Crowe who was also directing, even say hello to a grip, let alone introduce himself and shake hands with him. And here was Austrian star

Oskar Werner jumping up to greet the French grips. I'd already liked him from our chat together; now I loved him.

Soon, Bob Parrish entered and spied Werner and me at the table with the grips. By now our caterer, Henriette Marello, had served us our hors d'oeuvres, so everyone at the table was eating. Parrish came over to greet Werner, and I stood up and offered the director my place. I knew what Werner needed to say and I thought it would be easier for them both if I weren't there. I took my plate to another table. At the end of an hour, the crew was drifting back to the set, and the last two persons to leave were Parrish and Oskar Werner. Werner headed for his chauffeur-driven car and I caught up to Parrish. "Oskar's going to the hotel," he said. "He's not going to do a makeup test today, and you shouldn't rehearse with him. I've got to talk to Zanuck, and I won't be able to do that for a few hours."

The next morning in Parrish's trailer, tended by his no-nonsense Russian-French assistant, Marina Gromoff, I learned from Parrish that Werner was on his way back to Paris and that English actor Marius Goring was heading toward us from London at that very moment. I knew Marius Goring's work. He had been the young orchestra conductor with whom Moira Shearer fell in love in Michael Powell's *The Red Shoes*. He was a decent actor, but he wasn't German and he wasn't Oskar Werner. A few days later, on September 18, *The Hollywood Reporter* quoted Werner as saying exactly what he'd told me: "None of the script changes agreed upon have been made, and I refused to glorify a Nazi officer."

Parrish told me that he'd agreed totally with Werner's approach to the role, but when Parrish telephoned Zanuck and exposed the problem, Zanuck categorically refused to make any concessions to the actor. "You have to put up with that shit from Cary Grant," Parrish reported Zanuck as saying, "You don't have to put up with it from some second-rate German actor."

"You know," Parrish said to me, "you start a movie and you think you've got some good elements together, and all of a sudden you lose an element, then maybe another, and soon you don't have all the things you had when you started. And the picture you thought you had isn't the one you're making." He said it wistfully, then exited his trailer.

The following year, the Austrian-born "second-rate German actor" was nominated for an Oscar for his work in Stanley Kramer's *Ship of*

Fools, along with his costar, Simone Signoret. In it, Werner displayed a touching and tragic poignancy that was the very heart of the film. The haunting, illuminated look in his blue eyes that I saw when I met him is there on the screen, and continues to be in my mind's eye forty years later. In his final moments of the movie, he has a heart attack that is extraordinarily realistic and almost unbearable to watch. It is a paradigm of what acting is all about. After *Up from the Beach*, I never heard anything more about Marius Goring, and I remember nothing about the look in his eyes.

In making a movie, every day's work is unpredictable. An arc light explodes, a plane passes overhead, a mike shadow crosses an actor's face, the camera bumps a pebble on its dolly movement, and you start over again. Add the ever-changing Normandy weather to these variables, and the probability of getting to the final sequence of the day as planned is often remote. Yet on a given cold day, with the director trying to figure out how to get the actors to perform without clouds of vapor coming from their mouths, we adhered to our schedule and moved the company at the end of the day to a remote country bridge. Robertson, Demick, Buttons, and a dozen French character actors were to cross it with the setting sun behind them. On the safari-like move to the location, I was one of the first to arrive. It was desolate and bitter cold. The company would have to work quickly, for in an hour and a half we would lose the light. In a region like that, once the sun left the sky, the grass froze.

The moment I got out of the production car, I heard a desperate yowling coming from the bridge. One of the real-life soldiers being used as an extra that day made his way down to the bridge and returned, walking straight to me with a handful of wet, matted, shivering baby cat of the most common garden variety, obviously abandoned. The animal looked me straight in the eye, concluded I was his last chance for survival, and gave a final plaintive wail before giving way to a violent case of the shakes. I carried him to the car, placed him on the seat, and told the driver to keep the heater going.

While originally my intention had been only to save the cat, not to adopt him, it was crusty old character actress Françoise Rosay at dinner one night who pinned the badge of ownership on me. "Monsieur Becker!" she intoned with authority, "That animal must not be abandoned a second time!" She was a large woman with snow-white hair and piercing, though uneven, eyes that flashed the wrath of all the Gallic gods. "Do you hear me?" she thundered in the voice she used to reach the upper balconies. I could only mutter a vanquished "Oui, madame" back.

Thus began my life with Calvados. Despite a magnificent white diamond that extended from his forehead to the base of his stomach, and despite the occasional black tiger stripe, his overall color was tawny and reminiscent of brandy. He was definitely a Calvados. He would travel with me from film to film and country to country, and come to be known by all the French film crews as "the movie cat," even though he never appeared in front of the cameras.

On location, the quiet but certain war between Cliff Robertson and Irina Demick was increasing. It was subtle. It had to be on Cliff's part, since he knew she was the producer's girl friend. I was probably the first to notice the escalation. They never wanted to rehearse their scenes together. Each one would rehearse with me and then meet up at the camera. Bob Parrish would give a few instructions, then say, "Do you want to rehearse?" and Cliff would answer, "No, let's just shoot it."

Finally, one day things exploded. Cliff had been darkening his makeup gradually throughout the filming. He was becoming more and more "rugged," occasionally smearing dirt on his face as well. Irina's makeup had become slightly lighter, probably just through some inadvertence on the part of her makeup man.

"I can't light this scene!" Walter Wottitz, the cinematographer, stated to Parrish one morning, with both Cliff and Irina standing in front of the camera. "I've got cowboys and Indians here! I can't light them both." And suddenly it was a showdown. Parrish took Wottitz aside and spoke to him, but it was obvious as Wottitz continued to shake his head, that there was nothing technically he could do. One of the two actors would have to go back to the trailer and get the makeup changed. Parrish elected to tell Irina that she would have to darken her makeup slightly.

"All right!" she said, "I'll change it!" And she stormed off with her makeup man. I rejoined her in her trailer, to make sure that when the job was done she wouldn't forget her lines. "Cliff's been doing this purposely from the beginning," she said in anger and frustration. "It's because of my relationship with Darryl." Her eyes went moist. "Let's just get this over with!" she snapped to her makeup man, refusing to let a tear fall.

We finished all the exterior locations just in time. It was late October in northern France, the trees were baring, and the weather was getting gray and cold with rain and occasional hail. For its final task, the art department had to wire artificial leaves on the semi-denuded trees, since the Normandy invasion had occurred in June. Then we all returned to Paris to do the studio work. At this point, Cliff and Irina were barely speaking. Parrish was concerned. The two stars still had their big love scene to shoot together, and how do you shoot a love scene when the actors aren't even talking to each other?

An enormous set had been built at the studio at Épinay-sur-Seine, a northern suburb of Paris. The sand dunes of the Normandy coast had been brilliantly re-created, and a huge trap in the stage floor with water gave added depth for the edge of the Channel waters. We had done a night shoot on the real coast, showing the arrival of the villagers, and now we were in closer for several days, and what was supposed to be the most tender scene in the picture.

Parrish shot Cliff as he made his way across the dunes to where Irina, alone, was sitting, looking out to sea. He sat down next to her and they exchanged a few lines of dialogue. Then Irina lay back in the sand, and Cliff lay down next to her. Following that, they had three pages of intimate, tender dialogue that terminated in a kiss. Then, this being 1964 and an American film, the honorable sergeant rose and left. The scene was first and foremost a love scene, the only one in the picture. But for Parrish, it was something else besides; it was the understanding between the Americans and the French that the entire picture was trying to explain in so many different ways.

Parrish did his master shot, bringing Cliff into the scene, then running through to the kiss at the end and taking Cliff out again. It went without incident. Now Parrish moved in with the camera to do individual close-ups, each one of which would take about half a day to shoot. Irina's close-up was first. Camera and lights were adjusted and we began to rehearse. I lay down just off camera, in the spot where Cliff would be and cued Irina her lines. The lighting men and Parrish continued their work, until all was ready.

"Okay," said Parrish to the assistant director, "Go get Cliff. We're ready."

"Can we do it without Cliff?" interjected Irina. "I'd rather have Frawley read the lines."

"Sure, we can do that," said Parrish.

And he went ahead and shot her close-up for the entire three pages of dialogue with me next to her, off camera, playing Cliff.

When Parrish had two good takes in the can, he thanked her, told her how terrific the scene was, and with Cliff's stand-in in place, they began to change the camera angle and light for the complementary close-up. About an hour later, Cliff was brought to the stage, and he lay down in the sand. This time I was lying where Irina would be, off camera, and I read her lines to Cliff.

"Okay, let's shoot it," said Parrish. "Go get Irina."

Cliff jumped in immediately. "I'd rather do it with Frawley. I mean, he's here and I'm used to his voice."

"Fine with me," said Parrish.

"Let's shoot it!" said Cliff.

We did. With me lying just off camera for the three pages of intimate dialogue, and with Cliff being as loving and tender as he could be. The close-up culminated in his movement forward for the kiss. Then the "Cut!" from Parrish just as Cliff reached toward me. And that's how we filmed the big love scene of the movie. The two actors were together only for the long shot and the kiss. Everything else, all the close shots, all the tenderness and affection between the two characters, all the intimacy, all the passion, both Cliff and Irina played to me.

Red Buttons approached me on the set just days before we finished shooting. "Hey, Frawley, you know what Thursday is?" I had no idea. "It's Thanksgiving!" he said. "We should all do something together, go out to a good restaurant, all the Americans on the movie, and have a good Thanksgiving dinner!"

"The French don't celebrate Thanksgiving," I said. He stared at me, completely miffed. I almost said, "They celebrate Bastille Day," but decided to let it pass. I told him that I frequented a great little restaurant where I knew the owner personally, and I would call to see if we could get a reservation for Thursday night. It was Monday, and that didn't leave much time for a special order of a turkey. Buttons just shrugged and said, "See what you can do."

Chez Laurent, a small restaurant on rue des Acacias, was just down from the Arc de Triomphe and off the avenue de la Grande-Armée. With two small, intimate rooms decorated with country French antiques and gently lit with old brass table lamps, the restaurant had become my favorite. The taxi drivers often confused it with the grand and expensive Laurent on avenue Gabriel, near the Élysée palace, so the exact address always had to be specified. My Chez Laurent boasted a wonderful sea bass with tarragon, a giant standing rib roast with tomato-flavored mustard, an excellent rosé wine from the Ardèche region, and at the front bar, most incredibly, some specially bottled scotch only for that restaurant from a tiny distiller in Scotland. Madame Laurent said her ovens weren't big enough for a turkey, but would talk to her local baker and let me know. I was not surprised, having gone through enough Christmases in Paris to know that turkeys and geese were always taken to the large bakers' ovens the day before, since the ordinary kitchen oven could not handle anything bigger than a duck. You simply retrieved the bird from the baker's at the appointed hour, carried it home and set it down, steaming, on your table. It was a process I spared explaining to my American actor friends, and was grateful when Madame Laurent called me back to say everything was under control.

That Thursday, the American movie business descended on Madame Laurent's tiny restaurant: Bob and Kathie Parrish, Cliff Robertson, Broderick Crawford, Red Buttons and his wife, the film's ex-colonel technical consultant, Roy Everson, who was Cliff's stand-in and our token Englishman, and I. We all met at the bar in the front of the restaurant and stood for a few minutes imbibing Madame Laurent's excellent scotch. Broderick Crawford stated it was absolutely the best scotch he'd ever tasted, and I figured he knew. To his delight, there was a bottle with his name on it. At my behest, Madame Laurent had a calligrapher inscribe his name on the label, something she usually did for Christmas gifts. We were then all ushered into the upstairs room, especially reserved for us, Crawford calling for two more bottles of scotch to be sent up to the table immediately. He was going to save the one with his name on it.

It was a wonderful dinner. The *marquise au chocolat* dessert had us in ecstasy. The movie was nearly over, the atmosphere was convivial, everyone was relaxed. I realized that even Robertson had accepted me, and sat laughing and joking with me. He was obviously in the warm holiday mood and he'd received a visit in Normandy from Dina Merrill before we left, so he seemed quite content. Of all of those present, the only one whose friendship I valued and kept over the years was Bob Parrish.

We dawdled over coffee and *fraise des bois*, a wonderful liqueur made from wild strawberries. Then Madame Laurent appeared and we all burst into applause for her culinary talents. She carried her *livre d'or* with her that she reserved for only her most important dignitaries. She asked if the actors would sign it. As well-oiled as they were on scotch, *rosé d'Ardèche*, and wild strawberry liqueur, I think they would have signed an espionage confession. The book was presented to Broderick Crawford first, who made some humorous dedication and signed it, then to Red Buttons, who did the same, and finally to Cliff. He looked at the statements both actors had written, and scrawled, "These guys can joke, but they both won Oscars! I didn't," and signed his name. Four years later, when Cliff Robertson won the best actor Oscar for *Charly*, I told Madame Laurent to frame the ironic inscription, but she didn't want to tear the page out of her book.

Bob Parrish is gone now. So are Broderick Crawford and Oskar Werner at an untimely early age. The movie was released in France as *Le Jour d'après* (The Day After, a working title that had been used for a short while before *Up from the Beach* became official). Though the film is a far cry from being the sequel to *The Longest Day* as Zanuck had hoped, for him it may still have been the story of what happened to that beautiful French girl with the bicycle. But no matter whose story it was, *Up from the Beach* has virtually vanished, even from video status. Perhaps now, with memories in hand, this is all that is left, all that is written about the film. Maybe my final job in the unending chain of changing professions that irritated my father so much is now simply this one: recorder.

CHAPTER THREE

~

Two Directors,
Both Alike in Dignity

20th Century Fox maintained two satellite offices in Europe: one in London, the other in Paris. The Paris office went by the name of Les Films du Siècle (literally, Films of the Century, a close approximation of the original title). Just before *Up from the Beach* finished shooting, Christian Ferry, the head of production, came to me on the set and told me that Darryl Zanuck wanted to put me on a retainer, since the studio had plans for other films in Paris. One of these was an upcoming comedy that was to star Audrey Hepburn. Zanuck wanted to make sure I would be available for that one, but it was still several months off.

Ferry had to explain to me what a retainer was. It seemed inconceivable to receive a paycheck and not to work. "Oh, you'll have a few assignments, I'm sure," he said. "There are some screen tests we'll be doing over the next few months on a few European actresses that Darryl is interested in. The tests will be in English, so you'll need to work with those girls."

I still didn't get it, not completely. "Completely" would come a couple of months later when I made my first visit to La Résidence d'Auteuil to rehearse with one of Zanuck's girls.

"You did a great job on *Up from the Beach*," Ferry continued. "Darryl wants to make you part of the Paris team."

"I haven't even met him," I replied.

"He knows all about you."

"So, whom do I thank for this? Parrish? Irina? Or you?"

"Oh, I think we all put in a good word," he said in a noncommittal, French way.

I'm sure they all did. Knowing how Zanuck had ignored Parrish's pleas to keep Oskar Werner on the film, my instincts told me this new job offer was mostly due to Irina.

Irina Demick. The star who never became a star. I would work with her again four years later in a big French film, *The Sicilian Clan*. She was always warm, generous, disarmingly open and honest, and she never seemed to take her role as an actress seriously. Now, through her doing, my career had advanced another notch. I called her at home to thank her. She never admitted that she had spoken to Zanuck, but she simply replied, "No, I should thank *you*. You were my only friend on the film. I never felt anyone else really accepted me."

Funny, I thought, what had been Cliff Robertson's nemesis had turned out to be my ally. And though I was slow to learn the first basic lesson of the film industry, learn it I did: advancement is made primarily through relations.

I signed my first "deal" with Edward Leggewie, a lethargic American who was the titular head of Les Films du Siècle, and for the next five weeks I received one hundred dollars a week for doing nothing more than calling in twice each week to see if they needed me for anything. The answer was always no. Finally, I was given the name, address, and phone number of a young lady in whom Zanuck was interested. I was to tutor her two or three times a week for an hour to an hour-and-a-half and make sure her English would be good enough for an eventual screen test, should Zanuck decide she would get one.

I called young Béatrice and set up an appointment by phone. Two days later, I made my way to that portion of the elegant 16th Quarter of Paris known as Auteuil. This was the area where *la grande bourgeoisie* and a few aristocratic families resided. Auteuil boasted Belle Epoque town houses and immaculate apartment buildings that came later, and Paris' famous racetrack in the Bois de Boulogne.

I walked down the long, carpeted hall of the third floor of La Résidence d'Auteuil and located the apartment. I rang the bell, and a moment later an absolutely stunning young blond girl, no more than twenty, opened the door. She wore a diaphanous chiffon peignoir over a diaphanous chiffon slip, none of it totally hiding her charms.

"Béatrice?" I asked. "Bonjour. I'm Frawley Becker."

She broke into a big smile. "Bonjour," she answered. "But Béatrice lives on the floor below." She smiled and shrugged, as if to say, "Wrong girl."

I excused myself and went back to the elevator. A moment later, I stood in front of the correct apartment, ringing the bell. The door opened and another beautiful blonde girl, about the same age, wearing, I swear, another diaphanous peignoir, stood there, smiling. "Béatrice?" I asked, a little cautiously.

"Frawley?" she answered. "Come in."

I entered a sparsely appointed apartment and Béatrice offered me a drink. I told her about my confusion of going to the wrong floor. "That's my fault," she said. I've only been here a few days. I probably mixed up the floors." I wondered how you mixed up the floors, and what was she going to do when we got to tenses? "Anyway, you're here for the English lesson. But I have to change first, don't you think?" And she exited into the bedroom. "There's some Schweppes and ice on the bar," she called to me. I poured a drink and wondered how many doors in La Résidence d'Auteuil held girls in diaphanous peignoirs.

I would learn later that it wasn't just Zanuck who had playmates there, but many of the big businessmen in Paris, presidents of large corporations, government officials. It was the same golden clientele that frequented Madame Claude's, the most famous upper-class brothel in the world, also situated in the 16th Quarter of Paris. Madame Claude had been a Resistance fighter during World War II, so when de Gaulle, who had spearheaded the Free French movement from London, came into power she was protected. This protection extended through the Pompidou regime and only dissolved late under Valéry Giscard d'Estaing. In 1965, Madame Claude was reigning gloriously. Her girls were not only beautiful, they were intelligent, they spoke several languages, and many of them had a certain class about them. You often saw one of them in a fashionable Champs-Élysées café, draped in a mink stole with elegant pearls around her neck, sipping an *apéritif* with a French diplomatic figure. Only her stunning beauty told you she was not the diplomat's wife. I saw Yul Brynner exit Madame Claude's one day, and the story went that private planes of her girls had been flown to Washington. Apparently, JFK and Kissinger were aware of this.

Only a dozen blocks away from Madame Claude's, then, was La Résidence d'Auteuil. And here girls who wouldn't think of working at Madame Claude's were lodged. The Résidence girls were the affairs, the *petites amies*, the young mistresses, as they had been for centuries; they had nothing, and yet everything, in common with *les filles de Madame Claude*.

As I suspected, Béatrice was not a great student. She was a slightly fleshy country girl who hadn't been in Paris long and was far too ingenuous for her own good. She told me more than I wanted to know about her. And Zanuck. She thought she was going to have a screen test, but that never materialized. Zanuck was given the perfect opportunity to back out of that obligation like a gentleman when Béatrice announced to me one day that she was pregnant by the young boyfriend from her home town. He had been making visits to the city to see her, and the poor girl didn't know what to do.

"Should I tell Darryl?" was her first question to me. And "Should I keep it?" was the second. I realized that any answers I might give her could put me in disfavor with Zanuck and decided to proceed cautiously. While I felt pretty certain that Zanuck's feelings for Irina Demick were real enough, I thought perhaps Béatrice was a mere dalliance to him. I didn't give the girl any direct advice, but simply pointed out the pros and cons of the situation. She decided on her own to tell Zanuck, and a few days later Béatrice phoned me to say that the movie potentate was going to take care of all the bills at a private *clinique* she was going to, and wasn't that *chic* of him and wasn't that marvelous? The next day, I was called by the Fox office to say that it wouldn't be necessary to continue Béatrice's English lessons, and I went back to collecting my retainer fee for no work and making my two phone calls a week.

Some months later, I was called by the Fox production office to coach some German actors who were dubbing their own voices in *The Blue Max*, already in the can. George Peppard and James Mason, both playing German pilots, posed no problem with their English, although one could ask why these Germans were speaking English (or American). For the smaller roles, I was told to see if I could get the German actors to be more comprehensible than when they shot the scenes.

A few days after we finished, I was called in again, and this time I met the legendary Darryl F. Zanuck. My mouth almost dropped when I saw him. He was the age of my father and had the same habit of keeping a cigar, lit or unlit, clamped in his mouth at all times. Like my father, his lips were thin, his cheeks slightly sunken. Both men, I thought, had a simian look to them. Zanuck shook hands with me without standing up. Christian Ferry and Edward Leggewie were both in the room when I got there.

"I think we need to redub this," Zanuck began, addressing the whole room. "Don't misunderstand," he said to me, "You did a good job. But now that I've run it, I'm not so sure we should have German actors doing the voices."

"But they're German in the film," Ferry reminded him.

"Yeah, I know. And maybe we'll use some of that here in Europe. But it's not right for America. Middle of the country, they've never been to Europe, they're not gonna understand these guys. We should revoice them with American actors." He said it with assurance and authority. I was surprised to sense a certain vulgarity in the man. Not because he was discarding a more European approach to a movie that took place entirely in Germany; in the end, he was probably right. It was more the manner in which he spoke, the directness, the lack of finesse, the pro-American stand, and the godawful power of the cigar.

"How American do you want them to be?" I asked.

"Well, you know, most of these guys are officers, so they should speak good English. The others don't have to speak so good." He laughed at what was perhaps, but only perhaps, a joke, revealing cigar-stained teeth. Again, it was my father.

Everyone just sort of nodded. I stared at him. Zanuck was a businessman, thinking about dollars and cents. That was how he'd saved the studio from disaster. I wondered where the maverick producer was who had startled all the studios of Hollywood almost two decades earlier when he'd made *Gentleman's Agreement* and *The Snake Pit*. Hollywood had considered the subject matter of both films anathema, but Zanuck took the daring plunge. And there was *All About Eve* and *The Grapes of Wrath*. The success of his films clearly showed that Zanuck had his finger on the pulse of the American audience.

"Well, that's it," he said and rose, and the meeting ended. There was no final handshake and he left the room.

Accordingly, I worked with American actors who revoiced the small German parts. Christian Ferry reported later that Zanuck was very satisfied with the result.

A few weeks after that, Fox set up another meeting with me, this time at the Hôtel George V to meet director William Wyler, who shortly was going to be directing *How to Steal a Million* with Audrey Hepburn and Peter O'Toole in Paris. Just off the Champs-Elysées and near the Arc de Triomphe, the Hôtel George V was one of a handful of elegant, expensive hotels that were top-of-the-line, and the one used most by rich American businessmen and film people. Wyler had a suite there, and it was producer Fred Kohlmar, himself something of a legend, who actually opened the door and admitted me. He gave me a warm smile and a handshake and said, "Bob Parrish speaks very highly of you." Then he put his arm around my shoulder and led me over to the sofa where Wyler was sitting with a couple of other men.

I knew I was meeting a famous director. This was the man who was responsible for many of the screen's classics. He'd won three best director Oscars, for *Mrs. Miniver, The Best Years of Our Lives*, and the remake of *Ben-Hur*. Blithely and fearlessly, I made my way toward him. The quality of not being in awe of this man or, indeed, of being star-struck with the actors I later worked with turned out to be a saving grace. I think I must always have gone into these meetings, or into a star's dressing room, with total calm, almost nonchalance. I never fawned or gushed with any of them, and I think this seeming indifference worked to my advantage. I was able just to sit and talk to them, and in most cases, it was what they wanted.

Though I hadn't seen any photographs of William Wyler, it was obvious which of the three men he was. The other two never took their eyes off him. He had thinning, silver-gray hair, a prominent nose, and huge ears that stood miles away from his head. I saw a beige hearing aid in one of his ears, and would learn later that he had sustained an explosion injury during World War II that affected his hearing. I was introduced to him and the other two gentlemen. I knew Wyler spoke some French, so I greeted him in French, even pronouncing Wyler as Veelair.

"Aren't you American?" he asked, puzzled, not rising.

"Yes," I replied, "but I know you were born in Alsace-Lorraine, so I thought you might like that greeting now that you're back in France."

"The kid's done his homework!" Wyler grinned to Kohlmar.

Kid again. At thirty-five. Oh, well.

"How did he get here again?" Wyler asked Kohlmar.

"Bob Parrish," Kohlmar reminded him.

"Oh, yes. That's right." Wyler turned back to me. "I left France when I was young and I've lived in the States ever since. So I only know a few phrases in French. But if you speak French, that's helpful. I'll be using French actors in some of the smaller roles." Then he asked me what I was doing in Paris, and I very briefly explained my studies in England, my work with the Department of the Army, and my producing the English-speaking Albee plays. Although I was extremely brief, supplying not more than a sentence or two on each of these phases, I felt I was losing him. He leaned back and said, "Fine, fine. All that's terrific. But how are you at handling drunks? I have Peter O'Toole, Hugh Griffith, and George C. Scott in this movie, and they're all drunks."

"Well," I said, "I just finished a movie with Broderick Crawford, James Robertson Justice, and Cliff Robertson."

"You got the job!" Wyler roared. And Kohlmar laughed behind him. Then Wyler stood up and said, "I think you'll do just fine." Kohlmar escorted me to the door. And though Cliff Robertson wasn't really a drunk, he'd established himself in *Up from the Beach* as not being the easiest actor in the world, and I figured that whatever problems he had, I'd throw him in with the drunks. And that's how I got my second feature film.

I called Bob Parrish in London to thank him for putting in a good word for me. Relations again, I thought. Parrish said that he'd had dinner with Wyler in London a few nights earlier and had brought my name up. Wyler had asked, "Why do I need a dialogue coach? We're shooting this in English."

"Because you can't *hear* the dialogue, Willie!" Parrish had shouted back. "Even your good ear is bad!"

Wyler took it good-naturedly. "Yeah, you're probably right."

The film, *How to Steal a Million*, was supposed to start shooting two weeks after my interview, but because of rewrites, Wyler and Kohlmar decided to push the start date off another three weeks. Suddenly, I had five weeks in front of me, and I was due to meet director Nicholas Ray, who was in Paris at the time and who was starting up another film, to be shot in Yugoslavia. My close friend, writer Marie-Gisèle Landes, had already set up a meeting with him before I had seen Wyler.

My French friends, all amateur *cinéastes*, were excited about my meeting Nicholas Ray, one of only three American directors who had worked with James Dean. *La Fureur de vivre*, the French translation for *Rebel without a Cause*, had been a huge artistic success as well as a commercial one in France. And the French measured the worth of a film, not as American filmmakers do by box office receipts, but by artistic value. *Les Cahiers du cinéma*, an intellectual journal that dealt only with the world's finest film artists, had devoted several articles to Nicholas Ray, whereas William Wyler, despite prolific work, Oscars, and popular American appeal, was almost totally ignored. For the French, *Rebel without a Cause* was a small *chef-d'oeuvre*. It also propelled Dean's career, and Nicholas Ray received an Oscar nomination for writing the 1955 screenplay. Other films of his that the French loved were *In a Lonely Place*, a quintessential film noir, and *Johnny Guitar*.

Nick Ray stood up and shook my hand as I came to the Île Saint-Louis café, where we had agreed to meet. My friend, Marie-Gisèle Landes, introduced us. Ray was tall and gaunt, with a marked, lined face and wild, flowing hair that was just starting to gray at the temples. When he smiled, his cheeks became accordion-pleated, the lines bespeaking a hundred indulgences. Alcohol, tobacco, gambling, womanizing, hashish were the ones I'd heard or later learned about. Rumors were that he'd been drinking heavily while shooting *King of Kings* in Spain. The other story that preceded him was the Hollywood one, that he'd come home one day to find his second wife, Gloria Grahame, in bed with his son from his first marriage. She later married the lad. Well, who wouldn't have deep lines in his face after that?

Both Nick and Marie-Gisèle were smoking Gitanes, Marie-Gisèle out of habit, Ray out of faddism. In those days, cafés, restaurants, and most public places were filled with the acrid odor of the black tobacco of Gitanes, Gauloises, and anything Turkish or Egyptian. Ray was staying in the apartment of his friend, writer James Jones. Marie-Gisèle also lived in the area. Of the two islands smack in the middle of the Seine, the Île Saint-Louis had its own particular environment, a village within a city, and "Île" inhabitants had a special bonding. Many of the more successful writers, artists, and actors lived in apartments there, eschewing, as they still do today, the impecunious artists and writers of the Left Bank. Several years earlier Marie-Gisèle Landes had written her first novel at twenty-one, finished it in the south of France, posted it in a manila envelope to the Gallimard publishing company in Paris— *comme ça*, without a phone call or inquiry letter, or knowing anyone on the inside—and the novel was published. It had great success, which frightened the hell out of her, to the point where she now spent all her time doing interviews of celebrities for French magazines, and her second novel would not come until twenty years after the first.

"Have you heard of *The Doctor and the Devils?*" Ray began.

"No," I replied.

"It's one of Dylan Thomas's rare scripts. It's Gothic, even a bit macabre, set in Victorian England. And full of dark poetry. I'd like you to take a look at it, tell me what you think." He slid a manuscript across the table to me.

Me tell Nicholas Ray what I thought?

"Who adapted it?" I asked.

"The latest revisions are mine."

I opened up the script. The front page had "First Draft by Nicholas Ray, based on the screenplay by Dylan Thomas," and to this day it's the one script I wish I'd held on to. I was fascinated by the material. A mixture of horror and beauty, fear and fantasy. So much more interesting than Harry Kurnitz's charming but commercially pat *How to Steal a Million* that awaited me. And Nick's script didn't actually end, not by commercial standards. The final line of Nick's, as best as I can now remember it, was a description of a shot of the lead character: "And we do, indeed, see him again, one last time, but perhaps not in the place or the time we expect." Now this is not at all the precise language in which movie scripts are written. Scene by scene, scripts must be technically detailed. So what did Ray have in mind? Would he jump from a linear story to an abstract image? Was the final sequence to be improvised? Or did he have something very specific in mind that he didn't want the actors and crew to know? Or didn't he himself know how he wanted to end the film?

I met with him the next day in the same café, this time without Marie-Gisèle. We discussed the screenplay. I can't tell you what I said, but whatever it was, I must have pushed all the right buttons. Nick closed his eyes as he listened to me, occasionally smiling, nodding, encouraging me to continue. When I had nothing more to say, he waited a long, long, endlessly long moment, then he opened his eyes and said, "Of course, I want you to do the picture with me. You understand it." Then he told me he was going to be shooting the film entirely in Yugoslavia. He wanted me to be the dialogue coach, but in the interim he had some meetings in Paris and wanted me to go along and translate for him. These meetings were mostly for financing and distribution, though the biggest financing was coming from the Yugoslavian government. And he wanted to get a French writer to tweak the script a bit. "I'd like you to set up some meetings with me with some French actors. I've got Laurence Harvey and Geraldine Chaplin in the two leads, but everything else is wide open. Then I'd like you to come to Yugoslavia with me and help me with the casting."

"As a dialogue coach? You mean, check their English?"

"As a casting director. Later on, you'll be the coach."

"But I don't know anything about Yugoslavian actors."

"We'll get a projection room for you at the studio in Belgrade and you'll look at film clips. Then you'll call in the actors you think are interesting and I'll talk to them." Ray told me he'd rather have me with my theater background than a formal casting director with pre-set ideas at that stage. Later, he said, the casting director could take over.

And that was how Nicholas Ray worked. Gut reaction. He'd gotten a good feeling from me, and was giving me a wide range of things to do. It was heady, it was exciting, it was what I imagined creativity to be all about. Already Wyler seemed stodgy and archaic. Because of my commitment to Fox for the Wyler film, I told Nick I couldn't promise him more than a month's work. That was fine. Many movies, he said, were in rewrite so long that you could do a whole other movie first.

The next month was one of the most fascinating of my life. I was with Nick almost daily, with night and day bleeding into each other. He never seemed to sleep, this man. Not conventionally. He would work on well into the night, hold long, late interviews with French writers to whom he would pose the question, "What is this film about?"

Then the writer would answer by narrating the incidents in the screen-play, while Nick closed his eyes and listened as he had done with me. Then there would be an interminable silence during which nothing happened and we were sure he'd fallen asleep. Finally he would open his eyes and through his drifting Gitanes smoke say, "No, no, not the plot. I know the plot. What is this *about?*"

During the day there were meetings with French producers and dis-tributors, all of them impressed with him, but no one offering any con-crete deal. "It's my time," Nick would say to me, alone. "It's my time to hit it again. I'm due. One of these guys has to bite!"

In our spare moments, I presented wonderful French actors to him. The great Jean Vilar of the Théâtre National Populaire, singer-actor Philippe Clay, and a young, boyish actor by the name of Michel Gon-zales who had played the brother in the French stage version of *The Miracle Worker*, and who was the only French actor I knew in 1965 who was employing Lee Strasberg's "method." Gonzales remained in a behind-closed-doors tête-à-tête with Ray for over an hour, one evening at the Hôtel Prince de Galles, where Nick had taken a suite. When they emerged, Michel's baby face was flushed as he moved to the phone to call his agent. Ray had just offered him the role of the ju-venile, Billy, in the movie and said he would build the part. He pulled me aside. "Second time in my life that's happened," he confided. "I don't need to do a test on him. He's all feeling. The only other time I've encountered that was with Dean. All I had to do was talk to him and I knew. Same thing here."

A few days later, we left for Belgrade. I settled in at the studio and be-gan to look at film clips of Yugoslavian movies. I called in many actors and interviewed them. Only two remain in my mind today. Though they were both in their twenties then, they subsequently became na-tional treasures over the ensuing years. Boris Dvornik and Milena Dravić were the two I fell I love with. They were both beautiful, ac-complished, and showed great sensitivity in their performances. They seemed amazed that I, an American, would even know who they were. They sat with me quietly, partly from timidity, partly from language bar-rier, but I sensed the artist in both of them. Later, I set up meetings for them with Nick, who said he might be able to use them both in small roles. I began to feel I was beginning to help him move forward.

One night we went to the theater and saw *Tango*, a remarkable play written by Polish writer Slawomir Mrozek. Mrozek had fled the communists of his native country and taken up residence in Italy. This was the first of many of his plays to be produced throughout Europe and eventually in the United States. Though neither Nick nor I understood a word of Serbo-Croatian, we laughed uproariously at the latter-day and much darker *You Can't Take It with You*. Later, in a restaurant, we sat drinking beer and eating *raznjici*, small pork sausages cooked with onions and then served with freshly chopped onions on top of them, when suddenly Nick revealed the secret of his insight into actors. "When I was doing theater in New York years ago, I did some acting," he said. "Not because I ever wanted to be an actor. I always wanted to be a director. But I did it because I wanted to have insight later into the actor's problems. Elia Kazan and I both did that."

"I knew about Kazan," I replied. "With the Group Theatre. His name is in the original cast list of *Golden Boy*. He played the fight manager, Fuselli."

Nick smiled, pleased that I knew that. "Have you ever thought about writing?" he asked abruptly. The question was almost a non sequitur.

"Maybe, one day," I replied.

"You should write. Anything. Plays, for sure. But you should definitely write."

I don't know how he arrived at that from my mentioning Kazan's acting in the Group Theatre, but those were the kinds of little connections his rapid mind was always making. Lightning associations. He would be the first of three people, all fairly prestigious, to encourage me to write. The second was Audrey Hepburn, just months later, and the third was writer Lawrence Durrell, after I moved to Los Angeles. After Durrell, I stopped fighting it; apparently the gods knew better than I did.

A telephone call from Paris came through for me at my hotel and the Fox office informed me that *How to Steal a Million* had been "pushed" again, because of rewrites. A delay of yet another week. Nick was delighted that I could spend more time with him, and then posed the question I had been dreading. "Are you sure you want to do that picture?" he asked.

Sure? No, I wasn't sure. I wanted to stay and work with the man who never slept. What fascinated me about Ray was how his methods, his instincts, came so much closer to the theater world I knew than to film, which I was only just learning. This special craziness of Ray's was one of the essential differences between him and Wyler. In any case, a week later and with a heavy heart, I did return to Paris, my decision being to stay with the Wyler film. I had, *après tout*, made a commitment.

In a twist of fate, the film I wasn't interested in got made and the film I was interested in didn't. We were deep into filming *How to Steal a Million* at the Studios de Boulogne when I heard that *The Doctor and the Devils* had fallen apart. It was reported that Laurence Harvey, Geraldine Chaplin, Italian actor Raf Vallone, and young Michel Gonzales were on the set in Zagreb the first day of scheduled filming, and Nick was in New York, trying to raise the money that the Yugoslavian government had failed to produce in the allotted time. Nick had postponed the start of the film several times, and it was a miracle he'd been able to hold onto his actors. Finally, from New York, he told the assistant director, Lou Brandt, "You start!" which was an insane order, since actors must work with the director of the picture. Nick continued pursuing money in New York, and quickly earned the label of "madman" among the actors and crew. Discouraged by his antics and more postponements, they eventually all went home. Nick told me much later that after several more days he succeeded in getting the money in place, but by then it was too late. Nick was a fine director and a fine writer, and a fascinating man with rare vision. But he was no businessman, and his "time to hit it again" didn't happen that time around. Though I didn't know it, his life was sliding downward, and he was earning the reputation of being erratic, desperate, even deranged. As it turned out, he would never make another major motion picture. The fascinating Nicholas Ray script I read is probably lost to the world now, although twenty years later, in 1985, another version of *The Doctor and the Devils* was brought to the screen with a different screenplay and with Mel Brooks producing. Though it had a stellar English cast, Dylan Thomas's poetry was missing and there was nothing particularly magical in the writing. Almost no one saw the movie at the time. I found it recently in my local video store in the horror section.

CHAPTER FOUR

~

The First Lady

I was crossing rue de Silly (pronounced *see-yee*), going from one half of the Studios de Boulogne to the other, when I saw William Wyler standing talking to a thin, young lady in pedal pushers. She wore no makeup, and my first thought was that she was some new film technician. I was about to pass them both when Wyler called me. I stopped and he introduced me to Audrey Hepburn. It took me several moments for the realization to set in, for the familiar and beautiful face on the screen was not the one I was looking at. There were no long lashes, accented eyebrows, or elegant hairdos. There were small lines around her eyes, and she looked a little older than I expected.

As we spoke, she smiled that generous smile of hers that I would subsequently come to know as one of the warmest in the world. I realized there was actually great beauty in her face, the beauty that some women have when you see them first thing in the morning without makeup. Her features were fine and classic; they just hadn't been accentuated for the camera, the way I knew them. I felt like a fool for not recognizing her instantly. That distinctive, aristocratic long line of a neck should have told me right away. She said she was delighted that I was on the film, and suggested that the best time to rehearse would be after her makeup and hair were done each morning. Then, she said, we could either work in her dressing room, or in her trailer on the stage, or just sitting on the set.

"I'm usually there before the director," she said and threw an impish look at Wyler.

"You should be," was his answer. She tilted her head back in a laugh, showing a straight, shining line of perfect teeth. It was obvious that both Audrey and Wyler had, over the years, established a relationship that was relaxed within the work they were doing. Under his tutelage, she had garnered a best actress Oscar in 1953 for *Roman Holiday*, her first Hollywood film. There seemed to be mutual respect between them, although in the course of shooting *How to Steal a Million*, there would be a few deceptions for Audrey. Only her immense patience with him prevented these deceptions from becoming major incidents.

We proceeded as Audrey had requested. She had a three-hour preparation period for hair and makeup. This was sometimes followed by wardrobe, so that she was totally ready to go on the stroke of twelve noon, which was the normal call time. She would sit in her chair on the set and I would sit with her, running lines, before any of the technicians arrived and before Wyler appeared. It was a professionalism on her part that I would see with very few other actors over the years. Only the great French actor, Jean Gabin, had the same approach: to be ready before anyone else.

12 noon until 7:30 P.M. were normal French studio hours (I think they still are), with no official break for lunch. Most technicians arrived at eleven to have an early lunch that would carry them through the day. Others ate during the shoot if they weren't needed on the set, which was often, because cinematographer Charles Lang always took a long time to light the set. He actually never really finished lighting the set, but after two hours, assistant director Paul Feyder, one of Françoise Rosay's sons, would gently needle him and say, "Are we ready, Charlie? I'd like to call in Wyler and the actors."

"Yeah, I guess so," Lang would reply. And he'd go on fine-tuning his lighting during rehearsals and between takes. He'd remind Audrey to keep her chin up, because his lighting would mask any lines under her eyes that way. Between Lang and Alberto de Rossi, Audrey's Italian makeup man, Audrey looked stunning. But Lang never really finished lighting a set. He just stopped when Wyler stopped, sometimes on the twentieth take.

Why a 12:00 to 7:30 shooting schedule? This was traditional for the French. When the French film industry began to develop, there were no movie actors per se, so theater actors had to be drawn upon. And they worked in the theater at night, where the curtain rang up at nine o'clock. Performances ended around midnight, then the actors would sup late in a bistro, usually in the central marketplace in the heart of Paris, and go to bed at two in the morning. Then they'd arrive at the movie studio the next day at 11:00, ready for makeup and wardrobe, and the filming would begin at noon.

There was another reason for these hours: the French themselves. Unlike Americans, the French have never sacrificed their quality of living outside the movie business because of their work. Wyler would soon enough discover this, much to his surprise and dismay. On the first day of filming, which involved an auction scene, Wyler shot until 9:30 at night and the second day until 10:00. On the third day, at a little before 7 P.M., he started to set up a shot that everyone on the crew knew would go on till 10 P.M. again. Three nights in a row to work extra hours was too much for the French. Paul Joly, the French production manager, and Bill Kaplan, the American production supervisor, approached Wyler while assistant director Paul Feyder, sensing a showdown, sent for producer Fred Kohlmar. They all congregated in a corner of the stage.

"Monsieur Vee-lair," Joly began, pronouncing the director's name as I had when I first met him at the hotel, "we didn't want to bother you the first day of filming, when you went two hours over schedule. And we didn't want to bother you the second day, when you shot two and a half hours over schedule. But now you are preparing a shot that will take us over schedule again by two or three hours."

"Yeah, so?" asked Wyler.

"You cannot do that. By French law."

"Why not? If we go past 7:30, we'll pay the overtime."

"No, the crew will decide if we go beyond 7:30. They will vote and decide. That is also French law." Paul Feyder took over, explaining tactfully that by seven in the evening Wyler had to let the production manager know if he wanted to shoot overtime, and if so, how much overtime. Joly would inform the crew and they would vote on it. And by 7:15 Wyler would know what their answer was.

"But they're getting overtime!" Wyler's voice was rising.

"That's not always important, Monsieur Vee-lair," Joly retorted. "They want to go home and spend time with their families, or go out with friends. *That* is important."

Wyler was apoplectic, his face flushed. He called Charlie Lang over to find out how long it would take to light the new setup, then told Joly he wanted to shoot until nine o'clock. Joly very quickly made the rounds of various department heads on the set. I voted with the French crew, because I was being paid in French francs, like any other locally hired person. We voted to work until 9 P.M., but the next two nights of that week, when Wyler asked for overtime, the crew refused. Enough, after all, was enough. By the end of the first week, Wyler was unhappy, if not dyspeptic. This wasn't the way movies were made in Hollywood, where you could shoot as many hours as you wanted, and only the director and producer decided.

"After all," shrugged Joly, "this is why we fought the revolution in 1789."

Audrey added, "You can't blame them, Willie. They want to have a good dinner and a good bottle of wine. Not all of life is work."

Wyler grumbled and moved away. But a few of the crew members had overheard Audrey's reply, and they passed the word around quickly. It was an early insight into her humanity, a humanity that would surface many more times on the film, and eventually swell up a few years later as she tackled her task with UNICEF and worked with children of poverty-stricken nations, a humanity that never forgot the common man. Ironically, Audrey herself hadn't complained about the long hours, even though her complicated makeup and hair schedule required her to be at the studio three hours before the rest of the crew, or that her hours were the longest of anyone's.

I met Peter O'Toole on the stairs of the studio. He was descending with his entourage, which consisted of his makeup man, his coiffeur, and his somewhat seedy assistant cum body guard, Peter Perkins. They had all just been examining the dressing room suite O'Toole was assigned to. "I was on my way up to meet you," I said.

"And you are?" he asked on a slightly theatrical tone, midstairs, face to face with me.

"Frawley Becker. I'm the dialogue coach."

"A very essential man," he declaimed. "Are you an actor?"

"No."

"Then we shall get along famously." And he continued down the stairs with the entourage in his wake. I quickly followed.

"When would you like to rehearse, Mr. O'Toole?"

He stopped on a dime, turned to me and raised his finger like a class instructor. "Peter. It is always Peter," he corrected. Then he giggled. "Mr. O'Toole is some other family member. Come to me tomorrow during makeup. We can rehearse then." And he turned a second time and sailed away. I wondered if he was still playing Lawrence of Arabia.

As it turned out, he *was* acting for me. When I got to know him better, I saw that his everyday speech did not always consist of the theatrical tones he'd used when we met. His origins were working class, and there were often traces of that in his speech, though I'm not sure now he wasn't exaggerating them for fun. When he rehearsed, the sounds were pure, trained, with a classic ring. In *The Night of the Generals*, which I would do next with him, there were moments where he brilliantly used his ability to declaim to give his Nazi character both authority and pomposity. It was amazing over the next nine months and both films to see him slip in and out of these two manners of speaking, the low and the high, almost as if he had a dybbuk inside him, and both he and the dybbuk each had a voice. And then there was that giggle. He seemed to be amused at so many situations around him, at the whole movie business, perhaps.

Both Audrey and Peter were at the height of their careers when I met them. The year before, Audrey had done *My Fair Lady* and Peter *Becket*. The year before that, Peter had startled the world as Lawrence. Both performers had become major stars overnight on a first film, and though he was Irish and she Belgian-born of English and Dutch parents, Hollywood would claim them both. As I came to know them, I saw also the humanity that united them, his from his roots in the working class, hers from aristocracy, her mother being a Dutch baroness. It is only those trapped in the middle who are caught shy of humanity. She was a water nymph, a gamine, a princess; he was the common man who became the crowned king. Their chemistry together was not so far removed from that special chemistry ignited by highbrow Katharine Hepburn and everyman Spencer Tracy, and it's a pity Audrey and Peter were never reunited in another film.

They had something else in common, as they discovered in one of their conversations on the set. Something even the movie trivia maniacs in years to come would not know.

"Willie!" cried Audrey to Wyler one day, "This isn't Peter's and my first film together!" And O'Toole, delighted with their newly discovered secret, giggled his giggle.

"We were both in *The Lavender Hill Mob!*"

"Audrey had one line and I was an extra!" added Peter.

"You've both come a long way," answered Wyler, then added, "I think." They guffawed.

The Lavender Hill Mob was a 1951 Ealing comedy. A very young Audrey Hepburn has one line with Alec Guinness in the opening scene, but she is definitely noticeable. Peter is another matter, however. You have to do a real "Where's Waldo?" to find him. I think you see him as an English policeman, one of the two who jump in the river to save Guinness. He's in the background later in the police station, with wet hair and a towel as Guinness is questioned. In a doubly ironic turn, Guinness would come to be a supporting actor to O'Toole a decade later in *Lawrence of Arabia*, and Stanley Holloway, Guinness' costar in *The Lavender Hill Mob*, would come to be a supporting actor to Hepburn in *My Fair Lady*.

Peter O'Toole's reputation for drinking, as stated by Wyler and others, wasn't entirely deserved. During the filming of *How to Steal a Million*, I never saw him under the influence of alcohol. As we neared the end of the day, he often opened a bottle of champagne on the set at 7 P.M. and sat sipping a glass of foamy bubbles waiting for the last shot that involved him. It was rarely more than a glass, and he invariably shared the champagne, often Dom Pérignon, with one of his entourage. His hours away from the set were quite another matter. He was a frequent visitor to the Paris night spots, particularly Chez Castel, the most fashionable *boîte* on the Left Bank, and his name sometimes appeared in the French press, who reported him as being in drunken disturbances there. But whatever he did at night never seemed to affect his performance during the day. The lines around his eyes sometimes gave him away, and Audrey once remarked to me, as Peter appeared on the set, all smiles and removing the dark glasses he frequently wore, "What *does* he do with his nights?" Rehearsing with Peter in his dressing room while his makeup was being applied, and before any of the film crew had any contact with him, I saw the antidote of tomato juice, raw egg yolks, and Worcestershire sauce being swizzled down each morning after. Then, bright-eyed and declaiming in his theatrical—nay, Shakespearean—voice, he would stride magnificently to the set.

"I give him two, three more years. Five at the most," his assistant, Peter Perkins, confided in me at the Studios de Boulogne bar where we'd bumped into each other over coffee. The coarse, often vulgar, Perkins was an odd pairing to O'Toole, and everyone on the French crew wondered what affinities the two men had. The theory ran that O'Toole owed him a huge favor and had given him a cushy job as a nebulously defined protector. I saw him more as a parasite or an albatross around Peter's neck. Perkins was a large man with a large head full of thick features. His clothes were almost always wrinkled, his shoes almost always suede. He had Soho written all over him. I hadn't liked what he'd just said about Peter, because he always accompanied the actor to the night spots and, as I later learned, aided and abetted his drinking. An enabler, a codependent we would say decades later; a cohort in crime, this vulgar man. "It'll do him in, his drinking," Perkins continued mercilessly. "He'll lose his looks. It'll show up on the screen, in his face. Like I said, three to five years. And that gives me just a few years, too, to make my fortune." He smiled and showed me his bad working-class English teeth. I don't think I disliked anyone as intensely as I did him at that moment. It was a terrible prognostication, one that would eventually, and alas, have some truth in it. Though Peter O'Toole would, indeed, lose his handsome looks too early in life and show marked dissipation in his face, he would move on in later years to some extraordinarily eccentric character roles in *The Ruling Class*, *The Stunt Man*, and *My Favorite Year*, all of which yielded Oscar nominations. He and Richard Burton tie the record as the actors most nominated but never receiving the best actor Oscar. Seven nominations in all for each of them. In 2002, Peter would finally receive a special Academy Award for lifetime achievement.

I was told by the assistant director that George C. Scott had arrived and was in his trailer at the end of the stage. I went to meet him to work out a rehearsal schedule. I knocked on the door and the resonant, firm voice behind it told me to come in. I did, and I discovered that he was alone, which in itself was unusual, for a movie star almost always has someone with him—a makeup or hair artist, a secretary, a production assistant. I introduced myself, shook hands with Scott, and sat down to discuss a schedule. He stared at me a long moment, then said, "I've never worked with a dialogue coach before."

Was there resentment? Or defensiveness? Was he testing me? He was a known New York theater actor, and I felt the question might have contained, "Why do you think I need a dialogue coach?" I laughed, trying to ease the moment, and told him that I was working with Audrey and Peter. Then, remembering O'Toole's comment, I added, "I'm not an actor, so I won't suggest a reading. But I can run lines with you, if you want."

"Did the production send you?"

"The production? No."

"Did Wyler send you? Or Kohlmar?" There was definite irritation in his voice now.

"No. They hired me, of course, but no. I knew you were coming in today, so I just came over."

"Do you know how long I've been hanging around? A month."

"There are worse places to be than Paris, aren't there?"

"Paris is great, that's not the point." Then he said that Wyler had told him when he arrived that they had rewrites to do. After a few days they sent him back to New York. A few weeks after that, he was brought back. "I haven't seen anyone since the first time. No news, no explanations. Last night, I got a call from the production office that they wanted me here today. What kind of treatment is that? I need to talk to Wyler and Kohlmar."

There was a note to this conversation that was reminiscent of the one I'd had with Oskar Werner on *Up from the Beach* when he said he had to talk to Bob Parrish. I smelled trouble. "I'll let the 1st A.D. know," I said noncommittally. Scott grunted approval. There was really nothing further to say, and I could have just left, but somewhere I sensed that the guy felt alone and neglected and was chafing from the big Hollywood mechanism I was just beginning to see in operation. "I saw you on the stage," I blurted out. "In New York."

"In what?"

"*Desire under the Elms*." He stared at me passively. "At Circle in the Square. José Quintero's production. With you and Colleen Dewhurst and Rip Torn. It was pretty electrifying, and God knows O'Neill isn't easy to do!" I had seen the show only a couple of years earlier when I was in New York with Colette de Jouvenel and Paola de Rohan-Chabot, when we were interviewing actors and I was meeting with Edward Albee. Scott finally managed a curled lip that perhaps in a close-up would have passed for a smile.

"Thank you," he said simply. "I don't think these people ever heard of O'Neill." It was a dig at Wyler and Kohlmar and probably much of Hollywood as well. Seeing him on the stage, I knew Scott was a superb actor. He'd been nominated for best supporting roles in *Anatomy of a Murder* and in *The Hustler*. (Unbelievably, he was not nominated for *Dr. Strangelove* in 1964.) There was something about everything he did that had a grandiose quality, larger than life, that would eventually lead him to *Patton* and the main Oscar five years later. But in 1965 he was still being relegated to supporting roles. And for this one, he was obviously festering from neglect.

"Look," he said, "none of this is your fault. You seem okay, the only one I've met so far who is. But they brought me here too early and then never let me know what was going on. And that wasn't right, you know what I mean?" He stood up, signaling that our meeting was over. "See if you can find me the A.D., will you?" I said I would and made my way to the door. "And thanks," he added, a fillip to his annoyance. "Thanks for your comments."

What happened the rest of the afternoon and the next day I learned only in pieces through Paul Feyder, the 1st assistant director. Almost immediately after I left, Scott saw him and said he wasn't feeling well. He took his driver and car and went back to his hotel. Since I had detected no alcohol on him in his trailer, I had no idea how "sick" he was. The following morning, with the same scene of Scott's scheduled, he didn't show up and instead we shot with Audrey and Hugh Griffith. Paul Feyder told me that when Scott telephoned the studio that morning to say he was still sick, Kohlmar and Wyler, in disbelief, sent a doctor to the hotel to examine him. Apparently, Scott refused to see him, at which point Wyler and Kohlmar told him he was off the film. I'm sure Scott found that very wry, since in all the time he'd been waiting and ignored, he probably felt he'd never really been *on* the film. Later in the afternoon I heard he was being replaced by Eli Wallach, who would be arriving from New York in two days. My instincts had been correct when I'd remembered Oskar Werner in talking to Scott. Two films now, and in each a brilliant actor was replaced, one because the producer had remained intransigent, the other because the director and producer hadn't treated him with respect. Was this the way with all Hollywood movies, I wondered? The guillotine at any time? With a heavy hand always on the lever? And talented stars expendable?

Wallach arrived like a West Indies hurricane. We were locked in a closed set—Wyler, Charlie Lang, Audrey and Eli, the editor, the script girl, the assistant director, and I. The rest of the crew was outside in the café eating sandwiches and drinking *vin blanc sec*. The A.D. and I had already been through the process several times of watching Wyler block out a new scene. The process was always long and laborious, often taking an hour and a half to complete. Whatever talent Wyler had, it didn't seem to be in an overview. It wasn't a case of allowing the actors to ad lib movement, which might have been justifiable. He simply never knew what to do. The actors would mill about, try different movements and pieces of business, but it was all hit and miss, without direction. This had been the case with the first scenes shot with Audrey and Peter and Audrey and Griffith, but the spaces we had worked in were not terribly large. Now Audrey was in the great, open living room and hallway entrance of an elegant Paris house, so a choreography was called upon to navigate the players around the set. After a half-hour of aimlessness, Hurricane Eli set in. He suddenly said, "Willie, suppose Audrey is standing here, trying to avoid me!" And he placed her near a column. "And I've just come in, and I drop my bag on this hallway chair and I sit on the sofa over here! I see her in the mirror and I move for her, only I bump right into the mirror!" He dashed to the full-length mirror, bumped into it, then dashed to Audrey just as she was trying to slip out of the house, unseen. "We say the lines fast, she checks her watch, and then she's out!" The whole thing was a mad rush and both Wyler and Audrey were laughing. It was obvious that the scene, dead on its feet the first half hour, suddenly became alive. Wallach blocked it again, and Wyler, Lang, and editor Bob Swink picked an angle for the master shot. Then the set was opened and the lighting guys began to rig their lights and the grips began to lay dolly track and the actors went back to their dressing rooms.

I joined Eli in his dressing room. I told him how much I liked what he'd just done. "Well, someone had to block it out," he replied. "Willie wasn't doing anything."

"It's been that way all along," I said.

"I'm used to the theater. Where you block out everything first."

"So am I." I told him how sorry I was that I wasn't in New York when he had done Tennessee Williams' *Camino Real*, but that I had seen him earlier in Anouilh's *Mademoiselle Colombe* with Julie Harris and Edna Best in Philadelphia.

"God, no one saw that!" he said, and went on with great animation to talk about both productions. I realized that I had made points with him as I had with Scott in identifying his stage work. Over the years, I've noticed how the actors who hail from the theater are all truly delighted when you talk about that part of their careers.

Years later, I walked into an elevator in Century City where there was just one person: Richard Dreyfuss. I smiled and said, "I've enjoyed your work."

"Oh? What have you seen?"

"*The Tenth Man, The Normal Heart, Three Hotels.*" I replied, naming the three times I'd seen him on the legitimate stage.

"Don't you go to the movies?" he quipped, and exited. But I knew he was pleased that I'd identified his serious work.

Incidents with Audrey began to abound. Incidents of that great humanity of hers that I'd noticed earlier. The first was on the set with Hugh Griffith, who had won the best supporting Oscar for *Ben-Hur* and shamelessly stolen scenes in *Tom Jones*. Both on screen and off, the man was a genius at rolling his eyes crazily and erupting into sudden spurts of anger. There was a note of unpredictability, even madness, in every role he created. He possessed a huge mustache and beard that were his trademark and that he was constantly fingering. He had a tendency to mumble, sputter, stammer, and growl his lines unintelligibly, often into these hirsute bushes of his. I was constantly by his side, correcting him, trying to clarify his diction, and he treated me like a fly on soup, waving me off with a dismissive hand and roaring vocal scales that had no meaning whatsoever. At first I thought these outbursts were some of his native Welsh until I realized he was spouting gibberish. He also frequently had a sniff of whiskey on him, so his garbled words were compounded by slur. Sometimes he would start moaning when he saw me approaching him with the open script in my hand. That is exactly what happened during a camera rehearsal with Audrey and him. He'd just made a garble of his lines and I started to approach him with the script.

"No, no!" he cried. "Not again! Go away! Go away!"

"Fine," I answered casually. "If that's what you want." And I made an about-face to my spot with the script girl, just behind the director.

"He's such an annoyance!" I heard Griffith say to Audrey.

"Well, you know, Hugh, it's not easy, doing what he's doing, correcting actors. It's not easy at all."

Griffith mumbled into his beard and I thought suddenly that I'd had the best defense attorney on the planet.

Another time, standing and conversing with her on the set before filming began, I noticed Wyler and another man make their way toward us. Wyler had a Hollywood attitude that dictated he not always acknowledge the crew members who worked under him. Only when he needed them for something specific would he address the script girl or the sound man or the prop man or me. Other times, we were all totally ignored. For a French crew that felt it was an insult to be spoken to without having first been wished a good morning, Wyler's attitude was tantamount to personal injury. This, added to his cavalier manner of filming overtime the first few days without taking the crew into consideration, made him unpopular, even disliked. Now Wyler was approaching Audrey and me with a gentleman who turned out to be a 20th Century Fox studio executive visiting the set. Wyler introduced him to Audrey, totally ignoring me, and proceeded to tell Audrey that it would be good if she could spend a few minutes with the executive later, between shots. Somewhere in the middle of Wyler's second line, she interrupted him.

"And *this*," she said with uncustomary loudness and a gesture towards me, "is Mr. Becker!"

There was a moment of embarrassed silence and the executive and I shook hands and said hello. Wyler made no apology, and a second later, continued what he was saying. Then we all broke up, Wyler and the studio man moving toward the camera and Audrey and I heading for her trailer. "Thank you," I said.

"I'm sorry that happened," she replied and leaned in and kissed me on the cheek. It was a good thing she walked into her trailer then, because I think my eyes were moist.

There was another incident on the set. We were rehearsing a scene where Audrey and Peter approach the statue of Venus that her grandfather had forged and that is thought to be by Cellini. She stands next to a woman, one of the museum visitors, to look at the statue and the invisible rays that make up the security system surrounding the statue. After the first rehearsal, Audrey walked a few feet away, where Grazia and Alberto de Rossi freshened up her hair and makeup. She commented to them that the French woman who was standing next to her in rehearsal probably hadn't bathed that day, because her body odor was strong. She said it in a matter-of-fact manner, not as a complaint. But Paul Feyder overheard her and changed the woman with another extra who, in the next rehearsal, was then standing next to Audrey. Audrey, of course, noticed the change and completed the rehearsal. Then she called Feyder over to her.

"What happened to that other woman who was next to me in the last rehearsal?"

"Well, Audrey," replied Feyder, "I overheard your remark about her. I knew she was offending you, so I changed her."

"She wasn't offending me. There are a lot of people in Paris who still don't have bathtubs and showers. She's probably one of them. If she's on camera next to me, she'll get a bump in her salary, and I'm sure she can use it. Please put her back."

"But—" Paul began.

"I am not offended. Please put her back."

Paul Feyder complied and the unwashed woman was placed in her original position. It took eight or ten takes to get the scene right, and Audrey performed next to her as if there were absolutely nothing out of the ordinary.

A tragedy occurred about halfway through the movie. Charles Boyer was doing a special guest appearance, and we'd already shot one of his scenes. But then, while at his hotel, he learned that his son had committed suicide in Hollywood. Boyer immediately flew back for the funeral. Our shooting schedule was changed again (it had changed when Wallach replaced Scott), and a week later Boyer returned to Paris. He was needed for a second scene that we would get to midafternoon.

Audrey walked up to me on the set around noon and asked, "What do you think I should say to Charles when I see him? (She pronounced his name the correct French way as "Sharl.") Should I tell him what a tragedy I think it was? Or is it better not to say anything?"

I was dumbfounded. Audrey Hepburn asking *me* what to say! "No," I replied, "I don't think you should do either. "He already knows what a tragedy it is. And you shouldn't ignore it, as if it didn't happen. I think you should keep it simple. Just go up to him and take his hand, or hug him, and say, 'I'm sorry.' Just that, nothing more. Then that will give him the opportunity to talk further, if that's what he wants to do."

"That's good advice," she said.

The next day Audrey came up to me again and thanked me. The moment with Boyer, she said, had been exactly right. I asked her why she had come to me for advice.

"Well," she said on a little laugh, "I certainly wouldn't have asked Willie! *He* wouldn't have known!" It was at this moment that I felt I wasn't just Audrey Hepburn's dialogue coach. I had become her friend. She started to walk away, then stopped. "You know, you should be writing."

"Why do you say that?"

"Just something I feel. You know people."

"Funny. A few months ago Nicholas Ray said I should be writing, too."

"Well, you see! I'm in good company!" And she went on her way, leaving me with a big question mark about my life.

In the mornings, after we'd rehearse, she'd sit in her chair on the set, waiting to be called. It was then that she'd dictate answers to fan letters to her secretary. And I'd watch her later as she personally signed every letter she dictated. I commented on that to her one day, because I knew that letters to fans are often signed by staff persons. "No," said Audrey, "I've always signed every letter personally that has my name on it. It's the least I can do for the fans who have taken the time to write to me. When I have extra time, I actually write out a thank-you note in longhand."

"That's pretty remarkable, " I said.

"No," she replied, "it isn't. I'm where I am today because of these fans."

And she treated the few who got to visit the set with the same respect. A group of four women were brought in one day by the film's publicist, and they spent ten minutes talking to Audrey. I think they represented some small publications. One woman, an American with a Hispanic accent, told her how much she'd loved Audrey's performance in *The Nun's Story*, for which Audrey had received a best actress nomination in 1959. Audrey thanked her in Spanish and for the next several minutes the two women spoke to each other in that language. This was nothing new for Audrey Hepburn. She spoke excellent French with the crew, and Italian with her makeup man and hairdresser. She'd even gotten her five-year-old son, Sean, to speak in French, Italian, and English. Another day, I walked by her chair, where several men were interviewing her. I heard her speaking a strange language, so I retraced my steps to pass behind her chair again. And then again. Until I recognized that she was speaking her childhood Dutch! That made five languages, by my count. And each time she was gracious to the people with whom she was conversing. I never saw condescension, "attitude," or ego, all of which became ubiquitous when I started working later in Hollywood with people who barely spoke one language. She treated every film technician, every journalist, every fellow actor the same way, with deference and respect.

"The crew is always a little nervous the first few days of shooting a movie," she told me. "They don't know yet if they can relax or joke with the actors, or how to treat them. But everyone forgets that *we* go through the same thing. I always wonder if the crew will like *me*, so the first two days I'm as much on edge as they are!" Then she laughed, throwing her head back and showing that beautiful line of even teeth. "Crazy, isn't it?" she said, her eyes fairly dancing, "We're all so concerned with the impression we make on each other."

The only time she was troubled was after a visit from her husband, Mel Ferrer. Theirs had been a golden beginning, and when they appeared together on Broadway in *Ondine* in 1954, the New York press spoke of a new theater couple, to take their place with Lunt and Fontanne, Olivier and Leigh, Cronyn and Tandy. Unfortunately, the careers of Hepburn and Ferrer did not advance at the same pace. There was nothing exceptional to Ferrer's abilities, his box office appeal waned, and Audrey became a superstar. The two of them would sit in a corner of the set or in her trailer during his short visits of a day or two. He'd leave, and Audrey would be engulfed for another day in the moodiness of their meeting. (Though no one knew it, their marriage was beginning to unravel.) Then, the moment passed and Audrey would be back to her gracious self, laughing and joking with the crew, the actors, and with Wyler.

"Willie!" she called to him one day, in the middle of rehearsing with me. "Do you know that I called you 'Mr. Wyler' for the whole first two movies I made with you?"

"Why'd you stop?" he answered like a shot. And she threw her head back on that glistening white laugh of hers.

When she laughed, there was no movie star in her, only someone completely disarmed, enjoying herself. After a take that Wyler wanted to print, I called his attention to the fact that in a rapid-fire line Audrey had referred to Eli Wallach's character as "David Leland" instead of "Davis Leland." Wyler stared at me. He hadn't heard it. Nor had the sound man, nor the A.D., nor the continuity girl. Even Audrey looked dubious. I stuck to my guns. "She said David," I repeated. Wyler asked the sound man to replay the take and there was total silence on the stage as everyone listened. There it was: David Leland.

Audrey turned to Wyler and said, "I'll dub the 'd'!" Then she delivered herself to the absurdity of the moment and laughed her infectious laugh again.

My nemesis, Hugh Griffith, completed his portion of the filming. But my worries were not over. He still had to dub certain lines in the sound studio for clarity. Some of his lines had been muttered so unclearly that they were unintelligible, and the sound studio is the place where you can correct this. Normally. In Griffith's case, it was nigh on to impossible. The actor who never was able to repeat a performance or hit his floor mark from one take to another found the French "looping" system baffling and insurmountable. It's actually an impeccable system. A specialized technician writes words on a moving band that passes under a small piece of a scene. Since the "loop" is circular, involving image and written band together, you can run it over and over. The words move from right to left and cross a bar which is the precise moment that word has to be spoken by the actor. Sometimes the word is stretttc- cchhhed out, so it must be said that way, at that exact length, to match the mouth on the screen. It was all too technical, too precise, for Griffith. He failed at each essay, growing more and more annoyed, finally bellowing in frustration that he wanted to leave. The editor told him to "loop" as best he could, and the editor would match the words to the mouth, even if it meant cutting each single word and splicing it side by side with the next word. It would entail hours more work for him, but there was no other solution.

While the projectionist was changing loops, Griffith paced the studio, mumbling wildly to himself. Welsh, I thought. Somewhere I thought I heard him say, "Llareggub Hill," from a line in *Under Milk Wood*. I commented on it, and he began to declaim madly to me, the walls, and the ghost of Dylan Thomas:

> It is the grass growing on Llareggub Hill,
> Dewfall, starfall,
> The sleep of birds in Milk Wood.

Then he turned to me, his crazy eyes almost popping out of their sockets. "Llareggub looks Welsh, double l and all," he said. "But that's Dylan's little joke, you see. He told me. It's actually 'Bugger all' backwards!" And he laughed a bit madly.

When the dubbing session was over, I said a grateful goodbye to the madman. We even shook hands, but then he waved the gesture down disparagingly on an utterance of disgust, as he had done many times with me on the set, and he left. Welsh poets notwithstanding, I was still a fly on the soup for him.

Though Wyler was no one's favorite person (and Audrey everyone's), I did at last get to see where his talent lay. We were shooting a scene on a set designed to look like the bar at the Ritz Hotel. Audrey and Peter meet there in a booth after they have successfully stolen the fake Cellini statue from the museum. Until that point Audrey, has mistaken Peter for a professional burglar, and during this scene she discovers he is instead a highly qualified private detective investigating art forgeries. He has a long list of degrees and a longer list of international museums where he is a consultant, and he rattles these off nonstop to her. After the dolly shot that brought us to the table with Peter and Audrey, Wyler moved in to a two-shot, to be followed by two close-ups.

He did fifteen or sixteen takes, not unusual for him, on the two-shot, but this time I saw him invent, fine-tune the actors, find new things on every take. After a dozen takes, he told Peter, "Suppose you don't look at her when you tell her what your degrees are. Suppose you look away, like it's not important." Peter snapped his fingers, as he saw the new concept working. On the following takes, he looked away from Audrey, throwing the lines about his credentials to the wind, while Audrey sat staring at him in awe. Though eventually none of those particular takes made it into the final cut, I saw Wyler's invention at every turn, and the excitement he created between the two performers. This must have been the quality that honed some of Bette Davis's performances. But I feel to this day that Wyler was incapable of blocking out a big scene in *How to Steal a Million*. Perhaps he was getting tired. He was not in good health. He'd been plagued with gastric problems (a curse in Paris), and his bad hearing seemed to grow worse. And while I didn't care for him as a human being, I'd finally seen, in a small, tight setting with only two actors, the much-touted talent of William Wyler.

Assistant director Paul Feyder had his own take on him. Feyder agreed with me that he showed great sensibility to his actors when he was in close. But he scoffed at everything else. "He shoots every scene the same way," Feyder analyzed. "Always a master shot, a three-quarter shot, a close two-shot, two over-the-shoulders, and two single close-ups. It never varies. Then he has a whole bunch of shots to pick from. You could make five movies out of what he shoots!" Wyler, of course, exemplified the big Hollywood picture, and as such, from a European point of view, there was much overshooting. And French cinema was following a different road at that time. The style of the New Wave was sparse, direct, honest, even brutal, with limited angles and underlit scenes. Night shots kept actors half-hidden, while Charlie Lang was busy creating a veritable photography studio on the streets of Neuilly to light Peter and Audrey as if a full moon were hitting them in the face. Godard, Malle, Truffaut, Chabrol, Rohmer, and later Costa-Gavras reigned between 1956, when the best foreign film category was created, and 1973. During that period, France won the Oscar seven times. For aspiring directors such as Paul Feyder, the extravagant, yet sterile, way Wyler shot was dismaying. His plodding coverage had another drawback: the film was totally off schedule. What started as a fifteen-week shoot ended in nineteen.

Towards mid-October, Wyler decided on a Friday that he was going to need Audrey for a scene the following Monday. She had left Paris on Thursday and was in her home in Switzerland for the few days she was not needed. When word came that she was to work Monday, she flew back Sunday evening and the following morning had her usual long makeup and hair work. At noon, she was ready, waiting in her dressing room. But Wyler got completely bogged down in a scene that didn't involve her. One o'clock came, two o'clock, four o'clock. Finally, near six, Paul Feyder got the official word from Wyler that he would never get to Audrey's scene that day. Paul had the unhappy task of telling her, and I was right on his heels when he went to her dressing room. "I just wish he'd told me sooner," was Audrey's reply. "I've been here all day." Feyder apologized profusely, knowing she had flown back earlier than was originally planned.

With not much left of the film to shoot, and less to worry about, I dared to say, "Why do you take this from him?"

Audrey sighed. "With any other director, I would have said something. But not with Willie. He directed my first picture. I owe him a lot."

"Don't you think you've paid him back by now?"

She smiled. "Now don't *you* start!" And she ushered me to the door. "By tomorrow morning, it'll be fine," she said, determined to smooth things over, even at her own expense.

Films are almost always shot out of order, the schedule being dictated by availability of actors, of sets or locations, even by the director's desire to shoot a certain scene. The actual heist in *How to Steal a Million* was shot last, although it occurs about three-quarters of the way through the film. Part of the problem was that writer Harry Kurnitz hadn't figured out everything about the actual robbery. He knew the boomerang would be used to set off the alarm in the closed museum, so we'd shot the scene in the park where Peter buys the boomerang from a vendor. But how Peter and Audrey were to get out of the locked broom closet once they were inside the museum still had to be resolved. So we shot everything that went before and everything that followed the heist, while Kurnitz further cogitated the matter. Finally, the pages came in, and we shot the actual stealing of the statue, when everything else was in the can. Audrey was on her hands and knees, disguised as a cleaning woman, scrubbing the museum floor when the alarms went off, and a few days later we filmed the final shots of the picture, the closet scene with Peter and Audrey cramped against each other in jig-saw puzzle positions. The gymnastics of these final two scenes were probably not without concern for Audrey, because by then it had been announced that she was pregnant.

It was November when the shoot ended. There was one last drink on the set offered by the production office to the entire crew and both Audrey and Peter attended, since they had been in the final shots made that last day. Everyone was relaxed and laughing, Wyler and Kohlmar were both convinced they had a hit on their hands, and the crew was pleased that the "Monsieur Vee-lair" experience was at last over. Before we all gathered for drinks, Audrey called me to her dressing room and presented me with a small box that bore the name of Van Cleef & Arpel's on it. They, along with Cartier and Boucheron, were the lead-ing jewelers in Paris. Inside the box was the most beautiful pair of cuff links I'd ever seen. They were round blue lapis lazuli stones, dotted with tiny, upraised gold specks.

"It's real gold," she said on that generous smile of hers, her eyes dancing.

There were so many things I could have said to her then, but every line going through my head sounded like some God-awful Hallmark greeting. I remembered my own voice advising Audrey to keep it sim-ple with Charles Boyer, so I just said, "Thank you." We leaned into each other at the same time and kissed each other on both cheeks, French style. I told her I would see her down on the stage and left.

With the box of cuff links in my jacket pocket, I went to the stage and was immediately accosted by Peter Perkins. "Peter wants to see you," he said and accompanied me to the long table where O'Toole was standing with his makeup and hair people.

"Come with me!" he said in that familiar, dramatic tone. I followed him to a corner of the stage. "This is for you," he said, and handed me a small, wrapped gift. I took off the paper and saw a box with the name Boucheron on it in gold letters. Inside was a pair of square, solid gold cuff links. "Turn them over!" he said, a command from Mount Olym-pus. I did. On the back of one was inscribed what looked like "To Fraw-ley," and on the back of the other was inscribed, "From O'Toole."

I made no mention of Audrey's gift. It was obvious neither actor had confided in the other on this matter. "This is beautiful! But they got the name wrong," I said, scrutinizing further. "They wrote 'To Trawley.'"

"Let me see that." Peter looked at the inscription and saw the mistake. "I'll have them correct it," he said, and started to take the box.

"Not on your life!" I yanked the box back from his hands.

"I love it this way, mistake and all!"

Peter grinned. "Alright, Trawley, luv, if that's what you want. Now come have a glass of Dom Pérignon with me!" And we went back to the table with the drinks. On our next film together, unless there was anyone around other than his immediate entourage who all knew the joke, he would address me as "Trawley, luv."

In the next seven years, when I was wearing a shirt with French cuffs, I alternated between these two beautiful sets of cuff links. In 1972, I moved back to the United States and took a ground-floor apartment at the east end of Hollywood, near the Los Feliz area. Two years later, the apartment was broken into and both sets of cuff links were stolen. With my art school training, I was able to paint a perfect replica of both sets of cuff links for the police. They used the paintings with their pawnshop team, but the gifts were never recovered. The police theorized that drug addicts from nearby Hollywood Boulevard had broken into my apartment and later sold the cuff links on the street, probably for ten dollars a pair, perhaps five.

Now that the film was over, I wanted to get away. Like Pagnol's Marius, I am drawn to the sea. I put my cat, Calvados, in his basket and headed for Trouville on the Normandy coast. It was almost winter, so I didn't need to make reservations, which is the way I prefer to travel most of the time. Trouville and Deauville are coastal cities just minutes from each other. Deauville has a casino and in the prewar years the city was the spot for elegant Parisians to visit, their suitcases packed with formal evening clothes, the de rigueur apparel for gambling. I much preferred the less fancy Trouville. The weather was typically Normandy gray when I arrived, with incipient rain in the clouds. I checked into an inexpensive beachfront hotel, set out food and the litter box for the cat, and with heavy waterproof jacket and gloves immediately headed for the beach.

Like Paris, everything was gray: the sky, the sand, the water, the closed cafés jutting out onto the beach, even the tiny cooked shrimp—*les petites grises*—sold on the walkway. Whipped by the wind, eyes watering, I trudged along in the sand, recalling Boudin's early impressionist painting of *Beach at Trouville*. *Un temps de poètes*, the French called the weather. Gray. Melancholic. The weather of the poets.

In the evening, I drove along the coast to nearby Honfleur, a fishing village, untouched at that time by any tourism, even French. It was from Honfleur that Champlain and de la Salle had set sail in the seventeenth century for the New World. Dominating Old Honfleur is the church of Saint Catherine. Its bell tower, too heavy to hoist onto the church, sits on the opposite side of the square. Below, at the end of several winding streets, lies the magnificent Old Port with its ancient structures holding cafés, restaurants with checked curtains, and artisans' shops.

I called my father from the P.T.T. in Trouville. "P.T.T." stood for *Postes, Télégraphes, Téléphones*. In those days, the Post Office operators would connect long distance calls, which were impossible to make elsewhere, except from the most expensive hotels. I told my father I was on the Normandy coast, not far from where the Allied Invasion had occurred, and that I'd just completed working on a movie with Audrey Hepburn.

"Katharine Hepburn?" he asked.

"No, Audrey," I answered. "*Roman Holiday, Sabrina, My Fair Lady.* You must know her."

"Of course, I know her!" he said, annoyed. "I just thought you said, 'Katharine Hepburn,' that's all. The connection isn't very good!" Like Wyler, my father was growing a little hard of hearing. "Are you still doing that coaching business?"

Still? He was a killer, my father. With one word he could leave you gelded for life. I hadn't spoken to him in about six months, so the implication was that because I'd changed jobs so many times in the past, he fully expected me to announce that I was doing something else by now. "Yes," I replied, "I'm still doing that. It's a good-paying job."

"Glad to hear it, son, glad to hear it. You deserve it. Call me if you need anything, you hear? Anything!"

That meant money, of course. Another reminder of times past. I had Agamemnon for a father. How could one man in so few words cause such havoc on a soul?

I would see Audrey once again, a year later. I received a call from the Fox office to tell me that there were some scenes from the picture that Audrey needed to dub in a sound studio. Mostly lines that were shot out of doors with obtrusive noises in the background. She was in Paris again and it didn't make sense to fly her to Hollywood, where Wyler was, to dub a dozen lines. And of course Wyler didn't want to come all the way to Paris for a few lines to be dubbed, even for the great lady of cinema. So I was called upon to take charge of the dubbing, and Audrey, gracious as always, agreed to that.

The sound studio was in Boulogne, where we had shot *How to Steal a Million*, and I was there a half hour early. When Audrey arrived, it was truly on a note of excitement. She rushed in and literally threw herself into my arms. "I'm so glad you're here!" she said. "You're the perfect person to do this!"

"You don't mind not having Wyler?"

"He'd never even hear the lines!" she said.

She looked great. More vivacious. Impish. Happy. Something had happened in the year that separated our work together—well, several things, actually. First she'd miscarried. I'd heard that shortly after the shooting of *How to Steal a Million* ended. I remembered wondering to what extent her emotionally tumultuous meetings with Mel Ferrer had had an adverse effect on her health. I wondered, too, about her working on her hands and knees as a scrubwoman in the final days of shooting; she was, after all, extremely thin and delicate. In any case, she bounced back after the miscarriage and threw herself into work immediately, shooting Stanley Donen's *Two for the Road*, a film easily twenty years before its time. It was here she met Albert Finney, seven years her junior, who apparently was a great catalyst in her life. He was out of the new group of actors and directors burgeoning in England that also included Tony Richardson, Tom Courtenay, and Richard Harris. Their approach was very down to earth, the opposite of what Wyler and Ferrer represented, the opposite of the Hollywood Audrey knew. And opposites fascinate.

"I don't know if Albert and I have a future together," dresser Marguerite Brachet quoted Audrey as having said, "but I do know there is no future for Mel and me." Whatever Finney's role had been, I was now looking at an ebullient Audrey Hepburn, one whose excitement could barely be contained by the walls of the sound studio.

She told me that she and Ferrer were through. "I'm going back to Hollywood to do this movie he's producing. I'm sure he's getting to do it because of my name, and that's all right. But this is my final gift to him. Then it will be over."

And that's exactly what happened. Audrey would receive another Oscar nomination for her role as the blind girl in *Wait Until Dark*, and Ferrer's career would dwindle once more. Then she would be off to Rome, where she later married psychiatrist Andrea Dotti, with whom she would have a second son, and remained absent from the screen until 1976, when she appeared opposite Sean Connery in *Robin and Marian*.

We stood side by side in the sound studio watching short "loops" as Audrey matched the words she had spoken a year earlier. "You're too early," I would say. Or "You're short." Or even, "Is the tone light enough?" Years later, I asked myself the question: for a few brief moments, and albeit without a camera, did I actually direct Audrey Hepburn?

At one point, as the sound man was changing loops, she leaned toward me and whispered, "Have you started writing?"

"Not yet," I answered.

"What are you waiting for?"

"I think I need to live some more first. Then I'll have something to write about."

"Don't wait too long."

When we were through with the looping, Audrey told me she needed to buy something for her son, Sean, and did I know of any place that was open on Sunday? I told her that all French markets were open till one o'clock, and that there were many stores near the studio, on Avenue Jean-Baptiste Clément. "I can take you there if you want."

"Would you? We can go together in my car, and then I'll bring you back afterwards."

Riding in the back seat next to her, Audrey related how she tried to get me on *Two for the Road*. "I told Stanley how helpful you'd been to me, and how much I would like you on the picture. But he said he never worked with a dialogue coach, and preferred not to have one. So there was nothing I could do."

I thanked her and told her that I'd worked five months with director Anatole Litvak since I'd seen her last, and Litvak loved working with a coach. Every director is different.

We stopped at a large corner store that had toys and games and the ubiquitous *Tintin* comic books in the window. Audrey and I walked into the store, and she spied it immediately, hanging way up near the ceiling. A gigantic stuffed dog with floppy ears. She laughed and said, "Look at that up there!"

"It's pretty big," I answered.

"Sean will love it! It's almost as big as he is!"

She bought it, and Audrey's driver took us back to the studio where my car was parked. Audrey and I kissed each other on the cheeks as we had a year earlier in her dressing room, and the last image I have of her, as the car pulled away to head back to the Hotel Lancaster, was Audrey with this huge stuffed animal, looking like a child herself, waving to me through the car window. Her face was luminous, her smile enormous.

There would be one final word from her. In the early '70s I made my way to Hollywood. My agent sent a script of mine to her for the lead. I knew nothing about this until later. Had I known, I wouldn't have advised his sending it because she was not "right" for the role, and also because I knew she was living her happy life as a mother in Rome with Dotti. She had earned the absence from the screen that she was giving herself. When the script came back, there was a handwritten note, like the handwritten notes she used to write to her fans. In blue ink on blue stationery, she thanked my agent for sending the script and appropriately declined it. She ended by saying she cherished fond memories of our work together in Paris. And that she thought the writing was excellent.

For a split second, I wondered what she had seen in me that my father hadn't.

CHAPTER FIVE

~

Peter the Great

A week or so before *How to Steal a Million* finished shooting, Peter O'Toole told me that he was scheduled to do his next film, *The Night of the Generals*, with Anatole Litvak. Most of it was to be shot in Paris.

"I'll mention you to Tola, if you want," he said. Tola was the affectionate shortening of Anatole. "I'd love for you to be on the film. We'll have a few giggles together."

"Thanks," I said. "Margot Capelier has mentioned my name to him, but it would mean so much more coming from you." Margot was the casting director on the Wyler film and was scheduled to do the Litvak movie as well.

"I'll make sure Tola sees you," Peter replied in that imperious, unchallengeable tone of his, and walked off.

The following day, word came to me on the set that Litvak wanted to see me. I made my way to his office just across the street. I met his secretary and friend of many years, Ann Selepegno, and was quickly ushered into Litvak's office. He rose to meet me and shook my hand. Litvak was of Russian origin and had married a beautiful French model, following an earlier marriage to actress Miriam Hopkins. There was an immediate warmth I sensed about Litvak, and though he was almost thirty years my senior, we were destined to become fast friends. As it turned out, we lived in the same quarter of Paris, and between films we would meet every couple of weeks in a tiny Russian restaurant, Nichevo, three blocks from my apartment.

"Everyone's been talking to me about you," he said. "Peter O'Toole, Margot, Annie. . . ." He was referring to Ann Selepegno, who, a close friend to Margot Capelier, had added her two cents' worth, without having even met me. "It looks like I'm going to have to hire you if I want to make this picture!"

"They all get ten percent of me," I parried.

"You shouldn't pay Peter. He makes enough."

And that's the way the meeting went: friendly, relaxed, warm, with the occasional joke here and there. Litvak liked to have a dialogue coach on his films. If he had confidence in the coach, as he did soon with me, he would actually have the coach rehearse entire scenes with the actors and discuss character and motivation, not just run lines or correct accents with them. The meeting was almost at an end, and Litvak rose and I followed suit. He caught me staring at him and said, "Yes?"

"I've been trying to figure out where I'd seen you before, and now I remember. You sat in the row in front of me at the Judy Garland concert at the Palais de Chaillot."

"Wasn't she marvelous?" Litvak extolled. "Such talent, such energy!" And he immediately sat back down to discuss that evening five years earlier when we both listened to what might have been the greatest female voice of the twentieth century. The evening had been an indelible one for me. I went to the concert with my friend, Georges Lair, the only French person I knew who had seen *Une Étoile est née* (*A Star Is Born*), and the two of us were well ensconced in our extraordinary seats smack in the center of the orchestra wondering why, as the theater filled up, most of the row in front of us remained empty. Then, just five minutes before the curtain, almost as if on cue, entered the procession of seat holders. First came Lars Schmidt, the Swedish producer, then his wife, Ingrid Bergman, then Anthony Perkins, then Simone Signoret and Yves Montand, and finally Sophie and Anatole Litvak. Litvak was directing *Goodbye Again* at the time, and Bergman, Perkins, and Montand were the stars. It's a little-known film, with a terrible title, about a middle-aged woman's affair with a young man. The script was written by Françoise Sagan and the original title, *Aimez-vous*

Brahms? should have been kept in English as *Do You Like Brahms?* a line uttered by Perkins to Bergman as he desperately tries to get her to go to a concert with him. Brahms's Third Symphony is used largely as the love theme of the picture, and Sagan put words to a portion of the third movement. Anthony Perkins actually made a recording in French of the song, *Quand tu dors près de moi,* and since he had a decent voice and was an international star, the record sold fairly well. Like the film, the song was romantic, sad, and bittersweet, three qualities the French love in their songs. I bought a copy of the 45-rpm record and, while I no longer have it, I'm sure it's a real collector's item now.

And Judy Garland was unbelievable. A force of nature. The year was 1960, five years after *A Star Is Born* was released, and she was at the height of her concert performances. She was belting out all the old favorites and occasionally doing a few dance steps. The combination of vocal strength, vulnerability, and poignancy for which Garland was known must have appealed to the French. Echoes of Mistinguett's showmanship and Piaf's pain. Garland had the blasé Parisians in the palm of her hand, and when she ended the show by sitting at the edge of the stage, dangling her legs over the orchestra pit and looking like a waif as she sang "Over the Rainbow," it was the coup de grâce. The audience was on its feet, cheering, raining bravas on her like manna from heaven. The frenzy only increased with each curtain call, and I stopped counting after eight. This was essentially the same concert that she would give some months later in New York, the double album recording of which, *Judy at Carnegie Hall,* would remain on the charts for an unprecedented ninety-four weeks and win several Grammy Awards, including best female vocal performance and album of the year.

Litvak and I reminisced the moment of her concert five years later in his office. He sat there, shaking his head of white hair in near disbelief, recalling the miracle performance.

A few weeks after meeting him, I worked on a screen test for him with Omar Sharif in the role of Inspector Grau for *The Night of the Generals.* "I'm not going to do the movie," Sharif told me. "I have to do this screen test because Sam Spiegel asked me to." It was pure politics. There was no way an Arab could play a German officer, he said.

Spiegel had been a long-time producer for Columbia Pictures, *The Night of the Generals* following many memorable films, including

Lawrence of Arabia, which had first introduced Sharif to American audiences. When Sharif signed with Columbia in London to do *Lawrence*, he was placed on a seven-picture contract at very nominal fees. As a result, both *Doctor Zhivago* and *Funny Girl* earned him little money. At the time of his screen test for *The Night of the Generals*, I didn't contradict Sharif about not playing a German officer and simply said, "Well, let's just make the test as good as we can then."

In February 1966, the entire company made its way to Warsaw for the first month's filming. Cognizant of his obligation to Spiegel, Omar Sharif had signed on. I later learned from Omar that marital problems and gambling squanders had also contributed to his decision. We were the first company from the West to film behind the Iron Curtain. Incredibly, I had been issued a special visa by the Polish consulate in Paris for my cat, Calvados, to travel with me. The official letter bore the consulate seal, a visa number, and began with, "The cat Calvados, belonging to Monsieur Frawley Becker. . . ." I loved that. The poet John Donne, the painter Rosa Bonheur, the cat Calvados. The consulate advised me to make sure the cat's visa was stamped at the border upon entering Poland. "Otherwise," they said, "they might accuse you of stealing a Polish cat when you try to leave." With that one statement, I was instantly thrust into the paranoia that was Poland under communism.

We were an international company of French, English, and Americans, and the cast was even more diverse. Peter O'Toole was Irish. Tom Courtenay, Donald Pleasence, Charles Gray, and Christopher Plummer were all English. Philippe Noiret was French, Joanna Pettet American, Coral Browne Australian, Gordon Jackson Scottish, and Omar Sharif Egyptian. And except for Noiret, they were all playing Germans.

"What kind of English should they be speaking?" I asked Sam Spiegel in Warsaw.

"Mid-Atlantic," he replied, dead serious.

"You mean Reykjavik, Iceland?" I asked.

He didn't get the joke. "It shouldn't be too English and it shouldn't be too American. It should be so everyone can understand them," he replied. Spiegel, Polish-born, and Litvak, Russian-born, both spoke with Slavic accents, so I figured with this Tower of Babel and a Mid-Atlantic approach, I really had my work cut out for me.

What he meant, of course, was that A's shouldn't be as broad as the English used them or as nasal as Americans did. The problem compounded with different words in both countries. Did you take the lift or did you take the elevator? Was Courtenay working under the hood of the car or under the bonnet? And did Charles Gray's schedule go as the American "skedjule" or the English "shedyool"? Though the script is credited to French writer Joseph Kessel and Paul Dehn, Gore Vidal was often at the studio in Paris, and I recall hearing that he rewrote some of the dialogue. Irwin Shaw came by the studio one day, and Spiegel immediately enlisted him to rewrite the love scene. These things would certainly account for the fact that there were all sorts of Americanisms in the script that didn't quite sound right in the mouths of the English playing Germans.

"'You must be joking!'" Donald Pleasence read the line from his script. "That sounds awfully American to me. 'Joking.' I don't think a German would say that. Especially in the '40s."

"How about 'You can't be serious!'" I asked.

Pleasence tried it out. "You can't be serious!"

"That's better, but don't say it as 'cahn't.' The A is too English."

And so it went, in fits and starts with the language. We were back to Zanuck's problem in *The Blue Max*, a problem that was never resolved whenever the bankable American and British stars played roles that were neither American nor British.

The first day of filming was a night scene with Gordon Jackson and Omar in front of Lazienki Palace, an eighteenth-century marvel most of which had miraculously remained intact through World War II. Omar's hair had been lightened, but his fawn-colored complexion still belied German origin. The night was limpid, the snow crisp, and the palace, bathed by powerful *brut* arc lamps, shimmered. Dolly track, one of Litvak's constant instruments, was laid down easily on the packed snow. It all went without a hitch, and joyously, at 2 A.M., we went back to the hotel to go to bed. And while we slept, a searing sun came out. By early afternoon all the snow had melted.

At four o'clock, Litvak announced he would not shoot because Warsaw's streets had been completely stripped. He spoke to Spiegel in London, who agreed to wait a day or two. Surely, it would not take more than that for the snow to return. Three days later, I was with the despondent director in his suite in the Hotel Europejski as he eyed the clean, spring-like streets below his window. Suddenly, Peter O'Toole burst into the room.

"Tola, let's shoot it!"

"We can't. There's no snow."

"The script says February in Warsaw. Well, it's February and we're in Warsaw, so let's shoot it!"

"If there's no snow, it'll just look like we shot it on the back lot somewhere." And his face turned into a mask of Slavic suffering. It seemed incredible that the famous Warsaw winter was not there for us. Then Litvak headed for the phone and another call to Spiegel while Peter and I looked down on the sunlit street below.

The next day, the snow still didn't arrive. What did arrive were the snow-making machines that Spiegel had had flown in. For the next three weeks, the streets of Warsaw were winterized into whiteness with Styrofoam. The air was cold and clear, but not a flurry of real snow fell, not in Warsaw in February 1966.

At last, we were back on the streets with one of those mornings that are anathema to lighting directors, the skies alternating between cloudy gray and sunny blue every ten minutes. I knocked on Peter's trailer and entered. He was sitting, being made up. "So foul and fair a day I have not seen!" I declaimed as I walked in, proud of finding a Shakespearean line that seemed appropriate to the weather. Peter stared at me as if he'd seen a disembodied spirit. Bill Lodge, the makeup man, stopped his work. "Scotti," the hairdresser, froze. Then Peter started a moan that mounted and mounted into a yell, an actual yell.

"Do you not know that you must never quote the Scottish gentleman?" he shouted at me.

"You mean Mac—?"

"*The Scottish gentleman!*" he cried in his most theatrical voice, correcting me before I could complete the name of Macbeth. "He must never be named! And never a line from that play may be spoken, except in the theater where it is being performed or rehearsed."

"What happens if . . . the play . . . is quoted?"

"Great misfortune follows!" he thundered like an oracle. There was a long moment of silence during which all three men glowered at me.

"I forgive you because you are American, and as such I assume you do not know the traditions of the English stage!"

The makeup man and the hairdresser returned to their work, and Peter to his normal tone of voice. He explained that the last time a line from "the Scottish gentleman" was quoted was during the filming of *Lord Jim*. And the day it was uttered, a boat of extras overturned on the river. He didn't mention if anyone was drowned, and I was afraid to ask.

The day of my hapless quote was the day we were scheduled to shoot a major sequence on one of the largest squares of the old town, the central portion of which had been meticulously reconstructed by the Poles, brick by brick, from the original museum blueprints, after the Germans were defeated. The scene had Omar Sharif as a military police inspector encountering O'Toole's Nazi General Tanz, who arrives dramatically and Teutonically, standing up in an open staff car. With binoculars, O'Toole bites out the commands for the demolition of some buildings on the square. Though parts of these buildings were set construction placed on unsalvageable and condemned shells and designed to crumble on explosion, the buildings were interspersed with noncondemned ones, so the effect was tricky. Flamethrowers were fired up, Polish resistance fighters were flushed out and shot, elderly citizens were herded off, and finally, several buildings were made to collapse before our eyes. In the midst of this mayhem, O'Toole disdainfully ignores Sharif, who has come to question him about a murdered prostitute, and commands his chauffeur to drive off through the smoke and rubble. There were a hundred places for "great misfortune" to occur. It didn't, however, and the superstition of the English theater suddenly collapsed like the buildings before me. After the complicated shot, Peter called my name. Sort of.

"Trawley, luv!" I hurried to the staff car at the edge of the set. I expected some further reference to the bad omen I'd unwittingly spoken earlier. "Did I get all the dickey-birds right?" he asked. He was using the cockney "rhyming slang" that was all the rage then. "Dickey birds" rhymed with "words," so what he was asking me was, "Did I get all the words right?"

"Yes, dead on," I said, wishing I could have found a rhyming slang equivalent.

"Make sure you correct me, if I'm wrong!" he barked. "Don't I always?" I threw back. On his smile, I realized the Macbeth incident was truly over. We never discussed "the Scottish gentleman" again.

In rhyming slang, O'Toole's gloves became "turtle doves," and "Where's my titfer?" (short for tit-for-tat) meant "Where's my hat?" He played the game gleefully, always hoping someone would stump him, but surrounded by Americans, French, Poles, and an Egyptian, only his English entourage understood the game. Though they all dabbled at it, no one played it so well as he did. (In the 1943 film *Mister Lucky*, Cary Grant used rhyming slang, saying he borrowed it from the Australians. For Grant, "pot and pan" was used for "man," "twist and twirl" for "girl.")

Wandering around the city in my off time, I was amazed to see, twenty years after World War II had ended, entire vast city blocks still razed to the ground. A charred, raven-black wasteland, where nothing had been reconstructed and where plant life refused to grow. That Hitler had almost obliterated a nation's capital, destroying most of it, was outside comprehension. There was no Marshall Plan here, no Americans to rebuild the Berlin or Frankfurt of Poland. What had been erected in other areas of the city by the Communists in those twenty years were overscaled, massive buildings that rose straight from the street in gray concrete walls with miniscule windows. The importance of man was dwarfed intentionally, imprisoning him in a canyon. There were still a few Jews in Warsaw in 1966, though most concentration camp survivors had fled to the new state of Israel. In the old city, I found one small Jewish restaurant that had not only the ubiquitous gefülte fish, but also sweet-and-sour carp, a dish I've never seen since. I ordered both. Black bread and butter, Wyborowa vodka, and sparkling mineral water, and all was right with the world.

Paranoia reigned everywhere. Every Pole looked on his neighbor Pole as a possible liaison to the Party. Black-marketing and selling Polish currency on the streets were both illegal and dangerous, but they occurred. The young bellhops at the Hotel Europejski, where the film crew was staying, offered to do anything for a Westerner, and they meant it, if a few dollars could be forthcoming. Claudie Thary, O'Toole's French dresser, asked Omar Sharif's Polish dresser how much she earned, and the girl replied, "I don't know how much it is in your money, but it is the equivalent of forty beets a week."

But in spite of all these things, there was something about the Polish spirit that I loved. The Poles on the crew instantly turned their Friday paychecks into bottles of vodka that they drank off the back of the prop and grip trucks. I was one of the few Westerners, and the only American, invited to join them. They never lost their laugh or their generosity or the hope in their eyes. One Sunday, I was to join Marek Piwowski, the local 2nd assistant director, at lunch in a restaurant, meeting him first at his parents' house. But when I got there, Marek, sleeping off his previous night's drinking somewhere else, hadn't yet arrived. My Polish consisted of only a handful of words, but coupled with German, I somehow made myself understood. When I pronounced Marek's name, the young man's father grabbed me by the arm and pulled me from the front door to the kitchen table. In minutes, Marek's mother brought out every bit of food that was in the refrigerator, while Marek's father alternately poured *zubrowka*, the most flavorful of all vodkas, and homemade *citronowka*. I was half sated and totally sloshed by time Marek arrived, whereupon he and I proceeded to a nearby bar for many uncounted afternoon beers. Was I acting like a Pole? You bet. But it was also French and Italian and Dutch and Yugoslavian and just about every nationality in Europe that knew that a good job with good money could never hold a candle to good food, good drink, and good company.

And despite the Communist regime, art incongruously flourished. There were more shops selling oil paintings than shops selling milk and cheese. There were over forty legitimate theaters in Warsaw, most of them performing in repertory. That meant you could practically see a different play every night of the year. Few people bought tickets to plays in advance, most customers lining up the night of the performance, much the way Westerners do for movies. And everything was on the boards! Classic Polish pageants, Chekhov, Pirandello, Pinter, Tennessee Williams, French farces, a brave and hilarious *My Fair Lady*, and that most remarkable Polish playwright, Slawomir Mrozek, whose *Tango* I had seen with Nicholas Ray the year before in Belgrade. I convinced Peter O'Toole to come see the play with me, and though neither of us could follow the Polish, we both sat laughing our heads off at this outrageously black comedy, the same way Nick and I had done hearing the play in Serbo-Croatian. The next day, I was told that Peter had called his manager, Jules Buck, in London to try to buy the rights so Peter could perform it on the London stage. He was one week too late; the English-speaking rights had just been sold.

After *Tango*, we returned to the hotel. Peter Perkins, still the actor's inseparable companion, had gone to the theater with us and made his way ahead to the desk for room keys. Peter and I stood in the lobby chatting about the play, when suddenly an incredible vision entered the front door of the hotel. In an elegant Chanel cardigan suit dotted with iridescent bugle beads and a fur coat over her shoulders, Marlene Dietrich, alone, made her way across the lobby. Every head turned to get a glimpse of the most famous legs in the world. Peter immediately advanced and kissed her on both cheeks. The stars exchanged greetings. Then, as much the gentleman as Audrey Hepburn had been the lady, Peter beckoned me and introduced me to Dietrich. She smiled at me as she had smiled at me a hundred times from the screen. Everything I knew of her famed beauty was there in that great, classic face: the renowned cheekbones, the chamois-like skin, the high forehead, the half-mast eyelids, the defined eyebrows. Even her simple "hello" to me exuded sex. She was sixty-four and looked thirty. She had just finished performing her one-woman show at one of the theaters, and I believe Peter had seen her a night or two before and gone backstage to meet her. Peter told her he'd just seen a remarkable play by Mrozek that I had taken him to, and Dietrich replied that she knew of the Polish playwright, but that her own evening performances precluded her from seeing his play. I mentioned that I had a ticket to see her the following evening.

"I hope you enjoy it," she said.

"How could I not?"

"You are very kind," she said simply. Then she excused herself and headed toward the desk of the hotel. Her exit was just as remarkable as her entrance, and again she was the cynosure of all eyes. One thing I had noticed about her that I mentioned to Peter was that her head was somewhat larger than normal in relationship to her body.

"That's why the camera loves her," he replied. "Richard Burton also has a large head. You don't notice it with either one of them on screen because the camera distorts. They look good and we who have normal-sized heads have to work twice as hard to be noticed." Then he thanked me for the play, said goodnight, and moved toward Perkins, waiting at the desk. I had a hard time imagining O'Toole not being noticed on screen, but I think his observation is actually correct.

The next night, I saw Marlene Dietrich on stage, in an act that had already been perfected in Las Vegas. She wore her skin-tight dress (I think, the one into which she had to be sewn every evening) with spangly paillettes and more bugle beads. A white fox fur wrap dripped from her arms onto the floor behind her. She sang "Falling in Love Again" and "Naughty Lola," "La Vie en rose" in French, and the rousting "See What the Boys in the Back Room Will Have." And, of course, I was waiting for her most famous song of all, which came about three-quarters of the way through the evening. She began singing "Lili Marlene," first in English and then in German, which I was hearing for the first time. Then something happened. Someone threw an apple on the stage. A moment later, a potato. Then another. And a beet. Dietrich stepped back and continued singing. Only moments before, the crowd had been enthusiastic. What happened? Suddenly, I remembered the blackened, razed city blocks twenty years after the war and made the Poland–Germany connection. And I remembered that a few days earlier I had found an old glass in an antique shop. On the side of the glass were some gold German letters, not uncommon for glasses sold at nineteenth-century fairs. I say "were" because someone, doubtless during the war, had taken a razor and scratched through most of the German lettering, effacing it and the beautiful glass as well. For a people who loved art so much to destroy it willfully was a sign of the deep-seated hatred the Poles held for everything German. On top of it all, the song had been a favorite of German soldiers. But didn't the audience know of Dietrich's work during World War II, entertaining American G.I.s everywhere? Though German-born, she had become an American citizen in 1939, and her allegiances had always been crystal clear. When she finished "Lili Marlene" there was a mixture of applause and boos, with the applause definitely winning out. Still, she did not sing again in German that evening. The produce that lay scattered on the stage remained there, totally ignored, right to Dietrich's final bow with an armful of flowers. The standing ovation at the curtain call was overwhelming, as it had been for her in Warsaw a year earlier without the vegetables, proof that the majority of the audience recognized her artistry, German language be damned.

At the end of the month, we returned to Paris, where the bulk of the film was to be shot. There I discovered great diversity in the acting styles of the actors who had not worked in Warsaw. Tom Courtenay was out of the Tony Richardson school of naturalistic acting and tended to mumble, while Charles Gray and Coral Browne were old hands in the theater and tended to declaim. Because he was eager and approachable, I was able to get Courtenay to project a little better, always being careful not to overrehearse him, because his style depended much on the truth of the moment. I told Litvak about the leaning Charles and Coral had toward the theatrical, and suggested that he, not I, tone them down, which he did. Coral Browne was another of those forces of nature with whom you just didn't argue. I think only film people, and probably only some of them, know her work today. The sophisticated lesbian who steals Susannah York away from Beryl Reid in *The Killing of Sister George*; the actress playing Gertrude in a production of *Hamlet* in the Soviet Union who becomes involved with expatriated Englishman Alan Bates in Schlesinger's *An Englishman Abroad*; and the eighty year-old Alice of Lewis Carroll's earlier infatuation receiving an honorary doctorate's degree in *Dreamchild*—all these were Coral Browne. She also married actor Vincent Price, which proves my point completely about her tendency toward the theatrical.

Looking at *The Night of the Generals* today, I see a pretty good film, although by present standards there is undeniably a certain theatricality to it. The one scene that stands out is the lunch scene where Sharif and Philippe Noiret, police inspectors both, one German, the other French, exchange information in the middle of the war. Noiret's tendency to underplay was met tone for tone by Sharif, with the result that this is the warmest, most intelligent, certainly most human moment in the entire picture. We shot it in an upstairs room at Le Pharamond restaurant, in what is now called the *marais* area.

La Semaine de Paris was a weekly publication in the form of a small booklet that listed every bit of entertainment the great city held, from grand opera to the nude Lido dancers. One day, I noticed that the classic French film, *Volpone*, after the Ben Jonson play, was showing in one of the Left Bank cinemas. It starred Harry Baur and Louis Jouvet, two of France's finest actors, both deceased. I'd heard that Peter O'Toole had once performed the role of Mosca, the Jouvet role, and thought he might be interested in seeing the movie. I told him about it in his dressing room, and he seemed quite excited to see the French version. I proposed that we make an evening of it, with dinner first at Chez Laurent, the little restaurant to which I had taken all the Americans on *Up from the Beach*. Peter was delighted with the prospects of the evening, the only damper for me being that his quasi–body guard and passe-partout, Peter Perkins, would again be coming along.

On the appointed evening, the three of us met at the little restaurant, Peter wearing dark glasses, as he often did, both on and off the set, and Perkins the dubious gray-green suede shoes he'd worn throughout *How to Steal a Million*. He was a lug of a man, beefy and graceless, with massive hands and feet. I introduced the two Peters to Madame Laurent and her daughters, Josiane and Gisèle, who were thrilled to host the great star of *Lawrence of Arabia*. We were seated downstairs, and Peter immediately ordered his staple, champagne. Perkins wanted to taste the scotch I'd told him about, and I think I had the same. Peter looked around, taking in the warmth and intimacy of the restaurant, its antiques and subtle lighting.

"Charming, Trawley, luv. It's absolutely charming." Perkins smiled his smile of bad teeth and lit a Players cigarette. I hadn't realized that my choice of restaurants might possibly be a test, but certainly Perkins had held back his smile until Peter had given his verbal approval. It was also a discreet restaurant, and though everyone there recognized Peter, and on rare occasion glanced over at him, not a single Frenchman came to bother him with a compliment or to request an autograph. I translated the menu, and both Peters chose the "giant standing rib roast," which came with a special tomato-flavored mustard and shoestring potatoes. We were well into this course when Peter, totally at ease, began telling some of his movie anecdotes. He was suddenly like a little boy again, giggling at this madman's profession we were all in, giggling at its absolute absurdity.

"It took forever to shoot *Lawrence*," he said. "Almost two years. Every time we did a shot that was no good, they had to sweep the sand, or else we'd move on to another dune, because we had the indentations of all those camel hooves where we'd just shot!" And on *Becket*, he spoke of the day on the beach with him and Richard Burton on horses. It had been one of the coldest days of filming, and Peter swore you could actually see the wind on the screen. And the horses kept moving because they were cold, too. "We rehearsed and rehearsed," he said. "We were all from the theater—Richard, Glenville, and I—so we rehearsed it like a scene in a play, all morning." When they broke for lunch, Peter said the studio was going crazy because they didn't have anything in the can. Then they came back from lunch and made one shot that lasted five minutes of screen time.

We found Peter's car and driver waiting at the restaurant door. He took us to the movie house on the Left Bank where *Volpone* was playing. We were twenty minutes early. At the front of the theater stood the manager. In spite of the dark glasses, O'Toole was immediately recognized. The manager tried to confirm that fact with me. I translated for Peter, who waggishly said, "Tell him he is mistaken. I am just an English tourist!" I translated back to the manager, who would have none of it. He waved his arms excitedly toward one of his showcases. By untimely coincidence, Peter's face stared at us all from a *Lord Jim* poster announcing the film for the following week. Peter giggled and, throwing him his best French with "*Ce n'est pas moi! Ce n'est pas moi!*" he darted across the street toward a small bar for refuge. Perkins and I ran after him.

"That was close!" he breathed, as we all lined up against the zinc-topped counter. I gave the barman our orders and a moment later the drinks arrived. So did *la patronne*, who had left her habitual place by the cash register and approached us with a pad and pencil. She addressed me, since she had heard me order in French, and asked if "Monsieur O'Toole" would sign an autograph for her. Before I could answer, the barman had extended another piece of paper and said, "*Pour moi aussi, s'il vous plaît!*" And a customer standing near us moved in with his folded newspaper to be signed. We were outnumbered.

Peter looked from one to the other, downed half his drink, and gave me a resigned look that seemed to say, "It is easier to reach Aqaba by land than to go to a little cinema house on the Left Bank!" Then he giggled that giggle I knew so well and said, "Tell them I shall be delighted to oblige!" And he did, indeed, give them all his autograph. I realized at that very instant when they were all in on him with their various pieces of paper and their cloying smiles that I was able to do something Peter O'Toole could not. I could live a life where strangers would never intrude. And I realized it was thus for all celebrities who perhaps wanted only to go out to dinner or see a movie or go to a shop, any shop, anywhere, and could not ever do any of these things without that intrusion.

After *Volpone*, the three of us again got into Peter's chauffeur-driven car. "You have been a wonderful host!" Peter exclaimed. I had, in fact, picked up the tab at both Chez Laurent and at the cinema, since I'd been the one who'd extended the invitation. "Now, you are to be my guest for drinks!" And he told the driver to take us all to Chez Castel, the most fashionable club of its day, which he frequented.

Standing at the crowded bar on the first floor, Perkins and I had a round of cognacs and Peter ordered champagne. There was an entire downstairs level as well, with another bar and a dance floor. Peter had thrown out the occasional *bonsoir* as we'd made our way from the door. Even if I hadn't already known from the newspaper reports that he was an habitué of the establishment, the "*bonsoir, M'sieur O'Toole*" that he invariably got in return from one and all would have told me. There was a second round of drinks. I think all of us were beginning to get a little fuzzy at this point. Suddenly, I took the proverbial bull by the horns. "So this is where you get into fights," I challenged.

"Fights?" he asked. "Fights? In the plural?"

"The Gospel according to *France-Soir*."

"One time, Trawley, luv! I swear it! The papers still continue to report it! And do you know what really happened?" I shook my head. "Don't move your face," he said. Then he took off his dark glasses and brought his face three inches from mine. I found myself engulfed by those incredible blue eyes of his, which were actually slightly watery. "These eyes of mine are very sensitive to light. Without the glasses, I should weep much of the time. This is also why I wear them on the set until it is time to shoot." He put the glasses back on. Then he told me how one night he was standing at the bar when some slightly tipsy Frenchman started talking to him. Peter didn't know the man, who soon began to gesticulate, and in so doing almost brushed Peter's face. Peter had stepped back, as much as anyone could step back when Chez Castel was crowded, and the stranger moved in, becoming belligerent. Again, his hands started waving and in the process, Peter's glasses were jostled. "I was afraid for my eyes," Peter said, "and I pushed him away.

He staggered and fell against several people. 'Don't touch me!' I shouted, just like General Tanz." He was referring to the character he was playing, a fanatic who couldn't stand anyone's touch. "That's all that happened, Trawley luv. Just once. It wasn't a fight." Of course the press had turned Peter into a boxer.

The following week, he invited me to join him and Omar at the races at Chantilly. On Sunday, with spring bursting around us, I accompanied Peter on the drive up. Chantilly is about thirty miles to the north of Paris, and is known for its eighteenth-century château, its parks, its racetrack, and its whipped cream. The tiny city was the first to whip Normandy cream to a froth that Parisians immediately insisted be placed on top of their coffee. And so *café chantilly* was born.

Omar was already at the bar when we arrived, a glass of champagne in his hand. It quickly became a champagne day for all of us. We just had time for a *croque-monsieur*, a glorified grilled ham and cheese sandwich, at the bar when the races started. Omar showed me a sheet of horses' names and asked me to pick one. Blindly I did, and he placed a bet for me when he went to place his own. Neither his horse nor mine nor Peter's won. Then it was Peter's turn. "Pick a horse, Trawley, luv!" he said, and I picked another for the next race, with exactly the same results. And that's the way the next two hours went, with both Peter and Omar taking turns at funding bets for me each time they placed one of their own. Though he giggled a lot, Peter lost more than he won. Omar won very little and I not a single franc. I think that afternoon was their way of thanking me for all the work I'd been doing on the film.

Riding back to Paris with Omar, he told me he was not financially independent. Heavy taxes, gambling, and race horses were partly the reason. But mostly, he said, it was because Spiegel had him under a "slave contract" that the actor had signed with him. Then Omar related the story of how he'd gotten his break on *Lawrence of Arabia*. Director David Lean had become disenchanted with French actor Maurice Ronet, who had been contracted to play the role of the Arab Ali. When Ronet refused to wear contact lenses to cover his blue eyes, Lean sent for a directory of Egyptian actors. Sharif's photo caught his attention, as did the fact that Sharif spoke English. Lean asked Sam Spiegel to go to Cairo and meet with the actor whom he was considering for a "small part not yet written." Spiegel and Sharif subsequently met and though the actor was already a big star in Egypt, he nevertheless agreed to meet the famous director in Jordan to be considered for "a small role." Once there, Lean tested him for two different characters, neither of which was the major role of Ali. Peter O'Toole performed with him for the screen test. Sharif thought it strange to be tested for a small part, not knowing what Lean really had in mind. Then late one afternoon Lean and Spiegel were on an outside patio of their hotel, and Lean was explaining how the first appearance of the character Ali should be made, coming from a great distance. At that precise moment, Omar wandered outside the hotel, himself appearing in the distance. Lean pointed to him and apparently said to Spiegel, "Like that actor over there." This was how Lean got Spiegel to agree to recast the essential role of Ali. Spiegel actually felt Sharif looked much better for the role than Ronet, though the producer was not too happy about having to pay off the French actor's contract. "If I hadn't gone to Jordan to meet Lean, I might still be making Egyptian films," Omar said in the car.

"Pure serendipity," I proffered.

"What is that?" he asked. He spoke English so well, I forgot that once in a while he'd hit a word he didn't know, and then his curiosity would take over. We'd had a long discussion on the set once as to why "zeal" was pronounced "zeel," but "zealous" was pronounced "zeh-luss" and not "zeel-luss."

"Serendipity is something that comes along quite by chance and is very pleasant."

"That's exactly what it was," he replied.

To this day, Omar Sharif's entrance into the picture is one of the most dramatic and mesmerizing recorded on camera, coming from such a great distance that the audience is not even sure someone is really out there in the wavering light of the desert. Critics everywhere commented on the moment. But Lean devised an exit that is also noteworthy, where Omar, walking away from Anthony Quinn, casts one final look at him over his shoulder and is immediately engulfed in shadows.

A night shoot was scheduled, the final shot of which was to be done in the streaked light of dawn. In the movie, the scene would play as the streaked light of evening, right after sunset. At the end of our night's shoot, we started to set up cameras and lights on rue Royale around 3:30

A.M. to light up the exterior of the restaurant Maxim's. In the shot, Peter, as General Tanz, exits the restaurant and approaches his car, where Courtenay as his chauffeur stands waiting. Peter then utters what he and I thought was the funniest line of an otherwise humorless film. A maniac about cleanliness who never removes his gloves, Tanz glances back at the most famous restaurant in the world and says, "An adequate restaurant. Very clean." We laughed at the line, although audiences never found it as funny as we did, probably because most people couldn't identify Maxim's from the outside (or the inside, for that matter).

It was the only shot that night for which Peter was needed. He arrived in proper wardrobe and makeup and, I believe, he'd been up the whole night, rather than awake at three o'clock for makeup and hair. "You know," he said to me, "when I was a little boy, I used to have to get up at five o'clock in the morning, and I had to walk a long, long way to the bus stop. Then the bus had to go an even longer way to take me to school. And I used to tell myself that I wanted to be an actor so I'd never have to get up at five o'clock again. Now I'm an actor and it's five o'clock in the morning, and here I am!"

We were into the final stretch of the film. Peter needed to go to England for the bicentennial celebration of the Bristol Old Vic, where he'd done some of his earliest acting. The evening was to honor him and all the other "old boys" and "old girls" of the company, and there was to be a musical revue of the theater's past. The day he left, we shot scenes with other actors, and the following day he was due on the set at twelve noon for the climactic scene where General Tanz shoots Sharif's Inspector Grau. When I arrived at eleven, I learned that Peter had not yet returned from London. The production manager, the A.D.s, and Litvak himself were frantic with concern. Soon word arrived from Philippe Attal, a 2nd assistant director, from Orly Airport that a private plane bearing O'Toole and Perkins had landed, and that they'd be at the studio in an hour. Relieved, Litvak started to plan his shots. Omar would arrive in the room first, and then, when O'Toole would be ready, Litvak could do the two-shots of them together. I stayed with Litvak on the set as the scene began to be prepared, and I asked Tom Pevsner, the 1st A.D., to inform me immediately when Peter arrived at the studio, since I wanted to freshen lines with him. Soon, word was brought that his car had arrived, but that the actor, by dint of too much drinking throughout the night, might not be able to perform. I immediately started for his dressing room and found him with Perkins and the chauffeur on the steps leading to the dressing room. I caught up to Peter in a déjà vu moment of my very first meeting with him on the studio stairs. He put his arm around me and I was instantly engulfed in all the fumes of all the fetid pubs of England. He told me what an extraordinary evening he'd had, how much talent there had been present, and how completely touched he'd been to have been part of it. I guessed that the ensuing party must have continued into morning. I imagined the race he and Perkins must have made to the airfield, to the private plane that brought the exhilarated but sleepless actor back to Paris. I imagined his eyes crackling with red filaments behind his dark glasses.

"So it was worth it?" I asked stupidly. I had no idea what to say. I'd never seen him inebriated like this and feared for the scene on stage.

"*Worth* it?" he queried, staring at me as if I were the strangest of beasts, "Of course it was *worth* it!" Guided by helping arms, he continued on to his dressing room.

At the door, an equally red-eyed Peter Perkins turned around to say, "Come back in a half hour." Then O'Toole literally fell into the arms of his hairdresser and makeup man, and the door closed.

Word could not be kept from Litvak about Peter's state. Young Attal had told the 1st A.D. that O'Toole had had to be transported from the plane to the waiting production car in a wheelchair, as the actor could barely stand. Litvak's brow knitted itself into a permanent look of worry that barely left him for the next several hours. "See how he is," he said to me.

"It isn't a half hour yet, Tola."

"As soon as it is, go find out. And come right to me. To Tom and me, no one else. We have to figure out what to shoot."

At the end of the half hour, I knocked on Peter's dressing room door. Perkins appeared in a dark, oblong opening and whispered, "Come back in an hour. He's sleeping."

"Sleeping?" I asked incredulously.

The makeup man and the hairdresser pushed their way out of the darkness. "We're going down to the bar for coffee," one of them said. "It'll be a while."

"He'll be all right," Perkins added. "He just needs a little nap."

I brought the news to Litvak, which was much like telling a nobleman Versailles had just been assailed. He paled to whiteness. "Will he be able to shoot?" he asked. I told him I honestly didn't know, but his hairdresser and makeup man assured me he would, and I tended to believe them. Litvak decided to do a close-up of Omar getting shot, though there was no Peter O'Toole around to pull the trigger.

It would be three hours, not one, before Peter would be in any condition to see anyone. Repeatedly, I appeared at the dressing room door, and repeatedly, I was informed to come back. On the fourth visit, I was admitted. There were many empty glasses of tomato juice–egg yolk–Worcestershire sauce concoctions, the O'Toole antidote for a hangover, which I'd heard somewhere was the same antidote Noel Coward had used. Naked as a jaybird, Peter stepped out of the shower, his fair skin as white as Irish linen, a skin the sun rarely touched. His wet hair plastered down on his forehead, he caught my eye. "Do I have any big speeches, Trawley luv?" I told him no, but that there was an exchange of dialogue nonetheless. "Then we shall have it!" he declaimed as he started into a pair of under shorts. I opened the script and began speaking Omar's lines to him.

On the stage, Litvak had filmed everything he could without Peter: Omar's arrival and dialogue in the outer office, his entrance into General Tanz's office, and Omar's close shot getting shot to death. At three o'clock, the camera stopped turning, the crew drifted little by little to the bar and then casually returned. Litvak was strangling over the loss of time. He had gone from worry to anger, from a white Russian to a red-in-the-face Russian. At this moment, I appeared at his side and told him I'd rehearsed with Peter and that he'd be fine.

At five o'clock, Peter strode onto the stage in his general's uniform, his putty Aryan nose and every hair in place. Everyone went still as he walked right up to Litvak and said, in almost heart-breaking contrition, "Tola, I'm so sorry!" Four words, but they were the right ones for a sentimental Russian. Litvak's anger dissolved instantly, his eyes went moist, and then the two of them, renowned director and actor alike, fell into each other's arms and embraced. I swear they both were sniffling before Peter broke away and apologized to Omar and the crew. Litvak reached for a handkerchief.

Then Litvak did several two-shots of Peter and Omar together with Omar telling Peter he was under arrest. Peter's performance was superb—hard, controlled, mad, ending with his stepping over Omar's body and exiting. There was no trace of the night before. If you rent the video, look at the rapid cutting and distinguish the individual shots. Peter, alone, fires the pistol in one shot, and Omar, alone, is shot in the stomach and falls to the floor in another. But when he does, Peter is actually sleeping off a hangover in his dressing room.

Much has been said over the years about Peter's drinking, but between *How to Steal a Million* and *The Night of the Generals*, I was with him for over eight months. In all that time, I never saw him drink during work, except for that glass of champagne on the set a half hour before the last shot of the day. And except for the day I've just related, I never saw him in any state other than the most professional one, knowing his lines, ready to create the most complex characters. And in those eight months, there were only two hours of production time lost because of him. It's something the press never printed.

Finally, after almost five months, we finished. One by one, as each star terminated, there would be a final drink at the long table at the edge of the stage. The Impressionist paintings that had been used in the museum scene where Peter has a near-psychotic episode looking at the self-portrait of Van Gogh all had to be destroyed. Major Paris artists had painted copies of the famous paintings and these copies were, in themselves, valuable. The same production designer, Alexandre Trauner, had used these artists to create the paintings in the museum set in *How to Steal a Million*, where again the beautiful works all had to be destroyed. Omar left for a bridge tournament, and Courtenay stated he was thinking about performing the small role of Malcolm in a production of "the Scottish gentleman" that a theater in Chichester was doing. Litvak tried to dissuade him, but in the end I think Tom did do the role. Noiret, his actress wife, Monique Chaumette, and I would dine together in a few days. Litvak still needed me for several weeks of dubbing. And finally it came time to say goodbye to Peter. With his arms around me in a monumental hug, he thanked me and I thanked him. Though we didn't have a word for what we were thanking each other, I'm sure it was more than professional collaboration. I told him it was only an au revoir, not an adieu.

I would see him a few months later in London, when I accompanied Litvak there to assist Peter in dubbing lines that were shot with outdoor sounds interfering. I would bring him a gift of a nineteenth-century French horse saddle that surprised him and recalled our Sunday at Chantilly. That would be the last time I would see him. We spoke once on the phone after that, when he was trying to get me on *The Lion in Winter*, but the English union laws wouldn't allow an American to work on a film in England, which was where the majority of the film was shot. I did, however, at his request, do enormous amounts of research on the period for him, poring over centuries-old esoteric tomes in the Bibliothèque Nationale in Paris. I sent him reams of information on Henry Plantagenet and Eleanor of Aquitaine and all the other characters in *The Lion in Winter*. In 2000, thirty-four years after we worked together, I saw a filmed interview of him for a documentary made by Richard Rush, the director of *The Stunt Man*, in honor of the twentieth anniversary of that film. Considerably aged, Peter looked most elegant and sat smoking a cigarette from a long cigarette holder, a fetish I'd not seen since the days of—who? Coward? Lunt? the Sitwells? It was deliciously démodé, but Peter carried it off with his habitual panache. He spoke to the camera as he would for a classical play, articulately and with great regalness, all vestiges of childhood working-class vanished. I saw he had become the natural theater heir to Olivier, Richardson, Redgrave, and Gielgud. They were English, of course, and Peter is Irish, but I think he's stolen their kingdom.

CHAPTER SIX

~

I, Jupiter; I, Rex
(with a nod to Cole Porter)

What made 20th Century Fox decide to make *A Flea in Her Ear*, a script based on the Feydeau turn-of-the-century farce? As a piece of theater, it's hilarious. Two Frenchmen look identical. One is an upper-class lawyer, the other a drunken porter in a brothel. When the lawyer and his wife end up trying to retrieve his suspenders from the brothel, the lawyer is instantly mistaken for the porter. As with all farces, there are a hundred twists, building ridiculously until the *scène obligatoire* where all sorts of characters run and hide from other characters and all the bedroom doors are slamming. This old chestnut had a riotous revival at the Old Vic with Albert Finney in the double roles of the lawyer and the porter in 1966.

The fun of the play is to watch the actor playing the lawyer exit one side of the stage and in half a minute (twenty lines, to be precise) enter the opposite side dressed as the drunken porter. While today that would probably be easily accomplished with Velcro tear-away clothes, it was not so easy in buttoned-down 1907, when the play was first performed, or even in 1966. Feydeau, a brilliant technician, wrote elaborate backstage directions in his original manuscript, placing a dozen dressers in a semicircle. The actor was to discard his coat with one, his foulard with another, don the porter's jacket with yet another, and so on, all the while running behind the scenery from one side of the stage to the other, then stagger back on, hair mussed and bottle in hand, as the look-alike porter.

But what was pure gold on stage became dull dross before the camera. The concept was wrong. There is no magic before the eyes of the viewer in the movie house, when, with one snip of the editor's scissors, a hero can instantly be transported to another time or place. Somehow, the movie executives missed that.

Then there was the casting of Rex Harrison, another mistake. Harrison's turn at comedy was deft, drawing room, sophisticated, the perennial cocktail glass in hand. Perfect for Shaw or Coward or Van Druten's *Bell, Book, and Candle.* Perfect as the constipated, pedantic snob, Henry Higgins. But a *farce?* If you can't fall on your face, you have no business doing Feydeau. Stan Laurel would have been a better choice.

Finally, there is a special stylized acting required as each character begins in reality and, with vicissitudes and momentum building, must mount the pitch to absolute lunacy. The cast, fine actors in their own right, knew little about falling on their faces. Besides Harrison, there was the eternal, suave lover, Louis Jourdan; out of *The Lion in Winter* in New York came dramatic actress Rosemary Harris; Rachel Roberts, Harrison's wife, was principally known for *This Sporting Life*, another drama; then there was Edward Hardwicke, son of Sir Cedric Hardwicke, and a pretty English ingenue named Isla Blair. A lone French actor from the Comédie Française, Georges Descrières, was the only one familiar with French farce, although Hardwicke and Blair came close. Add to this olla podrida another Comédie Française actor, Jacques Charon, in the capacity of director, speaking little English. He had directed the production of the play at the Old Vic with Finney, but this was his first attempt at film. Finally, there was Walter Thompson, the elderly Hollywood editor, who would walk through every shot with Charon ahead of time, so it could all "cut" together later. He, too, knew nothing about French farce.

It was an accident waiting to happen.

I was contacted by casting director Margot Capelier, who told me that Georges Descrières was about to be signed for the role of the irascible South American. I worked with Descrières one day and informed Capelier that he had an excellent ear and was a quick learn. They signed him up. Then I met with producer Fred Kohlmar, back in Paris for the movie, who said that Descrières was in the process of constructing a house on the island of Corsica, and would I mind going there with him for a week or so, to rehearse with him, all expenses paid?

"Would I *mind?*" I asked unbelievingly. "You mean, would I mind taking a vacation with him? We can only work an hour to an hour-and-a-half in the morning and maybe an hour in the afternoon. Then an actor doesn't hear you any more."

"Fine," said Kohlmar. "Then go swimming, work on a tan, I don't care." And smiling, he stood up and led me to the door, arm around my shoulders in the same fatherly gesture he'd used for the Wyler meeting two years earlier. "You're not a problem," he said. "Not like Mr. Harrison."

"What's the problem there?" I asked.

"*He* is. I have to send Jean Zay, the costume designer, to Portofino, where Harrison is vacationing. All of a sudden, two weeks from shooting, he doesn't like any of his costumes. Things we settled on long ago. Now we have to start all over."

"I'm sorry," I said. "I wonder if this is indicative of how he'll be through the picture."

"Probably. We've all heard the Rex Harrison stories. Go to Corsica and enjoy yourself."

A few days later, in the blaze of a white hot noon, I landed in Bastia, Corsica. Georges Descrières had preceded me by a couple of days, and met me at the airport with a rented car. We drove inland, cutting through miles of undeveloped fields of wildflowers and brush that had a faint, peppery perfume. "That's the *maquis*," he said, referring to the bushes, "that gives that odor. It's very particular to Corsica."

"*Maquis*. I thought that was the word used for the French Underground during World War II."

"That, too!" he laughed. "No connection that I know!" We drove through woods musky with pine and juniper. Then, on a turn in the road, it all changed. We came to the west side of the island, where reddish cliffs fell precipitously into the sea. Before me lay the breathtaking azure Mediterranean under a burning golden sun. We headed south along the coast, a coast that was rocky and, like all of Corsica in 1967, savage and wild. I'd later see other coasts, rockier and wilder still, in Brittany and Cornwall, but for now there was no sun like this sun, no sea like this sea, no island like this Corsica.

Just outside the town of Calvi, we pulled up to a lovely hotel dominating the rocks and the sea and a small, sandy beach below. Descrières was staying here, since his new house was in the most rudimentary stage possible, with concrete recently poured and wooden posts erected. I checked into the hotel and found my room on the front side, overlooking the sparkling clear blue water, with not a wave in sight. In minutes, I rejoined Georges on the terrace overlooking the same view, and we sat down to a two-hour lunch of cold crustaceans and local fish, with the coldest bottle of dry white wine the island had to offer.

In the afternoon, we rehearsed for about an hour, and we did so again the following morning. The work was tricky because the role required English with a Spanish accent. I had brought with me a recording I'd made in Paris of two real Spaniards reading his lines. We played it, and Georges, the perfect mimic, soon had replaced his French accent with a Spanish one. Then we went to the beach for about two hours, swam in the lulling, warm waters of the Mediterranean, and lunched again for two hours with a chilled bottle of Corsican wine.

And so it went for almost a week. Then one day Leslie Caron joined us for lunch. A friend of Georges', she had bumped into him in a shop and he had invited her to join us. She had divorced English theater director Peter Hall the year before and was alone. We spoke only French at the table, and it was a pleasure to hear the star of (chronologically) *An American in Paris*, *Lili*, and *Gigi* speaking her native tongue. She was charming, disarming, *très française*, and I fell in love with her overbite. We spoke about Mike Nichols' movie, *Who's Afraid of Virginia Woolf?* which had taken Europeans by surprise. Until then, the European film market had been dominated by the English, the Italians, and the last films of the French New Wave. Caron thought *Who's Afraid of Virginia Woolf?* was important, not simply because it broke the outdated Hays Code, but also because it looked like American films might be growing up.

"It is serious filmmaking," she said. She was right, of course. While we were lunching on the terrace in 1967, Warren Beatty and Arthur Penn were about to take London, Paris, and eventually Hollywood by storm with *Bonnie and Clyde*. *The Graduate*, *Midnight Cowboy*, and *Easy Rider* would follow and with them, the disillusioned and disenfranchised American antihero.

"Yes, and here *we* are," said Georges. "We are going to shoot *A Flea in Her Ear*. Where nothing is serious." He had crystallized another thing that was wrong with this movie: it was not in keeping with the burgeoning trend.

After lunch, I called my father in Rochester, New York. I knew how much he liked Caron on screen. "Guess whom I had lunch with today?"

"Who?" he asked.

"Leslie Caron," I answered, preening.

There was a long pause. "What's she doing these days?"

Like I said, he was a killer, my father. With one question, he had underlined all the instabilities of the motion picture business. I could almost hear him say, "When are you coming home and getting a real job?"

"You calling me from Paris?" he asked.

"No. I'm in Corsica."

"Where's Corsica?"

"It's an island in the Mediterranean, between France and Italy. It's French."

"I thought you said you just had lunch with Leslie Caron."

"I did. She's here in Corsica, too."

"Funny life you guys lead."

I don't know what else we spoke about. He asked if I needed money, and I told him I didn't, that I was doing just fine. I don't think he believed that; a father never believes his son doesn't need him. I'm sure his only concept of earning money was in the manner he'd lived his life: working for one company for forty years and getting a paycheck every week. My movie life was strange to him, as strange as . . . well, Corsica.

On my last lunch with Descrières on the hotel terrace, I sighted French opera singer Jane Rhodes and her husband, conductor Roberto Benzi. Georges leaned forward to confide in me. "There's a story floating around Paris that when she makes love, she bursts into song!"

"Come on!" I said. "Not true."

"It's what I heard," Georges insisted.

Rhodes and Benzi had left the table, gone into the hotel, and Georges and I were idling over strong French coffee and fresh fruit. Suddenly from an upstairs window I began to hear the strains of the

Seguidilla from *Carmen*, Rhodes's most famous role. Georges looked at me and raised an eyebrow.

> Près des remparts de Sév-ill-e
> Chez mon ami Lillas Pastia . . .

And then she hit a note that was definitely not in Bizet's score, a note that was, in every sense, piercing. There was a tremulous sound and then the aria again. Georges' lips curled in an I-told-you-so smile, and he lifted his coffee cup, like a glass in a toast, in my direction.

I met Rex Harrison and Rachel Roberts at the same time. They had adjoining dressing rooms, and Fred Kohlmar brought me in and introduced me. Roberts was Harrison's fourth wife, being preceded by Colette Thomas, Lilli Palmer, and Kay Kendall. He definitely had a penchant for actresses. From what I knew of the screen presences of the other wives, Roberts was a definite departure in type. She was outspoken, animated, and a touch loud. They were at the studio for wardrobe fittings, and Harrison was due to start filming in a few days. Kohlmar introduced me, and there were hellos all around, hers much warmer than his.

"Look here," Harrison said to Kohlmar, "do you think this hangs right?" He was referring to his 1900 jacket.

"Oh, Rex, it's perfect!" retorted Roberts before Kohlmar could answer. The producer agreed.

Harrison mouthed a "Hmmmm" that said he wasn't completely convinced. "You know what I need, Fred? I should have another full-length mirror. Then I could see the back and front at the same time."

"We'll get one right away," Kohlmar replied, then tactfully turned to Roberts. "Would you like one, too?"

"I'm fine, Fred. I know what the back of me looks like. Rex still needs to look at his."

We all laughed and Harrison uttered one of his famous series of yesses. There were usually two or three together, and I was told that if he ever uttered five in a row, he wasn't listening to you.

Kohlmar and I left together. "Have they been drinking?" I asked him. There had been a slight aroma of alcohol and peppermint in the air.

"I'm sure they have," was his reply. "They do it a lot. Didn't I tell you that?"

One by one, I met the lead actors. Except for Descrières, they seemed unusually cold, and in the end the only other friendships I formed on the film were with young Isla Blair and Edward Hardwicke. Isla was to become quite the stage actress over the years, and I saw her in 1989 performing opposite Derek Jacobi in *Byron* and again in 1990 opposite Richard Harris in Pirandello's *Henry IV*. At dinner in Los Angeles twenty years after the film, Isla told me that she had been terrified during the entire shoot of *A Flea in Her Ear*. "Am I imagining things?" she asked, "or was everyone really so unpleasant? Rosemary Harris was practically mean to me."

"We had a lot of *monstres sacrés* on the film," I answered.

Rosemary Harris had been unpleasant to someone else, too: her dresser, Claudie Thary. She was a small, mousy woman with a perpetually sad face and a furrowed brow that announced her lot to be an unhappy one. She had been Peter O'Toole's dresser on the two films we'd worked on together, and he'd adored her. He used to joke kindly with her, and then her pleated brow would relax and she'd smile, trying her best to keep her mouth closed because she had a visible hole where a tooth had been. But where O'Toole loved Claudie, Rosemary Harris couldn't stand her. I was in Harris' dressing room, running lines with her, as Claudie completed the touches on Harris' long-gowned costume, placing the skirt material in even folds.

"Oh, do stop puttering!" Harris said irritably, and then, possibly because Claudie didn't stop quickly enough, pushed her hand away. It was almost a slap. "You don't have to touch me so much!" Then, as Claudie moved away, her face sadder than ever, Harris turned to me and said, "I can't stand her to touch me." I was sure Claudie had heard her.

Harris must have complained to Kohlmar, because Claudie was reassigned to the younger actors, and a different dresser was given to Harris, one whose touch was apparently more tolerable.

Because she was a theater actress, Harris saw the wisdom of rehearsing with a dialogue coach, especially since the director's English was so poor. She was always civil to me, as was Louis Jourdan. I never knew what kind of a mood Rachel Roberts would be in, so rehearsals with her were sporadic. The real problem was Rex Harrison. On a daily basis I would appear to him, and on a daily basis he would tell me he didn't need to rehearse. If there were mistakes on the set, I would simply move to his side, whisper the correction, and point to the script. "Yes, yes, that's it," he'd reply. Then I'd mime a gesture to Jacques Charon to do another take and we would go again. I'm convinced it was pure ego on Harrison's part not to rehearse with me. What with Roberts's changing moods, Jourdan's impenetrable aloofness, Harris's coldness, and Harrison's refusal to rehearse whatsoever, I didn't get to spend a great deal of time at their sides. The compensation came at the camera. Jacques Charon knew his English was not good and so constantly kept me next to him, so I could translate to the actors.

"*Viens, chéri!*" he would call to me. A slightly rotund man who'd performed mostly servant roles in Molière with great hilarity, he addressed every man under forty, and a few over, as *chéri*. To the eternally unhomophobic Frenchmen, it was always a compliment. "Stay beside me," he would say, and I did, for every shot in the picture, as I became the bilingual hyphen between actor and director.

One day, Harrison had a problem with the way a scene was playing. He wanted to speed up the timing, and Charon, trying to retain the rhythm of farce, absolutely agreed. Harrison looked at my script and remarked to the director, "The dialogue is slowing the scene. The lines need to overlap." Then he turned to me and said, "How do you say 'overlap' in French?"

"*Chevaucher,*" I replied instantly. I'd learned the word from the sound man on my first movie. Harrison's eyes narrowed (he had puffy, narrow eyes anyway) as if to say, "Are you sure?"

"That's what we need," Harrison continued back to Charon. "Everyone's lines have to *chevaucher*, if that's the word."

If that's the word! I wanted to kick him.

"*Oui, oui, chevaucher!*" replied Charon. "That will pick up the timing. You are right!" Then Harrison, satisfied that he was saving the scene, moved off. Charon looked at me, his actor's antenna having caught everything. "Don't take his remark personally, *chéri*. He doesn't even know what he said. That's Rex."

Another day, we came to a scene where Harrison had almost a full page of monologue. In his lawyer's cap and robes, he was to deliver to the court a rousting speech about the honor of France. When I appeared at his dressing room that morning with my usual question about rehearsing, he answered, to my astonishment, that yes, perhaps I could be somewhat useful to him. In I went, and out went the hairdresser and makeup man, and since we were dealing with a monologue I couldn't cue him any other actor's lines. When he faltered, I would try to show him what the connecting ideas were between sentences so he could link them together. "Yes, yes, yes!" he'd say and try again. Bit by bit, we began to make our way through the long speech.

Suddenly, the connecting door was thrown open and Rachel Roberts stood there. She was in street clothes, for she was not scheduled to shoot that day. "Oh, Rach, dear," Harrison said, "I'm just running lines with old Frawl here!"

Old Frawl? Had we suddenly become chums? *Just* running lines? As if this were a normal occurrence?

"Don't let me bother you!" she said. "I just came in to meet with the accountant. I'll see you later tonight."

"Yes, yes, that's right."

"Is today the big speech?"

"Yes, it is rather."

She turned to me. "Make sure he learns it. He didn't know it last night." Then she gave him a broad grin on her one-upmanship and started to leave.

"Oh, Rach, dear!" he called, catching her on her turn in the doorway. She looked back at him. "I love the dress."

"Rex!" she glowered. "I've had this for two years!"

"It looks different somehow."

"No, it looks the same! The bloody dress looks the same! If you'd take your eyes out of the goddamned mirror once in a while, you might notice what I wear!" And she exited into her dressing room, slamming the door behind her. I felt the hinges shake.

Harrison turned to me, not missing a beat, "Now where were we? I hate interruptions."

Years later, after their divorce, I ran across Rachel Roberts at a dinner party in the Hollywood Hills, at a house on one of those serpentine streets above the Hollywood Bowl. As always, her moods were like quicksilver, and she would alternate between railing at the world and embracing it wholly. I knew little about alcoholism then (and less when we'd worked together in Paris), so I just attributed her mood swings at the party to a matter of nature. I waited for one of her more joyous moments before I approached her. "Rachel, do you remember me?" I asked.

A grin broke out on her face. "Yes, but where was it?"

"A *Flea in Her Ear*, in Paris. I was the dialogue coach."

She hugged me. "Of course. I knew you looked familiar! My God, I'd almost forgotten that film!"

"Why not? Everyone else has."

She roared with laughter. "I like you! Did I like you then?"

"You and Rex were pretty much in your own world at the time. I don't think you saw me. You guys were drinking a lot."

"Like fish. We were not happy together. He was a son of a bitch!" Then she looked around and shouted to the entire room. "Rex Harrison is a son of a bitch!" A few people laughed back. Then, in her normal tone she added to me, "He is, you know."

"If you're looking for an argument, pick another subject!" I answered. I knew it was a line from some movie, but it never seemed more appropriate than at that moment.

She roared again, and said a second time, "I like you!" Then she immediately left my side to have her empty glass filled, and just as immediately forgot me. During dinner, I sat at a small table and conversed quietly with Christopher Isherwood and the two younger men with him, while Rachel, at an adjacent table, inundated us all periodically with a laugh that was raucous and far too attention-demanding.

We were shooting a scene in front of the Pré Catalan restaurant in the Bois de Boulogne, at the edge of Paris. In a dither, Rosemary Harris leaves would-be lover Louis Jourdan as she runs for a carriage, telling him she has to find out why the brothel sent back her husband's braces. (Braces is the English word for suspenders, another lift-elevator dilemma.) As Harris exits the screen, the camera, which had been tracking along with both of them, moves in for a close-up of Jourdan's perplexed face. Jourdan is then supposed to say, "Braces? What does she mean by braces?" End of scene, cut. We rehearsed a few times and Jourdan seemed to have forgotten the last line, so I moved in to him and showed him the script.

"Yes, I know," he said.

Then we began to shoot. The same thing occurred. As his face filled the camera in a full close-up, his lips did not move and the line was not said. At the end of the take, I immediately told Charon that Jourdan had not said the last line.

"Are you sure?" he asked. "He told me he'd say it." Then the two of us went to the sound mixer at his little table by the dolly track. He replayed the sound and both Charon and I listened with headsets. At the end of the scene, nothing. "Run back the last piece," Charon told him "and bring the sound up to maximum." He did. Then we both heard the faintest mumbling, almost indiscernible but something that matched the number of syllables in Jourdan's line. "*Voilà!* There is your line!" Charon announced.

"Who can hear it?"

"He'll dub it in the sound studio."

"But why's he doing it like that? His face isn't even moving."

"Precisely. Look at me, *chéri!*" And then he said the same line aloud, animating it with exaggerated astonishment. His face quickly pleated, lines falling around the corners of his mouth and eyes. "It is a very big close-up, *n'est-ce pas?* And Monsieur Jourdan doesn't want these lines around his eyes and on his face! That is why he isn't moving. I am from the theater where we don't care about such things. It drives me crazy!"

"Is *everyone* on this film self-involved?" I asked.

"Of course. These are not easy people, I assure you." Then we made our way back to the camera. "*Très bien, Louis!*" Charon remarked, all smiles, and we continued the day's work.

But the acme of self-involvement was yet to come. A small portion of the Paris opera had been reconstructed in the studio, with some fifteen rows of the orchestra section and a half dozen boxes. Through the opera audience, the camera was first to single out the Descrières-Roberts couple, then continue on to pick up Jourdan, Harrison, and Harris sitting in a private box. Actors and extras alike were in elegant turn-of-the-century formal attire. There was no dialogue in the scene, just a shot of the principals listening to the opera. It took several hours to light the set and place some hundred-odd extras. Then it was time to bring in the lead actors. Each was led to the stage, except Rex Harrison, who was not ready. Everyone waited. And waited. Finally, word came that he wanted to speak to producer Fred Kohlmar. A few minutes later, Kohlmar came down to the set and conferred with Charon and the assistant director. The other four stars were then told they could return to their dressing rooms and the extras could all take a break. Harrison was apparently distressed that his dresser had supplied black cotton socks instead of black silk socks for the opera scene. Harrison refused to come to the stage in a costume he considered "inappropriate," and the dresser was, at that very moment, in a production car being whisked to a haberdashery on the Champs-Élysées. Since we were filming in the suburb of Boulogne, that meant the break would be at least an hour long. The lights were switched off and most of the crew flooded into the bar for a coffee, a sandwich, the *plat du jour*, or a glass of wine.

Eventually, the dresser returned with an assortment of black silk socks, Rex Harrison made his selection, and the crew reconvened. Lights were switched back on, extras repositioned, the four other principal actors again convoked, and finally, after a two-hour caesura, Mr. Harrison was accompanied to the stage. Unlike the two-hour wait for Peter O'Toole on *The Night of the Generals*, no apology was made this time to the director or to any of the other actors. Harrison took his place on a velour-tufted chair next to Rosemary Harris and Louis Jourdan in the theater box, and the camera moved in for a final rehearsal.

In the *theater box*? There was a riser almost three feet high directly in front of the three actors, representing the exterior of the box. It was impossible, either by eye or camera, to see what the principal actors wore below the waist. Harrison had known this. He could have worn sweat socks and bunny slippers. Yet he held up the entire company for close to two hours until he had black silk socks on his feet.

"The wait had nothing to do with how we were shooting the scene," Charon said to me later when all the enfants terribles were back in their dressing rooms. "Or even with the kind of socks appropriate at the opera. What it has to do with, is Mr. Harrison's letting everyone know that respect will be given to him. As I said, not easy, these people."

Harrison always went to see dailies, film that was shot the day before. I couldn't help but compare him to O'Toole, who never once went to see dailies. I think Peter didn't want any thoughts to trouble him about what he looked like, so he could concentrate on the character. To my knowledge, he always waited to see a cut version of the film, months after completing it. But there was Harrison, on a nightly basis, studying his image on the screen. It was another mirror.

Twice, the massive display of ego actually became entertaining. The first time was with Rosemary Harris in her dressing room, as she spoke of *The Lion in Winter*. I told her how I had done research for O'Toole for the upcoming film version of the play.

"Yes, Katie Hepburn's doing my role," she said. "Of course, she's much older. And older than Peter O'Toole. I wonder how that's going to *play*." Then she spoke of James Goldman's remarkable language in the play, the constant barbs Henry and Eleanor throw at each other. And suddenly she was on stage again at the Ambassador Theatre, declaiming in both roles.

> You go to Rome, we'll rise against you.
> Who will?
> Richard, Geoffrey, John, and Eleanor of Aquitaine!
> The day those stout hearts band together is the day that pigs get wings.
> There'll be pork in the treetops come morning!

Her arms were in the air, her chin lifted in defiance. Oh, Rosemary Harris was talented, all right! And I wished I had seen her and Robert Preston in New York. At least here, in her dressing room, I caught a scintilla of her Eleanor of Aquitaine.

A week later, another performance. This one, Harrison's at the wrap party held on the stage. Drinks were flowing, everyone was congratulating everyone else, ironically for work on a film that no one has heard of today. At one end of the stage was a four-piece French band playing some dated French songs. Drink assisting, crew members stood up from time to time to sing one of the songs amateurishly and off-key. Drink assisting still further, Rex Harrison eventually made his way to the band. He turned and said something to the musicians, who simply shook their Gallic heads in the negative. Then he turned around and, a cappella, began to sing *I've Grown Accustomed to Her Face*. The room went completely silent, not because everyone knew how he had made that song famous, but because he'd been the star of our movie and no one dared offer anything but reverent silence. The French didn't get the song, of course, but the few Anglo-Saxons there did. Suddenly, I was on Broadway. Self-centered, mordant, cold, condescending, Harrison was all these things. Yet at that moment, with Henry Higgins incarnate before me, I stood in awe of his talent. He finished the song, speaking the final two words, "Her face!" as he had a thousand times over, and everyone applauded. Swaying slightly from scotch, but with an enormous grin on her face, Rachel Roberts advanced toward him. Her eyes were moist. Had the song been for her? "Her face!" Roberts' face? She kissed him. Everyone applauded a second time. "You son of a bitch!" she said, her voice raw.

Whatever fire was shared between them, drink would eventually extinguish it, and both of them in the process. Roberts died of an accidental overdose of barbiturates in 1980, and Harrison succumbed to pancreatic cancer in 1990. But I'm sure both their livers were shot to hell.

A Flea in Her Ear was another movie that, upon completion, made me seek fresh air. I again headed for the windswept coast of Normandy with the cat for a few days. I read, I slept, I walked the beaches, I ate the glorious seafood, and I drank glass after glass of *cidre brut*. Then, when France had again invaded my soul and the charming actors of the movie were no longer with me, I returned to Paris. In my absence, my friend, Marie-Gisèle Landes, had been trying to reach me. Director Nicholas Ray was back in town and wanted to see me.

We met at Le Paris on the Champs-Élysées. Through his cigarette smoke, I spotted Ray's gaunt features and that unruly mop of salt-and-pepper hair when I walked in. We played a few moments of catch-up. I told him about the films I'd worked on, and he told me how he'd been bouncing around all over Europe. He owned a nightclub in Madrid and a house on the north German island of Sylt, and he'd been helping Polish director Andrzej Wajda cut a film. But nothing really tangible had happened in Nick's career. Then he spoke of his latest project. Had I heard of *Gösta Berling*? I hadn't.

"It was one of Garbo's silent films, made in Sweden. It's based on a novel by Selma Lagerlöf that's a Swedish classic. I think she got the Nobel Prize for it. I want to remake it," he said. "I've got Ingrid Thulin interested." The Swedish actress was well known in Europe, then, and was very gifted. American audiences saw her as Liv Ullman's older sister in Ingmar Bergman's 1973's best picture nominee, *Cries and Whispers*.

"What do you want me to do?" I asked.

"I thought we could work on a treatment together."

"*Write* it with you?"

"Yes. Isn't it time you started?"

I was flabbergasted. Two years earlier, Ray had remarked that he thought I should be writing, and now he actually wanted me on a project with him. As it turned out, Nick was debt-ridden at this point, and so had no money to pay me. That may also have been a reason why he asked me; obtaining a professional writer would have been costly for him. Since I had just completed a picture and had a lot of time and a little money in front of me, I agreed.

"Do you have an outline for it?" I asked.

"I have a copy of the novel in English," he answered and slid a well-worn hard-covered book toward me. "I'm sure you can get it in French, too, but I can lend you this one."

"Where are we going to work?"

"I'm staying at a hotel on the Île Saint-Louis. We could work there, or I thought maybe at your apartment."

A few days later, he came to my apartment on rue des Belles-Feuilles. The street contained one of the better markets of the 16th quarter and was rife with fresh produce and dairy merchants. Ambulatory carts that sold lettuce, herbs, or flowers added more color. In my small one-bedroom flat, Nick walked around, admiring the antiques and old prints I'd begun to collect. The first day, we worked in the afternoon, making an outline of the material. I thought it would take only a few hours, but the work went on through the evening and then into the night. He consumed many glasses of my red table wine. I remembered my earlier impression, that this man could seemingly go for days without sleeping or eating. At ten o'clock, I reminded him that being a mere mortal, I was getting hungry. We'd have to hurry to the corner restaurant, I said, if we still wanted to be served.

And so the routine began. We worked almost every day, long, long hours, his cigarette smoke stifling my small apartment. A dash for the nearby restaurant before it closed, then several more hours of work. We were writing a narrative treatment, but animating it with great spurts of dialogue that flowed out of Nick easily. Of the character Gösta Berling, a minister with earthly desires, he wrote, "Just because a man's collar is on backwards doesn't mean his pants are buttoned up." I was in love, totally in love, with Nick's creativity and what we were doing together. Yet I was not blind to the fact that he was broke and that I was buying almost all our lunches or dinners. I didn't care. I considered it tuition to school. And I didn't care when he spoke of his gambling debts at some of the clubs, and I lent him several hundred dollars that he probably used to go to other clubs, drink, and lose still more. I didn't care that I would never see that money again.

One day, we came to a crucial scene, where the countess speaks for the first time to the drunken man of God who will be her lover. "Why don't you try this one by yourself?" Nick said to me. He got up and moved to the door. "I'll catch up to you in a day or so. Call me when you've got something."

Just like that! Suddenly, I was on my own to write for the first time in my life. I attacked the scene with exhilaration, with energy leaping from me to the page, on a portable Olivetti with a French keyboard. I wrote how the young minister staggered out of an inn, drunk, and was tormented by town children who pulled at his clothes. How the hero fell in a heap on the snow in the town square, just as the countess's sleigh was passing by. How she stopped to stare at him, got out of the sleigh and walked up to him, shooing the children away. How he looked up at her with bleary eyes as she delivered a page-long tirade of how he was destroying his precious life. She ended her speech with, "You are a sorry sight for the children." I reread what I'd written. A frisson went through my body. Tennessee Williams couldn't have done it better.

The next day, Nick came back and I showed him the scene, two-and-a-half pages long. He read it carefully, not once but twice, squinting his eyes through the curtain of cigarette wisps. Then he took a pencil and began to cut. He kept the inn, the drunken stagger, the children, the collapse in the snow, and the sleigh arriving with the countess. Then he came to her wonderful monologue. He crossed out every bit of it, right down to the last line, and said, "This is all you need: 'You are a sorry sight for the children.'" He left that in.

And he was right. My monologue had moralized and, while it was a wonderful piece of theater and a great moment for an actress, the camera was also telling us the same thing visually. Brevity was the soul of wit that day, as Nicholas Ray taught me Polonius's priceless lesson.

We had finished some twenty-five pages of our treatment, a sort of first act, when Nick, who could never stay very long in one place, decided to take the pages to Ingrid Thulin in Stockholm while I was to continue outlining the second half and flesh in more scenes. Marie-Gisèle would accompany him there. On our way to the airport, Nick told me that Thulin's husband was the Swedish minister of the arts, so his support in the project would just about clinch the deal. The very name of Nicholas Ray opened any door in Europe, including the one to Thulin's home, which was where their meeting was to be, and where he and Marie-Gisèle were to spend the night. Nick was excited and confident when I let the two of them off at the old Orly airport. "You think I can do the second half by myself?" I asked him.

"Of course. You're a writer. And I'm a filmmaker!" On his crazy smile, he turned and entered the airport with Marie-Gisèle, his Gitanes cigarette hermetically sealed to his lips.

I never saw Nick again. Marie-Gisèle called me from Stockholm to tell me that Thulin's husband had checked on the rights to *Gösta Berling* and they had just recently been bought up by Swedish producer Lars Schmidt, although I don't think Schmidt ever took the piece to fruition. I guess Nick had assumed that the rights were in public domain. Then he took the phone. His voice was shaky when he said, "They both loved the idea of Thulin doing the role."

Where Nick went after that I never knew. Too many pins had been knocked out from under him too many times. The Europeans loved him, but had no money to give him. The Americans had money but in a world with an obsession over recent screen credits, he was yesterday's director. Sadly, I remembered what he'd said to me once, right before we went into a meeting with some French money-people, "It's my time to hit it again. I'm due."

Poor Nick would end up never making another major movie. He returned to the States the following year, made an unheralded, experimental film called *We Can't Go Home Again*, taught some classes in New York, and occasionally appeared as an actor in small roles. Sometime in the late '70s, Marie-Gisèle, who had married an American and was living in San Francisco, saw him there at a special screening of one of his films, with a question and answer period following. According to her, he had become a scarecrow. The newspaper photos I've seen of him during his last few years corroborate this image. His lean, marked face had sunken still further, he wore a black eye patch over his right eye, claiming he'd had an embolism, and his hair was white and wild as the wind. He looked like a harpy, a spector, a Greek Fury. He told Marie-Gisèle over coffee after the screening that he'd joined Alcoholics Anonymous. He said this as he lit up another cigarette, the smoke drifting up to his eye patch and his one good eye. Then he flew back to New York and in 1979 died of lung cancer at the Sloan-Kettering Institute. His final project, in collaboration with German director Wim Wenders, was a macabre daily account of Nick's gradual dying on film. He was never a studio man, yet many of the films he made in the Hollywood system show real genius. His last big film, an epic called 55 Days at Peking, was shot in 1963. Then for five years he wandered all over Europe and our paths crossed twice during that period. To this day, I am eternally grateful for his pushing me to write, and to this day he remains my epitome of a creative filmmaker. Even his self-destructiveness seemed to take on a poignant beauty. I ask myself today if Nick became what every great artist who has not said all he wants to say becomes: a tragic, lost soul destined to roam restlessly from one place to another.

CHAPTER SEVEN

∼

La Révolution Française—
Once More with Feeling

I was contacted by my friend, casting director Margot Capelier, who invited me to have lunch with her at the bar/restaurant down the street from the Studios de Billancourt. She told me that movie icon John Huston was going to direct a film version of Jean Giraudoux's play, *The Madwoman of Chaillot*, with Katharine Hepburn. I had seen Martita Hunt perform the play in Philadelphia many years before. Giraudoux was a favorite playwright of mine and a master of poetic drama.

"Who are the other madwomen?" I asked.

"Margaret Leighton will be Constance and Giulietta Masina will be Gabrielle. I'm not sure who the fourth one will be." (It was Dame Edith Evans.) I was ecstatic. Both ladies were great actresses. I had seen Margaret Leighton in Terence Rattigan's *Separate Tables*, playing both roles on the stage that were performed separately by Deborah Kerr and Rita Hayworth in the movie version. And who could forget Giulietta Masina's performance as the slightly dimwitted waif, Gelsomina, in Federico Fellini's haunting *La Strada*? The real-life wife of Fellini, she was told by the director from the stage of the Dorothy Chandler Pavilion when he received a special Oscar in 1993, "Please stop crying, Giulietta!"

"What great casting!" I cried. "Were they your idea?"

"The producers set most of them. It's a big cast. Charles Boyer, Yul Brynner, Danny Kaye. But they want two French actors for the love interest. Irma, the café waitress, and Roderick, her boyfriend. I suggested Perrin and the little Allégret."

Perrin was Jacques Perrin, a young, good-looking, and extremely sensitive actor who never was appreciated by the French. In the late '60s, the French public seemed to have found more comfort in the rough, tough guys portrayed by Alain Delon and Jean-Paul Belmondo. The theory went among cinéastes that France had been losing so many of its colonies (Algeria, Vietnam) that there was a national inferiority complex, and the public wanted to see a tough image on screen. Overlooked in *The Young Girls of Rochefort* and *Donkey Skin* (both with Catherine Deneuve), actor Perrin would become producer Perrin for the dynamite Costa-Gavras film *Z* in 1969, and would also be destined, at 28, to receive an Oscar on the stage of the Dorothy Chandler Pavilion. "The little Allégret" was Catherine Allégret. She didn't have quite the body of work young Perrin had, but she was the daughter of Simone Signoret and director Yves Allégret, bore her mother's distinctive looks, and was a very decent actress in her own right.

"They're perfect!" I rejoiced to Margot. With Hepburn, Leighton, and Masina, I could see a wonderful film shaping up.

"So Huston wants you to work with Perrin and Allégret, and he's going to do a screen test here in a few weeks, to see if they can handle the text in English."

"I'm available. I'd love to work with both of them."

"There's one little problem. You may not do the actual picture. Huston has his girlfriend with him, and I was told that he wants her to be the coach on the picture."

"Has she ever done that?"

"No. But she's his girlfriend." She laughed her deep little laugh. "What can I say? *C'est comme ça.* We've done several films together, you and I, and I know the work you do. You make *me* look good. Who knows? Maybe I can talk to Huston when he gets here." But she made it clear I wasn't to count on anything. For the moment, I was hired only for the test.

The next day, I received a call from 1st assistant director Paul Feyder, who told me the same thing Margot did. Paul was scheduled to do the screen test also, and he assured me he'd try to tell Huston how good my work was. But, he said, it would be pretty hard to dislodge *une petite amie*. Ah, that little word, *petite*. When employed, it changed *amie*, just a friend, into a lover girlfriend, and in this case, someone immovable.

I started rehearsing with both actors. Allégret's English was quite good, probably due to her mother's influence, and she could converse in English. Perrin was a different matter. He spoke almost no English. But that had also been the case with Philippe Noiret, and we ended up keeping his completely understandable English in *The Night of the Generals*. Perrin had a similarly good ear, a musical ear, an imitative ear. I met him at his apartment in the suburb of Courbevoie, near Place de la Défense. We rehearsed and rehearsed, and soon the young actor was walking around the apartment, gesturing, spouting the English, having fun with it. He had become completely liberated from the text, which had been one of my objectives. His mind was no longer on pronunciation, but on acting.

We often dined together. He was the quintessential young Frenchman, full of finesse, intelligence, and sensitivity, and always seemed totally relaxed. I'm still astonished he never became a leading man. You can see him in Italy's *Cinema Paradiso*, the best foreign film of 1988. He plays the young boy grown up at the end of the film, who returns to the cinema house he had frequented as a child and where his friendship with movie operator Philippe Noiret had developed. The critics lauded the picture and marveled at Noiret's performance, saying it was "his" picture. But after the character dies, and forty years transpire, the actor playing the little boy grown up into a graying adult must hold the film together in the last half-hour, or all the good work done by Noiret and the film itself fall apart. That actor was Jacques Perrin. His performance was solid, sensitive, understated, masterful.

I rehearsed Allégret and Perrin together the day before the screen test. I closed my eyes and listened only to the words. They were clear, completely comprehensible, and their French accents were charming without being hindering. The next day, at the Studios de Billancourt, Margot introduced me to John Huston. He was tall and owned a weather-worn face with concentric hammocks that sagged below his eyes. There was a slight stoop to his shoulders. I think it must have come from years of leaning over to talk to people who weren't as tall as he. Huston was another legend. He had directed his father, Walter Huston, to a best supporting Oscar in *The Treasure of Sierra Madre* (for which he himself received the best director award), and would later direct his daughter, Anjelica, to a best supporting Oscar in *Prizzi's Honor*. In between, he directed *The Asphalt Jungle*, *The African Queen*, and *Moulin Rouge*, penned *The Maltese Falcon*, and held pivotal acting roles in *The Cardinal* and *Chinatown*. What was this legend like in person? See *Myra Breckinridge*, an absolute howl of a film, and you'll see Huston playing and satirizing himself as a Texas sexagenarian, languidly drawling out his words.

"Oh, yes," said Huston as he shook hands with me, "you've been rehearsing Catherine and Jacques."

"Yes, I have," I said.

"And what do you think? Will we be able to understand them?" He had an attenuated Texas drawl that sounded like he had, as my father used to say, a hot potato in his mouth. I wanted to say that I understood the two French actors better than I did *him*, but, noblesse oblige, I let it go. I was, after all, still hoping for the job.

"I think so." I replied. "You'll see for yourself. Or you'll hear for yourself."

"They tell me you're pretty good."

"Who's 'they'?"

"Margot, the A.D., anyone French who's in the film business."

"Ah, what do *they* know?"

He smiled. "I think we'll get along just fine."

The test went well. Huston had an interesting and subtle way of directing. He put both actors at ease and more or less pretended to let them find their way through the scene. He told them they could move where they wanted, when they wanted, but when Allégret crossed the set at an inopportune moment, Huston said, "Is that where you want to cross, darling?"

"I think so," she replied. "I'm not sure."

"No, it's fine, it's fine. Exactly right. But maybe you might start a little earlier." She tried it his way. "Let me check it through the camera." Then, his eye glued to the lens, he said, "Maybe just a little bit sooner." Subtle, indirect, allowing the actors to explore, then gently guiding them into the picture he wanted, that was Huston.

The screen test took a little over two hours. Not once did Huston acknowledge me during this time or indicate whether or not he was pleased. His only comments were for the actors and the camera. At one point, indicating Perrin, I held up my hand to Huston. He understood immediately and gave me a silent head nod. I approached the actor to correct one of his sentences quickly. "*Bien sûr*," said Perrin. I ran the words twice with him, then stepped away from the camera. Again, without any acknowledgment, Huston simply continued the test.

Except for Perrin, we all met later in the studio bar. When I arrived, Huston and Margot were standing at the metal counter, talking to Simone Signoret and Yves Montand, Signoret's second husband. They had come to collect Catherine and to meet the director. Almost immediately, Huston's eye caught me and he beckoned me to join them. I did, and Margot introduced me to them. Huston immediately said, "This is the young man who rehearsed with Catherine. Of course, her English is very good. But Frawley just made it a little more comfortable for her."

Both Signoret and Montand were extremely gracious, thanking me for my work. Though I greeted them in French, we immediately switched to English in deference to Huston. Signoret said to me, "I might need you myself sometime," in perfect English. I reminded her that she'd won an Oscar performing in English in *Room at the Top*. Still gracious, she replied, "One can always use a little help in a second language." Montand was just as fluent as his wife, although his accent was not quite so subtle.

Catherine appeared and told her mother they were all running late. Goodbyes were said, Catherine embraced me on both cheeks, and then the first family of French theater and screen left. Huston put his arm around me and turned away from Margot, who, knowing every single person in the film business, began to talk to someone else at the bar.

"Catherine and Jacques were very good, both of them. I'm going to use them," Huston drawled. "And I'd like you to do the picture with me." Then, referring to the girlfriend we had never mentioned, he added, "And we'll find something else for *her* to do." I had the greatest respect in the world for him at that moment, not because he'd selected me for the job, but because he hadn't let a personal issue overshadow his professionalism. And because he knew I was aware of his personal life and dealt with that fact honestly and simply.

But there were clouds ahead. Huston and the producers, Ely Landau and Henry Weinstein, were at odds over the script. Apparently, Huston wanted to return more to the original Giraudoux play, and the producers kept wanting to change it. At least this is what Margot Capelier told me. About a week after the screen test, Huston left the picture and a young English director, Bryan Forbes, was brought in. He'd been approved by Hepburn, who was having her usual opinionated say in the matter. I was summoned to meet Bryan Forbes in his hotel suite. Though I had only been paid for the test, I'd been told by Huston and the production manager, Henri Jacquillard, that I'd been hired for the film. Suddenly, everything was up for grabs.

Though Forbes was polite, he was quite cold when he spoke to me. I was already missing the Texas drawl and the stooped shoulders. "I don't think I'm going to use the two actors you worked with" was his almost immediate opener. "They're French, for one thing. English isn't their first language." I told him that Allégret's real-life English was excellent, and that while Perrin's was not, he could certainly perform in it.

"Perhaps he could. Perhaps they both could. But how many takes will I have to do to get it right? And during that time, while they're fumbling over their lines, what happens to Katharine Hepburn's energy? What happens to her performance?" I replied that I didn't think either actor would be fumbling over lines, but I could see his mind was made up. He obviously didn't want two French actors in the roles.

The new broom swept clean. Allégret and Perrin were out the door. I never learned whether or not the producers had ever even told them they'd been cast after the Huston test. Nanette Newman and Richard Chamberlain replaced them. Three others, all handpicked by Huston, were swept out as well: Margot Capelier, Paul Feyder, and I. Though Margot would eventually be brought back in to cast small roles and received a screen credit for doing so, Feyder and I moved on to other projects.

Despite its almost top-heavy cast (and partially because of it), *The Madwoman of Chaillot* did not do well at the box office. As Leslie Caron had predicted a year earlier in Corsica, American film was growing up. There was a push in America for realism now. The same year *Madwoman* was shot, *Midnight Cowboy*, *Easy Rider*, and *Butch Cassidy and the Sundance Kid* were all being developed. It was too late for poetic drama.

And artistically, the movie is a bit of a mishmash. Giraudoux's intention to the play was missed. Witness the Ragpicker's famous "pimp" speech to Countess Aurelia (Hepburn). It is done dead seriously, even sadly, by Danny Kaye, who should have known better. There isn't a jot of Gallic irony to it. Even Hepburn seems more eccentric than a woman bruised so badly from a love loss that she has retreated into madness. The play is careful to suggest that the countess's counterplot to the businessmen-profiteers, locking them up for all eternity in her basement cellar, may be a madwoman's hallucination. But the film takes it literally, which makes all four madwomen, the waitress, and the young lover all criminals.

The 1st of May arrived with its usual promise of good fortune. A workman's holiday, it was the day you traditionally bought a few sprigs of lily of the valley and offered them to friends to wish them good luck. Vendors appeared like mushrooms overnight selling tiny bunches of the fragrant flower from makeshift stands at every metro exit in every *quartier* of the city. In 1968, however, it was a false sense of tranquility. It was a troubled decade; unrest had been everywhere on the globe, and would continue. In Paris there was a demonstration, the first in fourteen years on the workman's holiday, with tens of thousands of workers marching from la République to la Bastille.

The next day, in the suburb of Nanterre, the students, leftist to the man, made their own demonstration. The minister of education immediately closed the Nanterre University and announced he would discipline eight students, including the ringleader, Daniel Cohn-Bendit. On May 3, in solidarity, the students at the Paris Sorbonne demonstrated. The government then made a bad move, an irreparable gaffe that ignited student discontent and all that followed. Armed police officers and an armada of police wagons were sent to the Left Bank to quash the demonstration. Six hundred students were led from a locked Sorbonne into locked police wagons. But when the police tried to transport the students to local jails, thousands of other students surrounded the vehicles and banged on them with sticks. In panic, the police released tear gas. Responding in kind, the students began to break up street cobblestones and hurl them. Retaliation was immediate and incredibly brutal, with billy clubs raining on everyone. Then the students formed the first barricade out of cobblestones, spiked tree fencing, café chairs,

A very ecstatic *moi* over an advertisement of the Edward Albee plays on a Paris kiosk, June 1963.

Conversing with Countess Paola de Rohan-Chabot and Princess Grace of Monaco at the gala opening of the Albee plays at the Théâtre Charles de Rochefort in Paris, 1963.

Rehearsing Irina Demick and Cliff Robertson in *Up from the Beach* in Normandy, August 1964.

William Wyler directing Peter O'Toole and Audrey Hepburn in *How to Steal a Million,* outside the Hotel Ritz in Paris, 1965, with me (blurred) behind Peter.

Director Anatole Litvak and a uniformed Omar Sharif, sans his trademark mustache, check dialogue with me during *The Night of the Generals* in Paris, 1966.

The two titans of *The Night of the Generals*: director Anatole Litvak and producer Sam Spiegel, on the set at the Studios de Boulogne outside Paris, 1966. Photo from the private collection of Marina Gromoff.

Tom Courtenay, makeup man Bill Lodge, *moi toujours*, and Peter O'Toole in Paris between scenes of *The Night of the Generals*, 1966.

Sporting a campy *chapeau*, photographer-designer Cecil Beaton photographs French director Jacques Charon on the set of *A Flea in Her Ear* at the Studios de Boulogne, 1967. Photo from the private collection of Isla Blair.

My movie cat, Calvados, in the Parco di Principi Hotel with me during filming of *If It's Tuesday, This Must Be Belgium* in Rome, 1968.

In my new Fiat Spider at the Château de Roussan with Jean-François Maurin and Jacqueline Bisset, just outside St-Rémy-de-Provence, during the filming of *Secret World* in the fall of 1968.

Rehearsing the children for their bilingual roles in *Secret World* near St-Rémy-de-Provence, 1968.

Director Jacques Charon with me, editor Walter Thompson, and Rex Harrison as the drunken porter in *A Flea in Her Ear* in Paris, 1967.

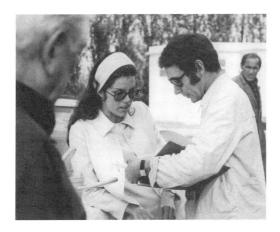

Making sure Samantha Eggar gets the lines right in *The Lady in the Car* outside Paris, with Marcel Bozzuffi in the background, 1969.

With director Anatole Litvak on a baggage cart in the Marseille train station, checking text for *The Lady in the Car*, 1969. Engrossed in work, we never saw the train pulling out.

On the set with Peter Ostrum for the final scenes of *Willy Wonka and the Chocolate Factory* in Munich, 1970.

Three of the five "kids" from *Willy Wonka and the Chocolate Factory* in New York, 1998. Left to right: Peter Ostrum (Charlie), Julie Dawn Cole (Veruca Salt), and Paris Themmen (Mike Teevee). Photo from the private collection of Paris Themmen.

René Clément directing Leslie Caron in *Is Paris Burning?* in 1966. Photo from the private collection of Johanna Clément.

Director René Clé-
ment flanked by two
of the many stars of *Is
Paris Burning?* Jean-
Paul Belmondo, left,
and Alain Delon,
right, in Paris, 1966.
Photo from the pri-
vate collection of Jo-
hanna Clément.

Aldo Ray with his
two boys, Eric and
Paul, around 1968.
Photo from the pri-
vate collection of
Louis DaRe.

With Ann-Margret at
the Los Angeles Inter-
national Airport, be-
tween set-ups for *The
Outside Man*, 1972.

Katharine Hepburn's only appearance at the Academy Awards, to present the Irving Thalberg Award to producer Lawrence Weingarten in April, 1974.

On the set of *Adam's Rib* with Spencer Tracy, Katharine Hepburn, Cole Porter, David Wayne, and producer Lawrence Weingarten, in the M-G-M studios, 1949. Photo from the private collection of Norma Pisar.

and car fenders, in an attempt to "hold" Boulevard Saint-Michel. It was suddenly the second act of *Les Misérables* playing out in reality.

Those arrested were taken to police stations throughout the city, where their names were recorded. At 2 A.M., at the Opéra police station, all the students but one were released. The one detained as long as was legally possible was Daniel Cohn-Bendit, whose name would forever be tied to the events of May 1968. Writer Michel Gomez reports in *Mai 68, au jour le jour* that a furious police officer said to Cohn-Bendit, "Little man, you're going to pay for this. It's a pity you didn't die with your parents in Auschwitz."

The second French Revolution had begun.

The month before, I had finished translating a script penned by French director Gérard Oury entitled *The Brain*. Three major stars had been cast in this upcoming gangster caper: David Niven, Jean-Paul Belmondo, and France's beloved Bourvil, a deft comic actor who always imbued his roles with immense humanity. Oury had heard about me and called me in for a meeting. He needed a translator for his script and also wanted a coach during filming. Some of the scenes, he said, would be shot in French, some in English. Later, there would be two versions distributed, one in each language. I delivered the *version anglaise* to him just two weeks after our meeting. We were set to start shooting in May, and I thought it was probably going to be great fun working with him and the stars he'd mentioned.

But then the student revolution started. The press criticized the police for brutalizing the students. Seven were actually brought to trial and four of them, between the ages of eighteen and twenty-two, were sentenced to two months of prison, an unusually severe punishment. Masses of students responded with further demonstrations, now with 1,500 students, now with five thousand, now fifteen, all shouting, "Free our comrades!" Barricades were set up everywhere on the Left Bank. More tear gas from the police, more cobblestones from the students. Eight hundred wounded on both sides, on the night of May 6.

"It is not possible to tolerate violence in the street," declared president Charles de Gaulle, blaming the students and turning a blind eye to the violence committed by the C.R.S., his state police. In response, forty thousand of the nation's youth marched up the Champs-Élysées and sang "L'Internationale," the communist hymn, in front of the tomb

of the Unknown Soldier. It was a slap in the face to Gaullist national-
ism. Socialist François Mitterand, who would become president in
1981, stated, "If Youth is not always right, the society that mocks it,
misjudges it, and strikes it, is always wrong."

Somewhere in all this, I tried to make a trip to a Left Bank bookstore,
innocently getting off the metro at the Mabillon station. I climbed the
steps to the street and heard the great din of mob shouting and bottles
crashing. Along with other people emerging from the subway exit, I was
suddenly in the midst of a riot, with students running in every direction
and helmeted police vehemently chasing and beating them. Three students ran into the group of us at the metro exit. A handful of policemen
were instantly on top of us all, pounding everyone in sight with cudgels.
A few very painful blows landed on my arm as I lifted it to protect my
face. Then the three students and most of us emerging from the metro
ran back down the stairs to the subway platform, the police on our heels.
I saw the students jump off the platform and start running willy-nilly
along the tracks into the black distance. It was a great risk because of the
third rail, but the students seemed to prefer that crazy risk to the billy
clubs. I huddled against the tile wall, not knowing which way to run,
when suddenly the police abandoned the pursuit and ran back up to the
street. I decided the bookstore could be visited another time and caught
the next train that came roaring obliviously into the station.

Then, suddenly, the student revolution took on a new aspect.
Leather-jacketed roughnecks from the working class suburbs and bour-
geois Parisian high school students joined the university students. So did
professors, medical students, law students, and five Nobel Prize winners.
Apartment residents came down to the streets to give food to those
manning the barricades, then poured basins of water from their windows
onto the police. Wall graffiti was inspired. "Under the cobblestones,"
said one, "lies the beach!" For the minister of education, the de Gaulle
government could do anything except recognize Cohn-Bendit—a
young upstart, a German, and a Jew all rolled into one. The state refused
to yield, the students refused to yield.

Gérard Oury's office called to state that the start date of *The Brain*
had been pushed back because of the student revolution. Oury had no
idea when he would be able to begin the film. I would not be needed
until some semblance of normalcy resumed.

The revolt escalated, becoming political. The Communist Party deplored the government's "ferocious repression" of the students. To de Gaulle's displeasure, Georges Pompidou, the *premier ministre*, decreed that the Sorbonne, closed by the police, would be reopened and the four sentenced students released. The next day, there was a celebratory march with François Mitterand and over a hundred thousand people. Led by Cohn-Bendit, the demonstrators made their serpentine way from la République to the Sorbonne. The renowned university was about to become the center of discussions between the enraged students and intellectuals such as Marguerite Duras and Jean-Paul Sartre.

The following day saw the first factory strike, near Nantes, the workers demanding better pay and a forty-hour week. In rapid succession, other strikes followed: Renault factory workers, the potassium mine workers in Alsace, the coal miners in the north. Then newspapers and postal services, bringing the total number of flash-flood strikers to six hundred thousand in four days. It was mid-May. No one said "student revolution" any more, only "revolution."

De Gaulle blamed the Communist Party for the strikes. He said he would quell the students completely, and do so by any means. Suddenly, the magazine *Paris Match* gave Cohn-Bendit a limousine and driver to take him safely to Berlin. Quickly, the minister of the interior signed a paper forbidding him to reenter France. And just as quickly there was yet another march in the Latin Quarter with the students waving the Communist flag and crying, "We are all German Jews!"

Displeased with media coverage, de Gaulle demanded control of radio and television. In response, mob violence broke out, with fires starting at the Paris stock exchange and buzz saws cutting down trees to form barricades. A police chief was killed in Lyon. The Paris metro trains stopped running, there was little milk for the children, and only a few bakers were making bread. There was no gasoline at the pumps, except for small amounts rationed to doctors. Garbage and trash piled up on the sidewalks, sometimes as high as the second floor. The City of Light was a city under siege.

Ten million workers were striking now. Stories of police torture circulated. "C.R.S.—S.S.!" went the shouts when de Gaulle's special police arrived. Almost no one went to work. Neither de Gaulle nor Pompidou could offer a program that was acceptable to the insurgents.

Power was completely afloat. Desperate, Pompidou called in the armed forces. Many of the soldiers were the same ages as the students and waited nervously with their weapons at the city's entrance gates. Would de Gaulle fire on his own people? On May 29, the Communists called for a massive demonstration. The politics of the entire country were suddenly pitted against two extremes: Gaullism and communism.

In the midst of this, de Gaulle and his wife disappeared. *Disappeared?* They fled the country by helicopter and landed at Baden-Baden, where de Gaulle was met by General Massu, commander of the French Forces in Germany. Whether de Gaulle's flight was to call these forces in to Paris and by martial law overturn the uprising or to demand refuge from the German government is still unclear. One hour later, he flew back to Paris, where the newspapers were proclaiming the imminent takeover by the former socialist prime minister, Pierre Mendès-France. Impervious, de Gaulle addressed his ministers, then the general public. He would not abdicate nor would he replace Georges Pompidou, but he would dissolve the National Assembly. The latter was a daring *coup de théâtre*, roughly the equivalent of an American president dissolving Congress. Using every bit of drama, nationalistic fervor, and the charisma for which he was known, de Gaulle called upon every man and woman to partake in a civilian action to back the government and reestablish order. In less than an hour, hundreds of thousands of cheering people, fed up with the strikes, were in the streets, this time in support of de Gaulle.

And then something happened. Something bizarre and very French. May is the month with the most French holidays, and whenever possible these are celebrated over a long weekend. Such was the case at the end of May with the Catholic holiday of Pentecost, and suddenly everyone had four days in front of him. Just as suddenly, gasoline mysteriously appeared at the pumps. The government had released its reserve. Cars packed with family and friends made their ways through the long lines, and after an hour had a full tank of gas. Then the cars took off for a calmer pastoral environment, country air, good regional food, and those wonderful little *vins du pays*.

In good spirits, the Parisians returned a few days later and went back to work. Most did; others trickled in over the next two weeks. The peeps of protest from a few obstinate strikers were silenced, not without the C.R.S. showing its habitual brutality. But by early June everyone was back to work and the revolution was over.

In mid-June, de Gaulle staged a great military procession down the Champs-Élysées. He pulled out most of the army's vehicles in a massive show of force, as if to say, "See what I could have done?" The citizens stood six deep on both sides of the café-lined avenue, with those in the back using cardboard periscopes with mirrors to see over the heads of those in front. With the Arc de Triomphe behind him, de Gaulle came riding down the avenue in an open car, arm in the air, his fingers forming the V-for-victory sign. It was the sign he had borrowed from Churchill and used during World War II as the head of the Free French, the sign he had used when Paris was liberated by the Allies. Emotions ran high that day as everyone remembered how de Gaulle had prevailed during the war and again through the recent events. The crowds cheered and cheered. And when it came time later to vote for new members of the National Assembly, a tidal wave would wash in an almost entirely pro–de Gaulle government.

But the last chapter is a sad one. Within a few weeks of the return to order, a tiny book appeared in a very limited number of copies, printed by some underground press. It was called, or referred to as, *Le Livre noir* (*The Black Book*) and was probably compiled by the student leaders. The book was an indictment of the police and named the key students and activists who had been arrested and brutally mistreated, some with crippling injuries. There were also the names of those who had totally "disappeared," the book claimed. These persons had little or no known families, at least in Paris, so there was no one to ask questions. The books circulated for a few days and then the government seized the ones that remained in the shops and as many as it could off the streets. I made the great mistake of lending my copy to a friend, who later said he misplaced it. Even at the time the book circulated, very few people knew about it. Today, when I ask anyone who lived through the Revolution of '68 what became of *Le Livre noir*, they say they haven't the slightest idea of what I'm talking about.

And perhaps they don't.

CHAPTER EIGHT

~

Strolling Players

While Paris was cooling down, I received a call from Tom Pevsner, now a production manager in London, with whom I'd worked on *The Night of the Generals*. He told me that an American film was going to be made, traveling all over Europe, and he'd recommended me to the producer, Stan Margulies. Though most of the actors would be American, the supporting cast would include Germans, Italians, and several other nationalities. He recalled that I spoke a little German and Italian as well as fluent French, and was I available? I told him I'd have to check with Gérard Oury's office on *The Brain*, which I was supposed to do.

"I think that's been pushed off for a while," Pevsner replied. And a call to Oury confirmed that he didn't know when they were going to be able to start shooting. Since I had a firm offer, he told me to take it and gave me his blessings. The next day, Stan Margulies from Wolper Pictures called and told me about *If It's Tuesday, This Must Be Belgium*, a spoof of the American tourist "doing" eight countries in eighteen days. I told him I thought it was a great title. "There aren't any really big stars," he said, "and it's going to be a logistical nightmare going from country to country, but we might all have a little fun doing it." I made my deal over the phone with Pevsner, and two weeks later I was on a plane to London.

There I met director Mel Stuart. He had previously directed only documentaries. One, *The Making of the President*, garnered an Emmy in 1960 and another, *Four Days in November*, in 1964 had received an Oscar nomination. Except for Sophia Loren, about whom he'd made an entertainment special, Stuart admitted he'd had little experience with live performers.

"How do you talk to actors?" was almost the first question he asked me. We were in his hotel room.

I was a little thrown. Either he was an innocent or he was in way over his head. "You just talk to them as people," I answered, "the way you're talking to me."

"How did you talk to Audrey Hepburn?"

"The same way I'm talking to you."

"Was she easy to work with?"

"Very."

"Supposing an actor doesn't agree with me, what do I do?"

"You talk about what's bothering him in the scene, and you work it out. You find a way to make him comfortable."

"But supposing we talk and we still disagree? Shouldn't we do it my way? I mean, I'm the director."

"What you might do is shoot the scene twice, once his way, once your way. An actor usually agrees to that. Then you can see both interpretations on the screen and decide later."

"That's a good idea," he said. "But I'll probably use my way."

The actors arrived from the States by plane, although Suzanne Pleshette, who was playing the lead, and her husband, Tom Gallagher, both stated they had a terrible phobia about flying and were thinking of making the return trip by ship. I met David L. Wolper, who turned out to be the prototype producer. Like Darryl F. Zanuck, Wolper had a cigar constantly clenched between his teeth, did not seem particularly sensitive, and shared Zanuck's interest in beautiful young women. Over the next two months, he spent a great deal of time running after Miss Belgium, Miss Holland, Miss Germany, and Miss Italy, to convince them to make brief appearances in the movie.

Playing the male lead opposite Suzanne Pleshette was a personable, little-known English actor, Ian McShane, who later moved to Los Angeles to guest star in a slew of television shows and appear at the Matrix

Theatre, an off-Broadway–sized house, in several plays. Once again, though my raison d'être for being on the film would be the non–English-speaking actors, I would actually spend more time rehearsing the American actors and Ian.

The supporting character actors, all of whom were or would become somewhat known, were an absolute hoot. Mildred Natwick hailed from the Broadway stage, her best-known plays having been *Waltz of the Toreadors* and *Barefoot in the Park*. Pamela Britton had been in the original production of *Brigadoon* and had starred opposite Frank Sinatra in *Anchors Aweigh*. Murray Hamilton would later play Mr. Robinson opposite Anne Bancroft in *The Graduate* and still later star in *Jaws*. Peggy Cass, Norman Fell, Marty Ingels, Sandy Baron, and Michael Constantine were all known as good comic supporting actors in New York and Hollywood. Without their knowing it, all of them were very much like the Americans they were spoofing on screen, and as we traveled from country to country, I would jot down some of their ad lib comments, often hilarious, on the country we were visiting. So did screenwriter David Shaw, Irwin Shaw's brother. Later, the two of us would compare notes and roar with laughter. David would insert some of the lines into the film, now voiced by the characters these same actors were playing. Many of the "voice over" lines that you hear as the tourists in the movie visit European monuments were actually stated at one time or another by the real-life actors. Life imitating art imitating life. The actors apparently never remembered they'd actually uttered the words their characters spoke.

But if the actors posed no problem in working, the director certainly did. Mel Stuart turned out to be a screamer. This was a daily event. He yelled at actors, he yelled at the cinematographer, he yelled at the 1st assistant director, Patrick O'Brien, and he yelled at his wife, Harriet, and two of their three children, Peter and Madeleine, whom he must have considered old enough to be yelled at. His third was still an infant. In the evenings, I would often see Mel storm out of the hotel lobby elevator in his scuffed white tennis shoes, screaming, but not looking, at his family who were running behind him in humble Japanese fashion. He would shout invective to the doorman in front of him and the family behind him all at the same time.

"May your earphones rot!" he shouted into the phone at the hotel operator in London, then he slammed the receiver down on the cradle.

David Shaw had been in Mel's hotel suite at the time and later recounted the story. It seemed that only Shaw and I escaped Mel's venom. Did he have respect for me, because of the name stars and directors I'd worked with? Or was it because I told him that if he raised his voice in that manner to me, I'd leave the film? In any case, before we left London, the first leg of the film, the actors had dubbed him "the Jewish Hitler."

The first scene we shot was of a poker game with Marty Ingels. Guest-starring with him were John Cassavetes and Ben Gazzara. It was a small moment, very fast, part of what would eventually be the opening background montage of our tourists. But Ingels was unsure of himself, and began to ask Mel about how he should play the scene. The director and the actor differed on the character, and soon Mel came to me to ask what he should do. Listening to him expose both sides of the issue, I thought it was Ingels who was right. I told Mel so. He was silent for a moment while he reflected. Then he said, "Okay, I'll let him do it his way. That way, next time he'll owe me a favor."

"I'm not sure that's the right reason," I said, a remark he totally ignored.

Because of his background as a documentary filmmaker, Mel insisted on shooting everything directly in actual locations, often with a hand-held camera. He, the cameraman, and I crowded into one corner of a tiny hotel bathroom, while the puzzled tourist that Murray Hamilton was playing stared at a *bidet* for the first time in his life and the Peggy Cass character quipped, "I'm telling you, Fred, it is not a planter." And while it had only been a few short years since the rear-projection technique used on a sound stage during *How to Steal a Million* for Audrey Hepburn and Peter O'Toole inside a car, with the car being rocked by stage grips and a film of Paris streets moving behind them, this would not be the technique Mel used. In the scenes of the moving tourist bus in the streets of London, with Ian McShane standing, mike in hand, at the front of the bus, it is the real streets of London one sees through the windows, not a projected film.

From London, the company traveled to Amsterdam. I flew back to Paris to grab Calvados, the wicker basket, and the cat's health certificates, and joined everyone in Amsterdam. For the crew, the cat, and me, the European trip the "tourists" in the movie made would not be easy. After England, the schedule read Holland, Belgium, Luxembourg, Germany, Switzerland, Lichtenstein, and Italy. Originally, the script ended in Paris, where the characters played by Pleshette and McShane finally consummate their love affair and where the other characters have their farewell dinner with stunning showgirls on the stage. I imagine Shaw was thinking of the Lido, and Paris would have been the perfect, beautiful end of the film. But because of the second French Revolution in May, Stan Margulies did not want to risk any uprisings recurring or having to halt shooting there.

"That's not going to happen," I told him. "De Gaulle has completely taken back the country."

"We can't take that chance," he answered. And I guess from a producer's point of view, he was right. It's unfortunate. After the visual glories of Amsterdam, Venice, and Rome, you miss Paris in the movie.

Only one day's filming in Holland with Mel screaming at the actors and the Dutch crew was enough for Suzanne Pleshette. All the actors had been complaining among themselves, and Murray Hamilton had already started to drink heavily. "You can't continue to shout at everyone," Suzanne told Mel. She later related the incident to me in the hotel lobby. "The weather's going to get hot soon and hotter as we move south. Someone's going to haul off and hit you, Mel, probably an Italian. Or else I will!" There were two things Suzanne was not short on: beauty and *chutzpah*. Apparently, Mel listened to her, and he lightened up for a couple of days. But before Holland was behind us, he was screaming again, and his family was still running ten respectful paces behind him.

From Holland we traveled to Belgium, filming as we actually traveled. The monotonously flat countryside didn't change when the borders did, and in one very funny moment of the film, the Peggy Cass character looks out onto this nondescript scenery that could have been the flatness of Kansas and asks nasally, "Where are we now, Fred?" Consulting the tour schedule, Murray Hamilton's character replies in his sourpuss best with the title of the movie, "If it's Tuesday, this must be Belgium." Unfortunately, this moment was cut from the final film, probably because the title needed no explanation. But somewhere there's an outtake with two priceless deliveries in it.

And Stan Margulies was right, the logistics were horrendous. Besides supervising production manager Tom Pevsner and 1st assistant director

Patrick O'Brien, each country we visited supplied a local production manager and 1st assistant director who had to prepare that country and supply local grips, electricians, and drivers. In each country, the key people spoke English in addition to their native tongue. The core production office people who started in London also continued from country to country, gathering local office persons as they went. What with personal baggage, technical equipment, raw stock, and exposed film, there were about three hundred items moving each time we changed countries. The joke went around that Suzanne Pleshette's bags alone counted for fifty pieces. Miraculously, not one piece of equipment nor one bag was ever lost, and just as miraculously every foot of film was accounted for at customs at each of the seven countries that followed England.

The other logistical nightmare was the fact that the crew was traveling through Europe in the summer. Should the schedule fall behind even for one day, say, in Holland in June, then all the reserved rooms in Italy in August, at the height of the real tourist season, would have to be changed. This is where Mel Stuart's fast-shooting documentary filmmaking paid off. Except for one shot missed in Holland, which he obtained in Belgium, he always completed the day's work. This is the only film I worked on in forty years that came in on schedule.

But the pace, the complexity, and above all, Mel's screaming were having their toll. In Germany and Switzerland, I often discovered lanky Patrick O'Brien at the hotel bar, needing more and more drinks to get him to that I-don't-give-a-damn point of no return. He was a quiet lad who started out in earnest to hold the show together, as all good A.D.'s must, and who, perhaps more than anyone else on the crew, received Mel's vehement venom each workday with silent suffering. The crew pained for him and the actors sympathized with him, but Mel continued to go after him, the way some animals will peck or claw at another that is weaker. And because Patrick would say nothing, Suzanne the protectress would sometimes rise to his defense. In front of everyone she would tell Mel to stop abusing him.

"Abusing him?" Mel would retort. "I'm just telling him what to do." And he'd add that Patrick couldn't figure it out for himself, which wasn't true.

Murray Hamilton was also drinking heavily. And Denis Whitehouse, a young assistant editor who was working as an assembly editor until the film reached the States, was dazed by the director's tantrums, which carried over from the set to the hotel rooms, where the editing machines had been set up.

From country to country we went, mostly by the picture bus in the film. Sometimes we traveled by train, and a couple of times, in spite of Suzanne Pleshette's anxieties, by short plane trips, one from Zurich to Venice, another from Venice to Rome.

Somewhere in Switzerland, I had a little verbal altercation with Pamela Britton's husband on the bus. A big guy, he was an ultraconservative American patriot who made remarks about the various cultures that, unlike those rolled off by our actors, weren't funny. Every European country we visited was a third world nation to him. Nothing was ever as good as it was in good old U.S.A. From across the aisle one day, I had been talking to Pamela about French theater acting, and her husband, seated next to her, had been listening. I was deploring modern French stage acting as reflecting too much influence from the turn of the century, and not being realistic enough.

"They're still patterning their acting after Sarah Bernhardt," I said. "That exaggerated, melodramatic acting."

Britton's husband piped up, "How can you say that? Sarah Bernhardt was the greatest actress in the world."

"Well, I don't know about that," I replied. "Certainly she had a style and made her mark. But I think it would be outdated today."

"She was the greatest actress in the world," he reiterated.

I shrugged. "Well, maybe the greatest actress France ever had."

"What are you talking about?" he asked indignantly. "Sarah Bernhardt was American. The greatest actress in the world was American." I could almost hear him say, "She'd have to be."

I remained calm. "No, she was French." I pronounced her name à la française. "Sair-rah Bairn-arr. There's a theater in Paris named after her. And she was Jewish."

"I never heard that!" His voice was rising.

Our doyenne of the theater, Mildred Natwick, leaned back from the seat in front of me. "Frawley's right, you know. She was French and Jewish, both." Ethel Barrymore could not have delivered the line with more authority. Pamela Britton could only smile a frozen musical-comedy smile, while her husband fumed silently and wrestled with the fact that somehow, somewhere something might be better than it was in America. In a way, he was what the movie was all about.

In an elaborate sequence in Switzerland, the youngest tourist, actress Hilarie Thompson, playing the teenage daughter of the Hamilton-Cass couple, has a secret date with a young American motorcyclist, Luke Halpin. While the adults end up at Fondue Fling Night, the kids go to an underground Hippie *cave* and listen to English musician Donovan strum a guitar and wail a particularly lugubrious song called "Lord of the Reedy River." Donovan was one of a handful of artists who made brief, sometimes subliminal, guest appearances in the movie. Besides Gazzara and Cassavetes, there were Joan Collins, Robert Vaughn, Virna Lisi, and *La Dolce Vita*'s Anita Ekberg, who all came and went, some with lines, some without. Donovan, excited by being in an American movie, told Wolper he wanted to write the title song of the picture. Wolper agreed and Donovan penned an equally lamenting, and lamentable, *If It's Tuesday, This Must Be Belgium*. Listen to it over the opening credits. What should have been a brisk allegro, the tourists excitedly on the move, was instead a painfully plodding largo.

There was also a mistake made in the relationship between the two adolescents, the only portion of the film that didn't ring true. It was 1968, and everywhere in Europe there were American hippies smoking pot and enjoying sex. But while Pleshette and McShane end up in bed by the end of the film, the adolescents don't. In reality, they would have beat Pleshette and McShane to it. And pot? Not a sign of it. While writer David Shaw nailed the middle-aged tourist, he missed the kids. Or was that an equally middle-aged executive decision?

Suddenly, we were at the Venice airport, then in vans that the Italian production office had organized and that took us to motorboats. As chance would have it, I was directed into the same boat as Marty Ingels and Sandy Baron, probably the two loudest and most insecure actors in the cast.

After the cold, immutable silence of the Swiss Alps (I understood why European doctors always sent hyperactives and cardiac cases to a place where nothing moved), I was looking forward to the lively beauty of Italy. Venice, especially, held a place in my dreams. I had heard many times that Venice was a city of romance and you really had to visit it with someone you loved. Until that moment, I had never been to this beautiful city, because when I was in love, I never had the money to go, and when I had the money, there was no one around to love. So there I finally was, arriving in Venice in a motorboat of wise-cracking strolling players, wondering whom I could kiss in a gondola under the Bridge of Sighs at sunset while the bells of the Campanile were ringing, who, so the legend went, would then love me forever.

The arrival catches you by surprise. By boat from the airport, you see Venice looming up from the water like a shimmering mirage. The distance across the water soon grows shorter, the buildings larger. Then you are near it, alongside it, and suddenly, as the motorboat makes a sharp turn, you are plunged into a waterway narrower than any alley you've ever seen, with sixteenth-century buildings shooting up on either side of you, so close you can almost touch them. That moment when you turn out of the sea into that waterway makes you catch your breath. Even the nightclub comedians in the boat were suddenly silent in awe. Past us slid walls and balconies and narrow pathways and twisting staircases, all umber and ochre and sienna, like the Renaissance paintings themselves. Many of the gesso walls were peeling. Centimeter by centimeter, they were tragically, ineluctably slipping into the sea.

Then came the comments.

"Isn't this something?"

"Nothing like this back home."

"But the canal's full of garbage." (That one made it into the movie.)

"Hey, Frawl, can't you just see *Romeo and Juliet* playing out here?" Baron called to me.

"Except that was Verona, Sandy." I tried to close my ears and just look.

And there was so much to look at. Not just the Doge's palace and the Piazza San Marco with its multidomed cathedral, and the beautiful glassware from the nearby island of Murano, but everything in the streets of the city. The streets? I was surprised to find that Venice was a walking city, that you could make your way from any part of it to any other part of it on foot; it just took longer than by gondola. And every turn you took in the streets threw you up against more beauty—inner courtyards, steps that brought you up to another street at a higher level, small bridges, shops hidden around corners, windows with artisan leather work, hand-blown glass, colorful printed papers with designs of winged Venetian lions that dated back to the sixteenth century.

One morning, Denis, the assistant editor, locked himself in his hotel room and refused to go to work. The screaming and shouting had simply been too much for him, and Tom Pevsner thought the boy might be having a nervous breakdown. Fearing that he might harm himself, Pevsner slept in Denis's hotel room that night and convinced him to return to work the next day.

Our stay in Venice was not long, because the producers wanted to move on to Rome to finish the film with all the actors, then return to Venice for the scenes that only involved Suzanne and Ian. It was August and the ancient capital was hot. Mel continued to scream, but the Italians never struck him, as Suzanne thought they might. Instead, they threw their heads back and laughed, then simply turned and walked off. Never off the film, mind you; they were too professional. But over two months had gone by since the screaming started in London, and there was emotional debris everywhere. I bumped into Denis one day in the lobby of the Hotel Parco di Principi, near the Villa Borghese.

"It's so hot," he said, his eyes distant.

"How are you doing, Denis?"

"Oh, I'm all right. I wish Mel wouldn't yell at me so much."

"He yells at everybody. Don't take it personally."

He continued to stare off in the distance, only looking at me occasionally. "Sometimes I can't think, he yells so loud."

"I'm sorry."

"I need a rest. Don't you think I should have a rest?"

"We all need one."

"God, it's hot," he said, and walked off in a daze.

And then there was 1st assistant director Patrick O'Brien. He and Murray Hamilton had become bar fixtures. I pulled Patrick off his stool one night and dragged him to a nearby trattoria. We ate and drank red wine, and I asked him why, over the past two months, he hadn't talked back to Mel or walked off the film. Mel had abused him mercilessly throughout the shoot.

"At first I was horrified at the way he was yelling at me," he said. "Then I was horrified at the way I accepted that. And then—" His eye grew distant as Denis's had. "And then, something funny happened. I realized I didn't mind the way he was treating me. Didn't mind the humiliation." He laughed. "Pretty sick, isn't it?"

I couldn't contradict him.

There was a short but wonderful scene at an outside Rome café where a young man strikes up a conversation with Mildred Natwick. When he explains he is a gigolo and asks for money to make love to her, she laughs uproariously. Sheepishly, the young man leaves. It was a cute little scene and gave Natwick her only real moment in the film. But at this point, Mel was completely annoyed with her, for reasons that neither I nor anyone else understood. I can only think that she may have asked him one serious question too many, perhaps about her character's motivation. He told me he would never put the gigolo scene in the movie, and he didn't. He also told me he had cut a lot of her lines in the group scenes in the editing room. Despite the fact that Mildred had billing immediately after Suzanne and Ian, she is almost nowhere to be found in the movie.

But the absolute gemstone of the film was shot in Rome, in a windowless basement where the production offices were located. The room had been dressed with hanging pieces of leather and shoes all over the place. No less than the great Italian film director, Vittorio de Sica, was to guest-star as a non–English-speaking Italian cobbler opposite non–Italian-speaking tourist Murray Hamilton, who wanted to have a pair of shoes made. I found de Sica in an office that was being used as a makeshift dressing room, and addressed him in Italian. He smiled and greeted me warmly, and since my Italian was only fair, we switched quickly to French. I immediately felt I had to speak to him of the realistic post–World War II Neoclassic Italian cinema, which he had spearheaded with *Shoeshine* and *The Bicycle Thief*, the former winning a special academy award in 1947, the latter receiving the same award in 1949. *The Bicycle Thief* is on most critics' international lists of the ten best films ever made. De Sica directed Sophia Loren to her Oscar for *Two Women* in 1961, the first of only two Oscars given for a foreign-language performance (the other being Roberto Benigni's in *Life Is Beautiful*). Then, almost twenty-five years after *Shoeshine*, de Sica's *The Garden of the Finzi-Continis* won the Oscar for best foreign film in 1971. But it was his early realistic films that would have a strong influence on Hollywood in later years. In Europe, de Sica was also sometimes seen as an actor.

He told me his early films were about displaced people, children and adults, because of the defeat of fascism at the end of the war. Somewhere, too, I proffered, the films had to do with survival. That was something rarely tested in Americans. "*È giusto*," he replied, and nodded.

He spoke English fairly well, but though he would perform his role in his native tongue, I nevertheless rehearsed with him so that his ear could become accustomed to the words in English that Murray Hamilton would say. During the rehearsal, one of those miraculous accidents that suddenly turns into something brilliant occurred. I delivered one of Hamilton's lines, and de Sica, groping momentarily for his text, stalled and repeated the last word I'd said before coming up with his line. I jumped on it. "That's good! The way you repeat the last few syllables of what you've just heard! That's what he'd do, the cobbler, if he didn't understand!" He loved the idea.

A little while later, he came down to the set, and Mel Stuart began to give him directions for the scene. First, he explained what de Sica already knew, that he was playing a poor cobbler who didn't speak English. De Sica smiled and nodded. "Yes, yes. Of course." I sensed instantly that he was annoyed. Then, Mel explained the shot. He was dollying back from the shop door where Hamilton would enter, precede him down the passageway, then pan over and pull back to reveal de Sica, seated, hammering. De Sica continued to smile and nod.

"But since your back is to the camera at first, I want you to be hammering from the beginning of the scene, even though the camera isn't on you yet, because you won't be able to see the camera."

De Sica nodded. "Of course, of course," he said.

Then we did a rehearsal. Mel called "Action!" and preceded Hamilton with the camera, back-tracking as the actor entered the shop and made his way down the passageway. There was no hammering. Hamilton continued, and the camera pulled back and turned. A split second before it revealed de Sica, he lifted his hammer and began to nail the shoe before him, the movement timed perfectly to the camera. It was as if he had eyes in the back of his head.

"Cut!" Mel cried. "He's too late!" He called me over. "I want him to start hammering earlier, from the beginning of the scene."

I was embarrassed. Mel was referring to de Sica in the third person, instead of speaking to him directly. I looked over at the Italian director. "*Si, si, j'ai compris*," he said.

And we started again. De Sica still didn't start hammering from the top of the scene, but when the camera pulled back to reveal him, he began a fraction earlier. This time the camera caught him on the second hammer blow. The rehearsal continued to the end of the scene. Then Mel made some camera adjustments. "Tell de Sica I want him to start hammering the moment Murray enters the door," he threw at me. I went up to de Sica and gave him a helpless look. His timing had been impeccable. With his back to the camera, he sensed where it was and what it was seeing every single second. De Sica winked at me before I could say a word. "Let's shoot it!" Mel called. Instantly de Sica's makeup man was on him, patting down moisture and making him camera-perfect. Mel walked up. "That was great, Vittorio. Very funny. Just start hammering earlier."

"Si, si, of course," de Sica replied, smiling, nodding. As soon as Mel walked away, he muttered, "*Che stronzo!*" to his makeup man. De Sica caught my eye. I was within earshot. "You understand, huh?" he said in French. I understood his tone of voice, but it wasn't until later when I asked an Italian crew member that I learned the expression meant, "What an asshole!" We did several takes of the master shot, and each time, back to the camera, de Sica would start hammering just before the camera discovered him. Then Mel moved in for closer coverage. Now, the heart of the scene counted and de Sica used the piece of verbal business we'd discussed in his dressing room. He used it at the perfect place. Hamilton, too, had had an inspiration. Playing the tourist, he figured that he would speak loudly to de Sica through most of the scene, since that's what the character would do to make a non–English-speaking person understand better.

"I'd like to buy a pair of shoes . . . the same color the salesman from Des Moines bought!" he shouted.

"Moynebawt, moynebawt," de Sica muttered, uncomprehending. The crew members doubled over in silent laughter. Mel completed his coverage with more angles and an insert shot of a shoe catalog, and the work was over. Well, almost. Mel thanked de Sica and shook his hand. The Italian director smiled and nodded, the way he had through the filming. Then he left. And Mel did exactly what I knew he would. He recorded a wild track with an A.D. hammering in de Sica's place; a wild track Mel could lay into the sound track so that the hammering would be heard from the moment Murray Hamilton walked in the door. And that's the way the scene plays in the movie. Mel got what he wanted. What he didn't get was de Sica's lesson in directing.

Our last scene in Rome was a big one. All the actors except Suzanne and Ian are eating a farewell dinner in an Italian nightclub, marveling over the food, even though it turns out that one dish is squid (not an American fad in 1968). The Italian showgirls were gorgeous in glittering but skimpy costumes, à la Folies Bergère. At one point, Mel wanted the girls to start dancing again and needed one of them to get the others started.

"What can she say to get them going again?" he asked me.

I barely paused. "Azione!" I suggested. It was a word we all knew, for every time Mel called "Action!" at the camera, the Italian assistant director would immediately yell, "Azione!" Mel bought it and with that single word one of the girls suddenly became a bit player instead of a background extra. And the testosterone level of the male crew members was way up during this scene. All eyes were on the girls, who were truly shaking their stuff. Several of the crew, lapsing into sudden jock talk, made macho remarks, mostly about their own prowess. Ugly Englishmen aren't much different from ugly Americans. While the camera was being turned around and the opposite side of the room lit, I mentioned the crew's reaction to the showgirl who had called, "Azione!" She laughed and said not too many of the girls would be interested. Then she pointed to one of the others. "That's my girlfriend," she said.

The actors left as they had arrived, suddenly and en masse and still making unintentionally funny remarks. I returned to Venice with the crew for the final scenes with Suzanne and Ian. With the exception of these scenes, If It's Tuesday, This Must Be Belgium was actually shot in continuity, since the crew was following the same path that the "tourists" were. In Venice again, we shot an interior scene of Suzanne and Ian on "the morning after" their lovemaking in a Rome hotel room. Since it was in an interior, you never knew we were in Venice when we filmed it. Then we shot a charming night scene by a canal where Ian tells Suzanne about his parents being London buskers (street entertainers). He did a little busker dance for her, which totally captured her. Ian was at his British best, and the scene ended with a kiss. During the night, Tom Pevsner asked Mel to give him a thirty-minute warning before final wrap. When Mel asked him why, Pevsner replied that Mel had been so noisy on the location that Pevsner had had to put up many of the neighborhood residents in hotel rooms, and he wanted to call them and tell them the filming was ending and that they could return to their homes. Mel blanched as he saw the cost of the scene mounting. The story was pure fiction. Pevsner's revenge, Tom called it.

Yet a better one awaited Mel. Shortly after O'Brien called, "It's a wrap!" the camera team "accidentally" dropped some empty film cans off their gondola into the canal, right in front of Mel. Dead serious, the guys moaned that it was the exposed film of the entire night's work. Mel's hand went to his head and his face lost color again, as he envisaged having to shoot the scene over the following night. We allowed him to age a few eons before we burst out laughing. The moment was hardly retribution for over two months of vocal abuse.

When the movie was released, it made back its money, but wasn't a huge success. Stan Margulies told me later that it did well on both coasts, and poorly in the middle of the country. New York and L.A. saw the movie for what it was: a spoof. But the middle of the country, he said, didn't get the jokes. They were the people who would think a yodeling act and Fondue Fling Night in Switzerland would be terrific fun, he specified. Having visited the middle of the country a great deal, I question his analysis. But then producers always have a reason beyond the film itself to explain why it isn't a blockbuster.

During the course of the film, Ian McShane and I had dinner together several times. Five years later, shortly after I moved to Los Angeles, our paths would cross again. Since I'd actually had a decent relationship with the screamer, Mel Stuart, I called him once I was settled in the city of automobiles. His wife, Harriet, answered the phone, and when I said I'd taken a small apartment in the Los Feliz area, she replied, "Oh. Well, that's a little out of things. But I'm sure Mel will be glad to see you." It would take me a while to understand that "things" meant the west side of the city, the only grounds possible, then as now, for people in the movie business. Mel returned my call and invited me to dinner at Por Favor, a Mexican restaurant on Santa Monica Boulevard in what is now West Hollywood. The food was no better than average, Wolfgang Puck not yet having arrived on the scene. Some time later, I learned that Ian McShane was also in town, I think for a television show. Mel gave me Ian's phone number and I called him. I made the mistake of inviting the English actor to dinner at my apartment. I thought it would have a much more personal touch if I did the cooking, and that as a European, he would appreciate that.

My first apartment was in the east end of Hollywood, just a few blocks from Los Feliz Boulevard. While some of the old art deco houses and apartment buildings there had a certain charm, my apartment, both outside and inside, certainly didn't. A tired, stucco, mom-and-pop building with eight units, it was probably built in the postwar early '50s, and was definitely on the shabby side. When Ian entered the door, I realized he wasn't a good enough actor to disguise his disappointment. The living room was small, with that horrible, variegated wall-to-wall shag carpeting so popular in the '70s and a Murphy bed folded up in one wall. The sofa was worn, partly covered with an Indian print imported from Pier One, and there was no dining room. The kitchen, happily, was large, as east-end Hollywood apartments went, and it was there that I served a home-made dinner to him and a young lady from the adjacent building. I think I made *boeuf bourguignon*. I'd bought a decent bottle of French wine, although I was on a pretty strict budget in those days. My friend, Pamela Davis, a bubbly and constant chatterer, gibble-gabbled away during the meal, and the longer Ian was there, the less conversational he became. The main course over, he suddenly bolted, blurting out something about having to be somewhere else, something that even my dialogue coach ears couldn't quite catch as he disappeared like a flash out the front door.

"Ian's gone!" Pamela needlessly chimed. I shrugged and we sat down again and ate the salad, the French cheese, and the home-made fruit salad with Cointreau. And we finished the wine, not giving an English farthing about our unfashionable surroundings.

CHAPTER NINE

~

Paid Holiday

The reasons I'd heard for making 20th Century Fox's *L'Échelle Blanche* (literally, *The White Ladder*) were varied, and as far as I know, all true. First, Fox had some money left at the end of the year on which it would be heavily taxed if it weren't used in film production. Second, an English fashion photographer, Robert Freeman, had made a short documentary entitled *The World of Fashion* (*mini-midi* in French), which apparently featured many young girls in miniskirts and various stages of dress and undress. Darryl F. Zanuck loved it. Very much in favor with him after that, Freeman was available to direct a feature film. Third, the Fox office told me of a budding young actress by the name of Jacqueline Bisset who wanted to fulfill her obligations on a contract with the studio so she could move on, with the career-changing *Airport* at Universal Studios waiting just ahead of her. She had a small track record behind her, having appeared in the romp *Casino Royale* and as Audrey Hepburn's roommate in *Two for the Road*. Then she gave strong support to Steve McQueen in the car-chasing *Bullitt* and made news when she replaced Mia Farrow opposite Frank Sinatra in *The Detective*. But while *L'Échelle Blanche* had no international name stars, it did offer Jackie her first lead role and the opportunity to move on. And fourth, a secretary at Fox's Paris office who had little knowledge of movies, reached into a file cabinet of never-before-read scripts, found one she liked, and gave it to her boss, say-ing, "We should make this."

For all these reasons, *L'Échelle Blanche* was about to be filmed in a small town in the south of France, in September 1968. The movie would be shot in both French and English, the way Gérard Oury had explained to me shooting would be done for *The Brain*.

I'd already saved a good amount of money making movies by then, and with more income in sight I decided to buy a new car. My ten-year old Renault Dauphine broke out with palsied shaking every time it reached forty-two miles an hour. No one had credit cards in France yet, the American buy-now-pay-later system was unknown, and so out of my savings I purchased a bright green convertible Fiat Spider, paying the full amount, as everyone did then, in one fell swoop. The day after the purchase, I left with the cat for St-Rémy-de-Provence. There was no freeway yet going south, so I took the national roads, cruising at a leisurely pace.

I spent a night on the road and the following day pulled into the courtyard of the Hôtel des Antiques, a charming and respectfully pre-served nineteenth-century landmark that was within walking distance of local shops and restaurants. Behind it sat an immense park, dotted with bungalow studio apartments with kitchenettes. It was here that I stayed for the first two weeks until the 1st assistant director, the ubiq-uitous Paul Feyder, and I rented a *mas*, which was the French provin-cial word for small farmhouse. It was old, had typical whitewashed walls, shutters, and a stone base. I would stay here for the remainder of the shoot, which turned out to be much shorter than any film I'd worked on until that point. The script was uncomplicated, with much of the filming in one location, and there were no superstars to hold up production.

St-Rémy-de-Provence is another little jewel of a town, of which France seems to have a plethora, that is relatively unknown outside of French travelers. There are cobblestone streets, lovely, tree-lined boulevards, and several colorful markets on central squares. The town lies midway between Arles and Avignon, and the whole region abounds in eighteenth- and nineteenth-century domains, Roman antiquities and arenas, and traces of Van Gogh. Here the senses reel from fields of lavender, thyme, rosemary, savory, and sage (the famous *herbes de*

Provence) while beyond the fields lie the distant mauve Alpilles mountain range. Add to this throughout September and October the changing leaves. Then add, at the end of each day, with the sun low in the sky, the tint of pure gold brushing the aromatic fields, the same gold that Van Gogh wanted so desperately to capture. Was I here to work? Or to dream? And for such a holiday, was I really to be paid by a film company? Or was I to pay them?

The perfect setting was soon matched by a delightful cast and crew. The actors, except for Jacqueline Bisset, were unknown to American audiences. Young and handsome Marc Porel and Pierre Zimmer would play quasilove interests for Jackie, although the understated relationship of the movie was really between her and an eleven-year-old boy, played by Jean-François Maurin. Finally, there was the elegant Giselle Pascal from the legitimate theater. Much of my work would be in getting her, Jean-François, and a few local children to play in English. But the truth was that in the entire cast there wasn't one ego, one tantrum, one drunk, one screamer, one actor holding up filming for black silk socks.

Jackie proved herself to be a sweetheart. She spoke fluent French (her mother's side) and could converse with the grips and electricians who generally spoke no English. There was no more language barrier with her than there was star barrier. No wonder the crew adored her. She would joke and laugh with them, knew them all by name, and always addressed them with the personal form of *tu*. Considering that she was the lead of the film, the fact that they addressed her back in kind was more than acceptance on the part of the crew; it was consecration. And what a beauty this lady was! In her very early twenties then, she had gray-green eyes and soft chestnut hair, and a face that could launch all the ships of Troy. The year 1968 was coming to a close, and the wardrobe designer outfitted Jackie in the latest Carnaby Street fashions of high boots and miniskirts, or silk blouses with flowing scarves and gossamer, ballooning pants. Either way, she was a vision. In July 1977, following the release of *The Deep*, she would grace *Newsweek*'s cover with the caption, "A Beauty Named Bisset." But what endeared Jackie the most to the crew was not her visible beauty, but the fact that she was warm and down to earth and took an interest in everyone.

L'Échelle Blanche was the epitome of what a European film is like and the antithesis of an American one. Both cast and crew worked together as if they were all one extended family. Much of the filming took place in and around the Château de Roussan, an intimate eighteenth-century treasure with an enormously long drive-up lined with peeling sycamores. The estate was vast, and whenever one scene was completed and we needed to move to another part of the grounds, everyone would grab some piece of equipment and walk with it, a practice forbidden by the American unions. I remember walking and talking with Jackie as we moved from the back of the château to the front. I carried a couple of folding chairs and Jackie carried the sound boom with the mike! Then there was a shot on the side of the road with young Jean-François Maurin looking at some leaves sadly, introspectively. Calling on his photographer's eye, director Bob Freeman suddenly decided he wanted the boy to be examining an insect on a leaf. This was news to the prop master, whose job it was to supply all hand props, even live ones. Since there were no insects in the script, he naturally had no jar of them on hand. He started to walk through the foliage at the side of the road, looking for a talented bug. Immediately, the ad hoc family flew into action, abandoning camera, cable, sound equipment, scripts. Cast and crew alike, everyone began to forage through the woods looking for the right insect.

"I found something."

"What is it?"

"A grasshopper."

"Bob doesn't want a grasshopper. Keep looking."

"I've got a caterpillar."

"Not poetic enough. He wants something with wings."

And so it went for the better part of an hour. Eventually the amateur entomologists found something that the director accepted—some sort of katydid, I think. The fact that it very much resembled the grasshopper rejected forty minutes earlier only reaffirmed the method with which all film casting is done.

I had a handful of children to coach. Besides Jean-François Maurin, there were two local French boys, also eleven, and an eight-year-old American model named Audrey Berindey. Each child had to be coached in a second language, but also because of their young years, they all had to learn something about acting as well. And since the director had virtually no experience along these lines, the task fell to me.

It was a wonderfully rewarding experience. Children's ears are pure, their imaginations without bounds. Sometimes, they merely aped the French or English words I pronounced, but from their own languages the children always knew what they were saying, so they acted their scenes fearlessly.

We had constant fun on the film and giggled a lot on the set. Jackie and I couldn't stop laughing over the possible readings of one of her lines, "He's such a bighead," which she says about Porel's character. "He's such a *big*-head" sounded too English. "He's such a big-*head*" made him sound like he had water on the brain. Splitting the stress evenly with "He's such a *big-head*" made you pause and wonder if he was a ram.

"Who wrote this line?" Jackie asked. In answer, one of the two screenwriters, Gérard Brach, saved from the ignominy of a file drawer by the Fox secretary, arrived a few days later. A short man with short arms, falsely intellectual and constantly apprehensive, he was the only pessimistic and neurotic Frenchman I met in my seventeen years in France. Like Wednesday's child, full of woe, he surely believed that though joy was better than sorrow, joy was not great. Fretting over his own dialogue (he had reason to!) he constantly changed words, then, uncertain of what he'd done, change them back again. That was in French, of course, and I'd alternately supply the English equivalent and then erase it. After a day or two of lolling around the set with his sweater and jacket sleeves hanging over his fingers, he announced that his best friend was coming to visit and advise him. And, indeed, Brach's friend arrived, only to abuse him verbally in public over and over, sometimes concerning his writing, sometimes his person. In one argument, he venomously threw out, "Oh, you! You with your tiny arms, what do you know?" Whatever this codependent abusive relationship was about, both tormentor and tormented seemed to thrive on it. They got drunk together and shouted at each other at night, then sat down to a quiet breakfast in the hotel park in the morning. Shades of Rimbaud and Verlaine, but sans their talent. I would later notice Brach's name as coscreenwriter with Roman Polanski on several movies. I can only think that the talented Polish filmmaker found an even more effective way of beating him.

Because it was 1968, and because young Marc Porel wanted so to be with the times, he would offer us a "hit" on a joint. That strangely sweet and acrid aroma of marijuana occasionally floated around the hotel park where he and Jackie sometimes walked in the evenings, and emanated down the hallway of the hotel. Since both of them were always in good spirits, it was impossible to know if this was from the languid atmosphere of the film, Provence, pot, or a little touch of amour.

Jackie and Marc were together almost every night at the Café des Arts, a warm and convivial bistro that soon became everyone's favorite hangout. It was a family-run restaurant, so the prices for their extraordinary fixed-price menus of five- and six-course meals were reasonable. Monsieur Silvio was the middle-aged patriarch restaurateur, and he had a natural bent for artists in general. The walls of his restaurant were lined with oil paintings of regional and itinerant artists, and he took to actors with the same fervor. Twelve years earlier, his restaurant had been the haunt for Anthony Quinn and Kirk Douglas while they filmed scenes for *Lust for Life* in the region. Often, an impoverished artist exchanged one of his paintings for one of Monsieur Silvio's meals, just as Van Gogh had done in nearby Arles. Patron of the arts and *patron* of the restaurant, Monsieur Silvio followed the filming closely and knew precisely where and what we were filming each day. "How did it go at the quarry today?" he would ask in the evening, or "Did you get all the shots on the road?" Eventually, Alain Franchet, the 2nd A.D., began to deliver the following day's call sheet to the restaurant every evening when he was making his rounds, for which Monsieur Silvio was absolutely enthralled. I dined with Jackie and Marc a couple of times at the Café des Arts, but so did others—Louis Wipf, the production manager, Paul Feyder, Giselle Pascal. It was all relaxing, warm, wonderful. It was a vacation.

Many of the actors, and anyone on the crew who could afford it, made the short trip to the nearby village of Les Baux-de-Provence, which sat on a spur of the Alpilles. There, deified by two of three possible stars in the *Guide Michelin*, was the renowned restaurant Oustaù de Baumanière, usually referred to more succinctly as Baumanière. The views of the Roman ruins and the village were reported to be breathtaking, while the restaurant itself was inside a sixteenth-century residence-turned-hotel. Where else could you begin a meal with ravioli stuffed with truffles and finish with caramelized fennel tart? Alas, after the purchase of the Spider, I was one of those who felt the bill would be a little too steep for me.

That has simply deferred my pleasure along these many years, and I have promised myself that my next visit to the south of France will finally take me to Baumanière, where I fully intend to feast my eyes, gorge myself, and dutifully pass out in a sixteenth-century hotel room, no matter what the cost. But back in 1968, all I could do was listen to Jackie, Marc, and the others, ecstatic over the very best of everything France had to offer in this one spot.

Then Michael Sarrazin arrived for a short visit with Jackie. Back in L.A., the two of them had been what the Hollywood press refers to as "an item." Sarrazin had starred with Jane Fonda in *They Shoot Horses, Don't They?* and narrowly missed the hustler role captured by Jon Voight in *Midnight Cowboy*. Suddenly Marc Porel and I were having dinner together every night, just the two of us. Marc didn't want to dine at the Café des Arts while Sarrazin was in town, so I drove him to La Fourchette, a simple restaurant with excellent fare at prices that fit my wallet, in nearby Avignon. I think this gesture on my part, taking Marc completely out of town once the day's filming ended, would endear me to him. He could relax with me, not worry about bumping into Sarrazin, and even once, when I caught him staring at his glass of red wine, he lifted his eyes to me and said, enormously moved, "*Je l'aime bien, tu sais.*" ("I like her a lot, you know.") When the film was over and Jackie returned to Los Angeles, Marc would occasionally phone me in Paris for dinner and then arrive in my apartment with the latest LP or 45-rpm record of artists we both enjoyed. And these would be his gifts to me, a constant thank you.

When Sarrazin left, Jackie and Marc were seen dining together again, but it was impossible to know (and, indeed, no one needed to know) whether or not the relationship was the same. But the film was already drawing to a close, and their two different professional careers lay in opposite corners of the world, so perhaps the decision was made for them.

One of the last scenes we shot was with Jackie reclining on Jean-François Maurin's bed, holding the young boy in her arms. It was a delicate scene, because it needed to skirt anything sexual between them and at the same time not take on a maternal aspect. Jackie's character, Wendy, was the only real friend the orphaned boy had in the film. The friendship would soon terminate with his suicide in his tree house. The child would place a plastic bag over his head and hold the bag tightly around his neck, suffocating. It was an obvious summing up of morose Gérard Brach's view on life, though I'm not sure that disturbing shot remained in the final cut. Jackie found exactly the right tone to the scene as she held the boy and talked to him. It was warm, loving, intelligent—an older friend guiding a younger friend. She was gentle and strong at the same time. It was the only scene in the movie that was written decently. When the take was over, I pulled her aside and said, "That was probably your best acting in the entire film."

She smiled. "All you need is good material. Given half a chance, I think I can deliver something decent." Those words would haunt me in years to come. With all the Hollywood films that followed, was Jackie given decent acting material or cast mostly for her stunning beauty? For me, her most memorable roles, performances that came up to that moment in L'Échelle Blanche, were as the Las Vegas showgirl on poppers and pills in The Grasshopper, the tragic Anna Karenina she did for TV, and of course, Truffaut's Day for Night.

Our last day of filming came and went, and for everyone the vacation was regrettably over. That night, I entered the Café des Arts to find most of the cast and crew there and every table taken. I waited at the bar, sipping a cloudy pastis, the obligatory regional apéritif, and nibbling from a plate of niçoise olives. Soon Monsieur Silvio came over. "So it's finished," he remarked, with his usual knowledge of the movie's schedule.

"Yes," I said. "It was too short."

"Like life," he replied. "I shall miss you all. I feel some of you are friends now."

When my table was ready, I attempted to pay the bartender for my drink, but he simply waved a finger in front of my face and said, "No, no. Compliments of Monsieur Silvio."

An hour and a half later, I called for my dinner bill. Monsieur Silvio's daughter appeared. "Not tonight," she said. "Monsieur Silvio offers you the meal." I was flabbergasted. All I could do was simply thank her and then seek out the restaurant owner to do the same. "Why?" I asked Monsieur Silvio. "You're supposed to be running a business."

"You have been eating here for two months. It's natural." I hugged him and kissed him on both cheeks, and he stood beaming at me, immensely happy. I later learned that everyone from the movie who was in his restaurant that night had his meal "offered" by Monsieur Silvio. As I said, he loved artists.

Back in Paris, much colder now, I stopped to see Jackie at the Royal Monceau Hotel near the Arc de Triomphe. She presented me to her mother, who was visiting. We all sat around and spoke French, reminisced on the film, and shared a final drink.

I don't know how much of a release *L'Échelle Blanche* finally had. I believe it came out in France under the title *La Promesse*, and I think Jackie herself told me in Los Angeles four years later that the film was released in the States as *Secret World*.

If Audrey Hepburn was the First Lady of film for me, certainly Jacqueline Bisset was a close second. She gave me a warm welcome in Los Angeles when I moved there in 1972. I visited her on the set and later at her home several times. Her two-story house abutted the canyon hills, and I was not surprised to find strong French provincial influences of rough stone walls and country antiques. And while Audrey encouraged me to write, it would be Jackie who would later speak of my work to others in the film industry. We also bumped into each other at the Formosa Café once, a terrible Chinese restaurant across from the old Goldwyn Studios, now Warner-Hollywood. I was lunching with Jean-Louis Trintignant in a booth and presented him to her, and we all immediately fell into speaking French. When Jackie moved on to another booth, Jean-Louis, accustomed like all Parisian men to having seen attractive women his whole life, turned to me and said, "*Qu'est-ce qu'elle est belle!*" ("How beautiful she is!")

Jean-Louis, you only caught a glimpse.

CHAPTER TEN

~

The Bad Boys of France

In the fall of 1968, a somewhat sensational murder occurred. That is, it became sensational as certain celebrities began to be implicated. A young man of Yugoslavian origin, Stefan Marković, was found wrapped in two heavy plastic mattress covers inside a burlap sack with a bullet in his head, at the bottom of a hillside in the Paris suburb of Élancourt. Though no longer in their employ, he had previously been the sometime chauffeur, bodyguard or stand-in, and friend and "confidence man" to young French actor Alain Delon and his actress wife, Nathalie. Delon was one of France's biggest stars. An international actor, he might have been seen by Americans in any number of films: with Toshire Mifune in *Red Sun*, opposite Shirley MacLaine in *The Yellow Rolls Royce* and Burt Lancaster in *The Leopard*, as part of an all-star cast in *Is Paris Burning?* as the pilot in *The Concorde, Airport '79*, and in a '60s classic suspense film, *Plein Soleil* (terribly translated as *Purple Noon*), remade three decades later as the American *The Talented Mr. Ripley*.

Delon had returned from the navy and Indochina in 1956 as a stunningly handsome young man with dark brown hair and cold, steel-blue eyes. Not yet twenty-one when he arrived in Paris, he soon began to turn up in places where movie people gathered. One of these was a wine-tasting festival not far from the Joinville film studio, where he caught the eye of the wife of film director Yves Allégret. The following day, Delon was presented to the director who, taken by the young man's beauty and offhand manner, immediately cast him in the small role of a young rogue opposite Edwige Feuillère, the *grande dame* of French theater and cinema, in *Quand la femme s'en mêle*. Four films later, renowned directors René Clément and Luchino Visconti would fall for Delon's ambiguous charm, his raffish air, his good looks, and his sexual magnetism. Clément would give the actor the lead in *Plein Soleil*, which was followed almost immediately by the lead in Visconti's *Rocco and His Brothers*. Both films would be instant classics, and together they would propel Delon into stardom. Visconti was known to have a weakness for beautiful, young men, and Clément, despite a Russian wife and later an English mistress, was also not unmoved by the boy's beauty. It was understandable. Who could refuse this good-looking, masculine young man who seemed to be just as much at ease with men as women? In a televised interview with Christine Ockrent in 1991, Delon would later say of himself, "Before or after I was twenty, I became conscious of the fact that I had a certain effect on the female species as well as the male, and of all ages. . . ." This was not immodesty. Others would say as much. In *Moi, Claudia, toi, Claudia*, actress Claudia Cardinale stated, "Alain was sure of himself, of his beauty, of his charm, and even more of his sexual power." And in *La Guerre à neuf ans*, Pascal Jardin penned, "He is the only man who holds me with his look, the only one who has sometimes given me the desire to be a woman in order to know him better." Bernard Violet, in his biography, *Les Mystères Delon*, cites René Clément as letting Delon discover a "special relationship between director and actor" with him, a phrase that in itself is ambiguous. Delon's romances with women were renowned, the most publicized being the one with Austrian actress Romy Schneider. There were also actresses Brigitte Auber, Francine Canovas, who would become wife and actress Nathalie Delon, and Mireille Darc. But the reputed equivocal sexuality of Delon's would come into play as l'affaire Marković began to unfold.

And not just Delon's sexuality but the sexuality of an entire world of celebrities and aristocrats. *Le beau monde*, the beautiful people. Privileged, chic, jet-setting, bored. It was a world with which I had once been quite familiar, when I was organizing Paris Playhouse with Colette de Jouvenel and Countess Paola de Rohan-Chabot. They toured the elegant watering holes of Paris, sometimes with me in tow, and they often dropped names of celebrities who liked to abandon themselves from time to time with one gender or the other, or both. *Bâteau à voile et à vapeur* ("sailboat and steamboat") was their picturesque expression signifying an AC/DC person.

Bisexuality was not just in the domain of aristocrats and celebrities. It was, and probably still is, somewhat pandemic in France, if not most of Europe. At Porte Dauphine, near Paris's Bois de Boulogne, during the years of which I write, there would always be a circle of parked cars at the square at night. In them or standing outside them were their male owners, single all. On any given evening, other cars with couples, some married, would arrive and slowly cruise the square, selecting a mate for the evening for both of them. A *ménage à trois* in France more often means two men and a woman, with the men sharing each other as well as the woman, whereas with homosexual panic so engrained in American men, it more often means to them, when thought of at all, as two women and a man. Alexandre Dumas *fils* is attributed with having put it as, "The chain of marriage is so heavy that it takes two, and often three, to carry it."

With the rich and beautiful people of Paris, however, so public a spot as Porte Dauphine would never serve as a meeting ground. Instead, it was the elegant "in" clubs like Chez Castel and Chez Régine and Bistingo, or Madame de's or Monsieur de's living room, and the sexual pairings, triplings, or group parties organized out of them. Bluebloods, artists, writers, models, and even politicians were the cast of characters. For some, *partouzes* (group sex) was the cry of the day. Somewhere in all this, the name of Claude Pompidou emerged. She was the wife of Georges Pompidou, the former *premier ministre* of France and the man everyone assumed would soon replace de Gaulle as president of the French Republic.

This, then, was the world in which handsome young Alain Delon, erstwhile common sailor, now brilliant celebrity, soon found himself. He had hired Stefan Marković in the fall of 1964, immediately after the young Yugoslav had finished a prison term for breaking and entering, and offered him private quarters within his own Paris townhouse that extended over several floors. Throughout his career, Delon was drawn largely to roles of gangsters, hit-men, ex-cons, and in his personal life seemed to hold the same fascination for the real bad boys of society.

Following the discovery of Marković's body, rumors began to circulate. Was Delon in any way involved? Was his wife, Nathalie? And if so, why? Marković had apparently been invited by Delon, or both Delons, into the social circle of special partygoers several times. In itself, this was not astonishing. French history had shown that kings and queens often had delicious dalliances with kitchen help, chambermaids, and stable boys. Why not a virile chauffeur with a Slavic accent? That would be amusing, *non?* What wasn't amusing was the rumor later that Marković had photographs of some of these liaisons and that could prove embarrassing. What wasn't amusing was that ugly word *chantage* (blackmail) that the press was beginning to use. If this were true, whom was Marković trying to blackmail? The Delons? Madame Pompidou? Other notable figures? And what certainly wasn't amusing was an unanswered crime and that young man's body with a bullet in the brain.

A few days after the discovery of Marković's body, two police inspectors questioned Delon in his Saint-Tropez villa, where he'd been staying during the filming of *La Piscine*. Later he would be questioned again, the newspaper headlines screaming, *"Delon Arrêté!"* While both times inspectors were probably just seeking information, in the public's mind Delon was being considered a possible suspect. When the actor was released, the police stated cryptically that the affair went far, very far.

What did that mean? Had Delon dropped a few very important names of pleasure-seekers, implying, but not saying, that the police needed to be careful because of the people they might have to deal with? It was no secret that Claude Pompidou frequently kept the company of film artists, including Delon. Had he evoked her name as a friend and partygoer? Another Yugoslav, Ackov, told the police how he and Marković had been to a group sex party where Marković identified a tall blonde lady to him as the prime minister's wife. And was it true that nude photos of her were already appearing here and there throughout Paris?

The affair went very far. Could that also mean the French Mafia? From his youth, Delon had had a friendship with "Mémé" Guérini, a veritable godfather in Marseille, and with François Marcantoni, an underworld figure whose friendship with Delon went back to his pre-Paris days. Marcantoni had been arrested many times and was suspected of having been involved in several murders. He'd had a rendezvous with Stefan Marković the night of his disappearance. Together they had planned a fixed poker game and a robbery. Both men had been involved with drug trafficking. Letters written by Marković just before his murder indicated how much the young man feared for his life, stating that if anything were to happen to him, those responsible would be Delon and Marcantoni. Other letters were full of rancor, showing that the close friendship with Delon had turned to animosity. And finally it was discovered that Stefan Marković had spent several amorous nights with Delon's wife, Nathalie, and that Delon knew of this. With each new twist, the looking-glass became "curiouser and curiouser."

Delon? Nathalie? Marcantoni? Guérini? The hidden French government? The Yugoslavian Mafia? The French Mafia? Who fired the shot? As in *Murder on the Orient Express*, where Hercule Poirot notes that there are too many clues, so in the Marković Affair were there too many suspects. Government figures who did not want to see Georges Pompidou as the next president fanned the flames of the scandal, turning an affair of morals into an affair of state. Valéry Giscard d'Estaing, a future president for the country, was one of the few politicians who remained faithful to Pompidou. For Delon and Marcantoni, the spotlight was off of them for a while.

The investigation went on for many months, with no official suspects. In the spring of 1969, Delon appeared in a question-and-answer session for the BBC program, *Twenty-Four Hours*. In it, Olivier Todd questioned Delon about murder, about sex orgies, about the Pompidous, and about Delon's homosexual leanings. On the latter, Delon replied, "And if it was true, what's wrong with that? What am I guilty of? . . ."

L'affaire Marković ran from the fall of 1968 into June 1969, when de Gaulle stepped down from power and the country voted in Georges Pompidou as the next president. At the celebratory reception in the gardens of the Élysée Palace, Claude Pompidou stood next to her husband, smiling and wearing spotless white gloves. She was tall, blonde, elegant, and above reproach. The new president's first act would be to sweep out the judges and police commissioners who had allowed his wife's name to be dragged into the whole sordid business. The nude photos of Madame Pompidou were then determined to be montage. The plastic mattress covers that had been used for Marković's body were part of 865 such sets. One of them was traced to a Paris dealer who, in May 1968, four months before the murder, had ordered such a set for one of her clients, François Marcantoni. But by the time this crucial identification was made, Georges Pompidou was president and the new judges appointed by him felt it best not to bring the affair into the limelight again. A young friend of Marković's, Uros Milicević, who had accompanied him on the night of his murder to his fatal rendezvous with Marcantoni and probably caught a glimpse of the underworld figure, would later be found shot to death in a Brussels hotel room, never having formally identified him. To this day, the murder of Stefan Marković remains on the books as a *non-lieu*, no sufficient grounds to prosecute.

In what would doubtless be the quirkiest coincidence of my career, I was called into the office of French producer Jacques Strauss just shortly after Delon did the BBC interview with Olivier Todd. I'd known Jacques from my days at 20th Century Fox. "We're going to make a movie called *The Sicilian Clan*. Henri Verneuil will direct it with the three biggest stars in France," Jacques told me. "You know who the three biggest stars in France are, don't you?" Before I could answer, he named them: Jean Gabin, Lino Ventura, and Alain Delon. They were, indeed, the biggest stars in the business, and any one of them could hold a film together, and had. Only Jean-Paul Belmondo and Jean-Louis Trintignant could be mentioned in the same breath. My old friend, Irina Demick, had also been cast and would supply a little love interest in the macho-dominated film. Gabin was to play Vittorio Manalese, the head of a Sicilian family of Mafia members, Ventura a detective, and Delon a ruthless killer on the run.

"Shades of the Marković Affair?" I queried.

"Oh, that's practically all over with. Besides, who knows what really happened?"

As it turned out, I was to be the dialogue coach for everyone *except* Delon. He had his own coach, a sometime American actor I knew, Steve Eckardt, who had worked with him previously. The film bears both our names at the front end of the credits, ironically next to a freeze-frame shot of Delon.

Jacques Strauss also explained that *The Sicilian Clan* would be shot in double version, French and English both. In the late '60s, most big French films were done this way for all the close shots. The French version would be used in Europe, the English for the rest of the world. If a French actor's English were good, his voice would remain in the final cut. If it were not, he would be revoiced by an American or English actor, but because the French actor's lips had formed English words in the first place, the dubbing would match undetected.

The first person I rehearsed was Lino Ventura, a big and solid man who, along with the other stars in the cast, had already made a reputation for playing tough guys with hearts of gold. With a prominent nose and square jaw, he looked like a former wrestler, which he was, who might have taken more than one beating in his life. I went to his sprawling suburban home, and he greeted me at the door. He told me he spoke some English (actually it was very decent) but that he really needed to rehearse. He had never before acted in English. We sat in a tufted bay window seat and began to work together. It struck me immediately that the movie's tough guy wasn't tough at all. He was soft-spoken, gentle, intelligent, and most obviously sensitive. We read through all his scenes for the entire picture, and at the end of an hour and a half I asked him why he wasn't playing roles that could exhibit that sensitivity and tenderness. He smiled and indicated his stocky build. "Look at me," he said. "I'm a prisoner of my roles."

I learned much later that Ventura had a daughter with Down syndrome, and that among his friends he was considered to be a fine and loving father. This must have accounted for his sensitivity in real life, a sensitivity he was not given the opportunity to portray often on screen.

Then I met the patriarch of the movie, indeed, of all French cinema. Jean Gabin had the reputation of being a *monstre sacré*. Stories abounded how he dismissed people summarily from films, literally sending them off the set in tears. A veritable lion when angered, he could roar a crew of sixty technicians into instant, petrified silence when he had to. His earliest roles in the '30s established him firmly as a leading man with such classics as Renoir's *Grand Illusion*, and he made a brief appearance in Hollywood in the early '40s.

I rehearsed with him in his dressing room at the Studios de Joinville. His manner was gruff and his voice gravelly, as they were with all the tough guy roles from all the working-class sections of Paris that he had performed. He had snow white hair now, and his face had deep lines in it, his thin lips set in steely resolution. "What a face!" Steve Eckardt, the other coach, said to me a few days later when we were both on the stage together. It was true. Gabin had one of the great faces in film history.

Gabin spoke only a little English, and with a heavy accent. He immediately told me the story of his first day in Hollywood, when he learned his lines in parrot fashion, imitating the assistant director who had said them for him. "What kina pie yagot?" he threw at me. And when I laughed, he added in French, "You understood me? Maybe my English isn't so bad, after all."

One of the first scenes we shot was in a warehouse of pinball machines that Gabin's character owned. It was a front for his Mafia operations. Ventura, playing the inspector, enters to question Gabin on the whereabouts of cop-killer Roger Sartet (Delon). Director Henri Verneuil rehearsed the scene briefly with the two stars, then dismissed them as the first shot was being put into place. When they were brought back in, Verneuil pointed out that he had the camera high up on a crane for the opening moment, and would start to lower it after Ventura had arrived at one of the pinball machines. But for his entrance, the camera would be shooting down on him and slightly from the back. Gabin smirked at Ventura, then pointed to the top of his own head, and Ventura laughed. Gabin was letting his costar know that the bald spot at the top of Ventura's head was going to be seen in the shot. This was the first I saw of Gabin's bonhomie and playfulness, which throughout the film, would pop up now and then, albeit only with people for whom he had the greatest professional respect.

The scene ready, Verneuil asked the two actors with which language they wanted to start. Once the crane lowered, the camera would finish in a medium-close shot for the dialogue. "Either one," said Ventura, completely relaxed.

"Let's do it in French first," said Gabin. "We might find something in our native language that we can use in both versions." And that's what we did. But over the weeks that followed, the order became interchangeable. I felt good about my work because, soon, both actors were comfortable in English, and every so often Gabin would tell the director, "Let's do the English first."

We had been filming for a week when Alain Delon came on the set for a scene with Ventura. If both Gabin and Ventura had great faces, so in a completely different way, did Delon. Everything about him immediately riveted your eyes to him. He was one of those stars whose handsomeness is just as striking in reality as on the screen. There was something cold about him, something removed, that I didn't see with the two older actors. He was totally in control of himself, sure and sensual in his movements, aware that crew members were all staring at him. What was it, I wondered, that compelled us so to him? The recent scandal? The equivocal sexuality? The danger? The animal in us all? If Gabin was the lion that roared, Delon was the panther that could pounce at any moment. Then Gabin cracked a joke and Delon smiled. A generous smile that relaxed his face and formed small lines around his eyes. Suddenly, he was warm and human and approachable and immensely appealing. This mercurial change from cold to warm and back again was doubtless part of Delon's fascination. You sensed you could trust him and not trust him at the same time. "The eternal marriage of angel and riff-raff," writer Jean Cau would say of him.

Throughout the rehearsal both Steve Eckhardt and I stood at close range, our scripts open, he for Delon, I for Ventura. When the rehearsal was over, director Henri Verneuil introduced Steve to Ventura and me to Delon. We shook hands, and Delon smiled again on meeting me. Since Steve would only be coming on the set the days Delon was shooting, I told the actor that I was there for the entire picture in case, for any reason, he might need me. As it turned out, my comment was prognosticatory. Quite a few times on the film, Steve, not a well man, became ill and then I worked directly with Delon.

I found myself to be even more riveted to this fallen angel than I had the first day, when the entire crew stopped to stare at him. He was polite, professional, making whatever changes I suggested, which usually consisted of shifting misplaced tonic accents, since his pronunciation was excellent. I'd seen him on the stage with Romy Schneider in a French translation of 'Tis Pity She's a Whore, an Elizabethan play about brother-sister incest. It was a daring move for a popular movie star, but he pulled it off, gaining my personal respect. It also said he took chances. But mostly there was an almost palpable sexuality that exuded from him, and behind that sexuality was the danger, the immense danger that excited far more than it repelled.

"Checking my neck, inspector?" Delon recited the line to me. It would be directed to Ventura and referred to the guillotine. Suddenly, I felt the Marković Affair was hovering over us and the line took on an added meaning.

"It's perfect," I said. "The pronunciation is perfect."

Some time later, we shot a scene with Delon and Irina, who, playing a young mobster's wife, is fascinated by and drawn to Roger Sartet, Delon's character. She questions him about killing someone. "When he falls, right there in front of you, what does it do to you?" she asks.

"Nothing," he replies, impassive.

I looked around at other crew members. Were they getting the same double entendre? The continuity girl, Lucile Costa, nodded to me. That was not the only occasion where the Marković Affair haunted *The Sicilian Clan*. There was a scene where Delon, as the hit man Sartet, manages to cut his way through the floor of a police wagon on its way to prison and escapes through the floor opening. The scene was apparently based on a real-life incident performed by a criminal known as René the Cane on his way to la Santé prison. But once Delon escapes through the floor he has to make his way to a waiting car, handcuffs still on him. Delon was concerned that some photographer might learn of the nature of the scene and photograph him in handcuffs, tying in the photo to the Marković murder. Fortunately, the production trucks and the crew formed a protective ring around the filming area, and the scene was shot quickly before any journalist could profit from the moment.

We went to Rome for a few scenes, including the encounter between Gabin and a well-known Italian character actor, Amedeo Nazzari. The scene was brief, the two old Mafia members meeting at the airport after many decades, and only recognizing each other when all the passengers have left the waiting area. Gabin and Nazzari had no more than a few words to say, but Nazzari had a terrible memory. And his eyes kept going inexplicably to the sound boom. Still, the scene was filmed without a problem. But when we returned to Paris, I had to spend an undue amount of time with Nazzari to get him to learn his lines. He'd always forget one line whenever he learned another. I told Verneuil about the problem, warning him that he might have to shoot Nazzari's speeches in pieces, and cut away, the way I had seen Bob Parrish do with Broderick Crawford when he'd been drinking.

The problem suddenly became compounded when Nazzari appeared on the set, ready to shoot. We began to rehearse, and the Italian actor stumbled through the scene, his look again distracted by the sound mike extended over his head. I went to him as soon as the rehearsal was over to refresh his memory. "What's that?" he asked, pointing to the overhead boom.

"The microphone," I answered. I thought it was a silly question.

"They're *recording* this?"

"Of course. That's what we did with you in Rome."

"I thought the microphone was just there for general atmosphere," he answered. "It was recording my *words?*"

And then I realized what was disturbing him. The Italians were known during the '60s for not taking live sound seriously, recording only a guide track, and sometimes not recording sound at all. Dialogue was dubbed in in a sound studio afterward. Now, for Nazzari, there was suddenly direct sound, bad memory, and two languages that weren't his. I did manage to get him through the scene, but once again I was just off camera, throwing him a line the moment I sensed his hesitation. Verneuil, unruffled, assured me afterward that the scene was just fine; still, he did a cutaway shot in protection.

Once the scene was over, Nazzari told me the story of how Fellini did all his movies without the sound really counting. Since he used actors of many different nationalities, as in *Satyricon,* he would give each actor a number to which he needed to count, and tell him the emotion. "'Twelve, anger,' he would say," Nazzari explained. "And then, in anger, the actor counts to twelve in his native language. Or 'seven, sadness,' and the actor counts to seven, very sad." Apparently, only Fellini knew what words he would later dub into the actor's mouth. And that was what Nazzari had expected in *The Sicilian Clan.*

Jean Gabin's professionalism was manifest. When a scene finished with a tight two-shot, followed by a close-up of Gabin, he would then be released from all further work for the day and told he could go home. But he never did. He always waited around, sometimes for two hours or more, just to throw his lines from off-camera to the actor who was then having his close-up shot. He didn't need to do that, of course, since the dialogue coach or an assistant director could do it for him. His staying at the studio was a courtesy to his fellow actor.

But the greatest test of his professionalism would come with me. There was a scene with one long monologue of Gabin's, as he stood before a map of Sicily, showing all the land he had bought up for his family. The monologue was almost a page long, and his speech showed his obsession over, and love for, his family. It was the justification of his character. "Vittorio's credo," I named it. Gabin worked on his English especially hard for this scene.

On the set, Verneuil told him that because of the length of the speech, he should first do it in French. Gabin agreed, and it was shot four or five times, with director and star fine-tuning the speech. Satisfied that he had two good takes in the can, Verneuil then called for the English version. Gabin stepped away and he and I went over to the canvas-backed chairs reserved for him and his aged dresser, Micheline. We ran the lines of the monologue several times while Verneuil and the crew waited. When Gabin seemed to have the speech at his command, we returned to the camera. He took up the same position by the wall map, the assistant director called, "*Le rouge!*" and the red light at the entrance door of the stage went on. The buzzer sounded, and Verneuil called, "*Partez!*" ("Go!")

Without hesitating, Gabin delivered the entire speech at breakneck speed. At the end of the scene, Verneuil yelled, "*Coupez!*" Then the director smiled, rose from his chair, threw his arms out, and said, "*Oh, Jean!*" with the intonation that the scene had been perfect. It looked like he was ready to embrace Gabin. I rushed to Verneuil's side and began to whisper my concerns in his ear. Though Gabin had not paused in his speech, there had been two fluffs in pronunciation. Something else had occurred as well. Gabin hadn't played the scene the same way he had in French. He had played it much bigger, his eyes rolling, his facial expressions much more exaggerated. He was overcompensating. How could Verneuil not have seen that?

Suddenly, the lion roared. "*Qu'est-ce que c'est? Qu'est-ce que c'est?*" Gabin demanded to know angrily, his voice exploding atomically. The crew was instantly frozen. I fully expected Verneuil to explain to Gabin what I had just whispered to him about the fluffs, but Verneuil, for reasons that I do not understand to this day, remained absolutely silent, although it certainly was his place, not mine, to tell the star of the picture that a take needed to be done over.

"*Voilà, Monsieur Gabin* . . ." I began, totally aware that the entire crew, not just Gabin, was watching me. I tried to keep my voice from trembling. I explained briefly about the two small fluffs and ended by saying that in rehearsal he had done the speech better. There was a death-silence. This is it, I thought. This is where I get roared off the set. Steve Eckardt would take over the film.

In a very calm, matter-of-fact manner, Gabin said, "Well, then, let's do another one." It was addressed to everyone present, Verneuil included. The technicians began to move back to their original places, Verneuil sat back down in his director's chair, and I very quietly corrected the two fluffs. Gabin repeated his speech without an error. Then I leaned in to him, lowered my voice, and with my life in my hands, I told him how he had hammed up the scene. I told him about his eyes, I told him about his grimaces, about his runaway speed. I told him he was overcompensating and that he had done none of those things in French. He looked me squarely in the eyes, and without any emotion whatsoever, called over to Verneuil, "Let's do it, Henri!"

We shot the English version a second time. The two fluffs were corrected, he slowed down a bit, and the grimaces were lessened. They were still there, but they were better. At the end of the take, Verneuil called, "*Coupez!*" and immediately looked at me. So did Gabin. So did the crew, to a man. The take hadn't been perfect, but I thought I'd better not push my luck. I gave a thumbs-up back to Verneuil. He got up from his chair, smiled at Gabin, and went to complete the hug he'd intended to give him the first time. The crew began to break the set up and I walked away from the camera on jello legs.

A few moments later, Gabin was seated in his chair, talking to Micheline. I waited for a pause, then approached him.

"I wanted to thank you, Monsieur Gabin."

"What for?" he asked.

"For not shouting me off the stage. For doing another take."

"But that's only natural, *mon petit*. Of everyone on the set, you are the only one who can hear what sounds right and what doesn't. No one else has the ear. Not even Henri. It is for me to thank you."

"I was letting him know what happened when you asked about it."

"You did the right thing. We are all making this movie together."

"You know, before I met you, I'd heard stories about the way you fired people off the set."

"I never fired anyone who was doing his job correctly. That's what you were doing," he declared. Next to him, Micheline, who had been his dresser for thirty years, nodded quietly. "I've been selling my potatoes for a long while," he said picturesquely, "and I know a professional when I see one." I thanked him. "Now tell me again why you thought my expressions were too big," the lion asked.

From then on, there was always a special warmth Gabin seemed to hold for me. I was flattered. Often, with his arm around my shoulders, he would lead me from the lights to his chair where we'd rehearse or just sit and talk. Unfortunately, this was short-lived. With just three weeks left to film, I suddenly became ill. I felt tired and had dizzy spells. The whites of my eyes were yellowing and my urine was darkening. My doctor ordered blood tests and they confirmed his suspicion that I had contracted hepatitis. Naïvely, I called the production office to say that I might have to be off the film for a few days.

If there is one thing the French know everything about and the Americans nothing, it is the liver. The production office knew instantly that I would be out for the remainder of the film, and the following day, my doctor told me I needed to stay in bed for six weeks. The liver, he said, restored itself, but only if there were a very rigid diet and complete bed rest. But complete. He ordered me to keep a bed pan next to the bed.

I remained in bed for exactly forty-four days. In the first two weeks, I rose only once a day for about ten minutes. In later weeks, I was allowed to get up twice, then three times, each time very briefly. I had no television set, so I read a great deal and did French crossword puzzles and slept a lot. The cat loved it; he had a twenty-four-hour bed partner now. I ate simple foods, all without fats or oils or butter. Chocolate was not allowed, nor was orange juice, though I never understood why. Wine was totally out of the question. Over the years, I'd learned from the French that indulging in overly rich foods, mayonnaise, heavy cream sauces, pâté, or a bit too much wine would result in a *crise de foie* (liver crisis) with accompanying headaches. When that happened, you simply put yourself on a little diet of broiled meats, steamed vegetables, cooked fruit compotes, and Vichy water. A few days of this regime and you were as good as new, ready to begin the gluttony all over. Married to Pierre Galante, then the editor of *Paris Match*, Olivia de Havilland wrote a book in 1962 called *Every Frenchman Has One*. The "one" is not what you think; it's the liver.

Hepatitis, of course, is far more serious than a simple *crise de foie*. My doctor came to see me once a week, climbing four flights of stairs and drawing blood to test my enzyme levels, which in the fourth week, began to decline. Friends occasionally visited, keeping their distance (the virus was infectious), and brought cooked food and emptied the cat box. Someone else visited, the only person from *The Sicilian Clan* to do so: Irina Demick. Elegantly attired, and looking very Russian with a black fur toque and matching muff, she actually dared to sit at the foot of the bed. On each visit, she brought flowers and we chatted for a while and then I'd rehearse the few lines she still had left to shoot. While I was ill, they filmed the long action sequence involving landing a hijacked jet on the freeway west of Paris, simulating a forced landing outside New York. A good ten minutes of film time essentially without dialogue. What little dialogue there was left in the picture, Irina explained, was being covered by Steve Eckardt. They all sent their best wishes, and Irina mentioned that Jean Gabin particularly wanted to be remembered to me. With the peculiar sense of justice that only the film industry has, the famous monologue of Gabin's in which I'd played such a pivotal role never made it into the movie. But it offered me the opportunity to get to know the legendary man inside the lion.

My father called me from Rochester, New York, after having received my letter explaining the illness.

"Your brother, Donald, caught hepatitis while he was stationed in Japan," was his opening line.

"I know," I said. "And I only have one brother so I know his name."

"What's that?" my father asked rhetorically. He was always saying, "What's that?" when he'd heard perfectly well. I decided to let it go. "How did you catch this, anyway?"

"Who knows? Unwashed food, maybe." I didn't mention possible sexual transmission.

"Your brother, Donald, caught it from a needle while he was working in the hospital. The needle was infected from a patient. But that wasn't his fault. As long as I live, I won't understand why you want to live in a foreign country."

"You can catch hepatitis anywhere. In the U.S., too."

"I don't know anyone who has it. Just you two and you both got it abroad. Who's taking care of your meals, anyway?" I told him friends brought food every day. "You shouldn't be living alone," he said. From anyone else, this would have been a non sequitur, but from my father it was Aristotelian logic.

I asked him how he was doing in Rochester. Since the death of my mother six years earlier, he'd given up the house they had been renting on the temperate Jersey shore and he'd moved to upstate New York. It was a self-destructive move warranted, he thought, by the fact that he still had two brothers living there. Subsequently, one moved away, the other died, and my father remained there and fought blizzards and treacherous, icy sidewalks the rest of his existence. But I wasn't going to argue his life, with the hope that he wouldn't argue mine. Of course, that rationale rarely works with parents.

"You still making movies? he asked. I told him I was. "And still coaching those actor people?"

"Yes."

"Funny way to make a living." I told him I wasn't necessarily going to do that for the rest of my life. As soon as I said that I regretted it, because it set him up for the obvious question. "Then what d'ya wanna do?" he asked. I could almost hear, "When you grow up" tacked on to the question.

I thought of Nicholas Ray's advice. And Audrey Hepburn's. "I might try my hand at writing," I said.

There was a long pause. Too long. "Your brother, Donald, wrote an article that was published in some medical journal," he said finally. "About one of his operations. You know, he sews up veins."

"Vascular surgery," I said.

"Yeah, that's right. I didn't understand what he wrote—after all, I'm just a dumb bunny—but he sent me a copy, anyway." Then came the perennial killer. "Of course, he doesn't make his living that way."

I realized that although my father had left school in the tenth grade, he possessed all the statesmanship of Disraeli, Richelieu, and Machiavelli rolled into one. I thanked him for his concern and somehow ended the conversation. I lay back in bed, pulled the cat up close to my chest, and hoped beyond hope that my enzyme levels hadn't gone up.

~

CHAPTER ELEVEN

The Friends Thou Hast

In the last two weeks of my horizontal encampment, I started to receive phone calls from Margot Capelier and Ann Selepegno, and even from Anatole Litvak, about a film Litvak was going to direct soon, *The Lady in the Car*. That was how we would all subsequently refer to it, although the full title was actually *The Lady in the Car with Glasses and a Gun*; it was based on a Sebastien Japrisot mystery novel. Japrisot was considered by some critics to be France's Agatha Christie. He put mystery into his own pen name, which was an anagram of his little-known real name, Jean-Baptiste Rossi. His stories always held some kind of surprise twist at the end. Unfortunately for the picture, the twist of *The Lady in the Car* required a long flashback in the last reel to explain everything that had gone before. A flashback that would take up 20 percent of the entire running time of the movie. This later proved to be fatal.

Margot told me that filming would be in Paris, on the Riviera, and many spots in between, as we followed the car in the story south. The big question was whether I'd be well in time to do the film. Litvak said he'd forego having me on the screen tests he was going to do, so long as I could be available for the film itself, and he sent a script to my apartment.

The premise of the story was a good one: a young lady drives her boss to the Paris airport and then, totally on a whim, decides not to return his car, but instead heads south toward the Riviera for an impromptu vacation. But along the way, she keeps bumping into people she's never seen before who all say they recognize her. Eventually, she makes it to the Riviera and a villa that more people say she has rented. In it there is a dead body, and she appears to be the murderer.

Margot sent me French actor Bernard Fresson, whose work in the theater I knew, to rehearse with me at home before his test. He was a stocky young man with sandy hair, who had also been in the Costa-Gavras movie, Z. He was testing for a major role in the picture, a truck driver who gets involved with Samantha Eggar, the title lady in the car, on her strange trip south. Fresson sat in a chair in a corner of the bedroom and I sat up in bed, and we rehearsed. Though Fresson's English was fairly good, he told me how much he hoped I would be at the screen test, scheduled in about ten days. Much was at stake for him.

My blood tests continued to improve until they were normal; I remained in bed another two days beyond the required amount, and then walked timorously around my neighborhood one day after that, warming myself in the July sun. My market street was bursting with summer vegetables and flowers, so I rejoiced in suddenly being immersed again in the bustle and *bonjours* of everyday life. The following morning, I drove to the studio for Fresson's test. I was pale, not as strong as I thought, and sat on an apple box on the stage through most of the test. The few hours of work there absolutely exhausted me. But I got Fresson through the test and the following day, after Litvak saw the dailies, he awarded the actor the role. Fresson immediately called his girlfriend and then me to announce the news.

A little shaky but working again, I met the two stars of the film, Samantha Eggar and Oliver Reed. Eggar had come to sudden stardom in William Wyler's *The Collector*, even receiving an Oscar nomination for her work, and in *Dr. Doolittle* opposite Rex Harrison. She was English, red-haired, strong-willed, and feisty. Her battles with Wyler were well known, and during the course of our film there would be occasional friction with Litvak. Never an outright fight, just a sudden, unpredictable response or an abrasive remark. It started with a rehearsal just outside Paris. Samantha drove the convertible picture car into the shot, in front of a restaurant. Lens finder to his eye, Litvak followed it, then wanted to see the rehearsal again with a different lens and called for the transportation captain to take the car back to its opening position.

"Come on, Tola! Don't you think I can do that?" Samantha called from the car, suddenly throwing it in reverse and racing it backward at forty miles an hour, scattering the team of drivers who were on their way to reset the car, and anyone else in the path. Litvak went white, and headed over to her.

"Don't do that again," he said calmly. "There are people here who are paid to move the car."

"I just wanted to show you I could drive it in reverse!" Samantha replied, all smiles and flashing eyes. It was obvious that the lady in the car was a headstrong one.

Much later, somewhere in Provence, the two of them had a little discussion on the set about character motivation for a particular scene. Litvak wanted Eggar to do it a certain way; Sam wasn't sure. "You can do it," Litvak said. "A good actress can do it," and he started back toward the camera.

"Sarcasm is a very low form of humor, Mr. Litvak!" she shot after him, dead serious. Those were the bristles, the barbs they exchanged. Always the European gentleman, Tola often left the last word to Sam.

Oliver Reed was unpredictable and standoffish, with bizarre outbursts of anger and pleasantness, all of which I would later come to recognize as characteristics of the emotionally unpredictable alcoholic. Some of his lines were delivered with a strange sort of eruption. His cue would be given, then there would be a split-second pause during which time no emotion appeared on his face. Then the pop! The line exploding out of his mouth with whatever emotion he wanted to convey. Many times his response was too big, out of control, his face distorted in sudden grimace like a Notre Dame gargoyle. And frequent bloodshot eyes bespoke excesses of the night before. That he was troubled, perhaps tormented, was obvious to us all. The French crew members had theories on the cause, some of them sexual. Whatever demons lodged within Reed, he appeared to be a man not at peace with himself. I often wondered what the French technicians thought of all these Anglo-Saxon actors who had drinking problems: Broderick Crawford, James Robertson Justice, Rex Harrison, Rachel Roberts, George C. Scott,

Hugh Griffith, Murray Hamilton, Oliver Reed. I never once saw a French actor under the influence of alcohol.

"*C'est du jambon!*" the continuity girl, Alice Ziller, remarked to me, sotto voce, after one particular rehearsal with Reed where he'd played his lines with such insane anger that his jaw muscles continued to tweak after he stopped speaking. Her phrase wasn't French at all. It was a standard joke among bilingual French crew members, *jambon* being French for ham. Although *cabotin* existed for bad actor, it just sounded a lot funnier to say an actor was *jambon* when he was being hammy. Or else, more kindly, they simply said he wasn't speaking "just."

"Was he this theatrical in *Oliver!?*" I asked Tola after the rehearsal where Reed had been knighted *jambon* forever. I was referring to Reed's role as Bill Sikes, where he'd received great reviews from the press. The critics compared him favorably to Robert Newton, who'd done the role in David Lean's 1948 version of *Oliver Twist* with Alec Guinness. But though Reed did well in *Oliver!* taking villainy to new heights, Newton was the better actor.

"It was a musical," Litvak said in answer to my question. "He could play it like an opera." Then he leaned in to me and lowered his voice. "Besides, I heard the editor made him look good." He meant that the editor had cut out all Reed's bad moments. Litvak probably figured he'd have to do the same.

Other performers were added to the mix. There was French actress Stéphane Audran, at that time the wife of film director Claude Chabrol. In America, Audran would later be seen in Luis Bunuel's *The Discreet Charm of the Bourgeoisie* and in the title role of *Babette's Feast*. There was English actor John McEnery, just following his extraordinary interpretation of Mercutio in Zeffirelli's *Romeo and Juliet*, and French character actor Marcel Bozzuffi, who had also appeared in *Z* and who, with a bullet in his back at the top of a New York subway staircase, personified *The French Connection*. Finally, there was Martine Kelly, a French-American actress who had just appeared in the Paris production of *Hair*.

I would soon become friends with Samantha Eggar. It happened almost by accident, as I was telling her about some of the excellent small restaurants in Paris, restaurants that most tourists or movie stars never got to discover.

"I would love to go to one of those!" she exclaimed.

"Well, I would have asked you sooner," I said, "but I assumed you were busy most nights."

"Everyone always thinks that! Just like no one ever asks Frank Sinatra out to dinner. Everyone assumes he's booked."

So that very night I took her to Le Berthoud, a charming, tiny restaurant near the Pantheon where I heard a great deal about Sam's personal life. She lived in Los Angeles, was married to Tom Stern, and had two children, a boy and a girl, both redheads. She was at a point where she felt her marriage could no longer survive. Divorce papers had been filed just before filming started, Stern claiming "extreme cruelty." Suddenly, I was her kindred soul, Sam's confidant, hearing more about her life than I needed or wanted to know. Compared to the cold façade she evinced on the set, Sam now seemed terribly vulnerable. It would take me a long while to discover that it was probably self-concern, not vulnerability, that I saw that night. We lingered over coffee, and soon found ourselves to be the last ones in the restaurant. I called for the check and paid it.

"I haven't closed a place in quite a while," she said as she slipped her arm through mine and we walked back to my Fiat convertible. I drove Sam back to her hotel, kissed her on both cheeks, and told her I would see her down on the levee.

The next day, there was quite a stir on the set. The *International Herald Tribune* spoke of the brutal murder of actress Sharon Tate and others in a house in Benedict Canyon. "My God!" Sam said, looking at the photograph of the dwelling. "I think that's the house I first lived in when I moved to Los Angeles!" Then she put down the newspaper and rehearsed her scene with Litvak, completely in control of herself.

Sam and I would have many more dinners together throughout the film, with long conversations about her marriage. Two years later, I made a brief trip to Los Angeles and stayed at the home of a friend. I called Sam, and she invited me to her house in Brentwood, which I had no difficulty in locating, because, as she had described, hers was the only house on the block with bright red shutters.

"Elliot Gould lives across the street," she told me, and I wondered for a moment if I might see Streisand walking about. We lunched in Sam's dining room on homemade *salade niçoise* and white wine, and it all seemed very pleasant. When I left that day, I had the impression that if I moved to Los Angeles, we would continue to be good friends.

The stills photographer, Paul Apoteker, had the saddest, longest face in the world. We were about one-third through the film when he stated he had almost no photos approved by Samantha for release. It was customary for contact sheets of all pictures taken on the set to be reviewed by the stars and the director. Anything they objected to would be crossed out with a red grease pencil. What was left could then be used by the publicist and the studio for press release. The primary function of the stills photographer, then, was to furnish usable photos. Despite having a reputation as one of the best in his line of work, Apoteker was despondent. Samantha apparently found herself not beautiful enough and drew red crosses through so many of the pictures that the photographer was left with almost nothing to work with. Stéphane Audran did the opposite, approving almost every shot taken of her. I consoled Apoteker, telling him that just because Samantha was hard on herself there was no reason for him to be the same. It did no good. He thought years of his reputation were disappearing on this one film.

It was our last day in the studio before we left Paris and struck out for the road. We were doing a slightly complicated camera shot of Samantha and Oliver. The camera had to dolly back to a fixed position where some of the dialogue played out, then dolly back to a second position for more dialogue, then dolly back yet a third time for a wide shot of the whole scene. Each time, at each of the floor markings where the camera was to pause, the focus puller had to adjust for a certain distance and had those figures on a paper in his hand. Two rehearsals went well and Litvak decided to shoot. On the second take, the scene had just begun when suddenly someone yelled, "*Coupez! Coupez!*"

Litvak turned around, void of color. "What is it?" he cried, displeased. The key grip, Minouche, had cut the take. This, of course, is something that would never happen in Los Angeles. The First Commandment is that the director, and only the director, may call, "Action!" and "Cut!" If that rule were broken in Hollywood, the violator would veritably, as the saying goes, never work in that town again.

Minouche stepped forward and began with, "*Voilà, Monsieur Litvak . . .*" much the same way I'd addressed Jean Gabin a couple of months earlier when everyone on the set froze. Minouche explained that he'd completely missed the second mark and had dollied back to the third position. He knew that the focus puller would not know that the camera was in the wrong position, and would not, therefore, compensate by turning the lens for the correct distance. The shot would be out of focus.

"You did the right thing! Thank you!" Litvak exploded at the top of his voice. Everyone laughed and the camera was reset. But before Litvak called "Action!" again he turned to the key grip and asked, "Minouche?" who nodded that all was ready. And each subsequent take was done the same way, with Litvak checking with the key grip just before setting the actors into motion. When the shot was in the can, Litvak put his arm around Minouche, telling him again that he'd made the right call, this time in gentler tones. The incident was an almost identical repeat of one during the filming of *The Night of the Generals*, where the continuity girl, again Alice Ziller, also had cut a take. She'd noticed that the license number on the front of a staff car dead on to camera was not the same number on the back of the vehicle. When the car drove off, the back was also visible. Litvak had told Ziller he'd planned to shoot the entire scene in one shot, so, seeing the two different license numbers she knew there was nothing else to cut away to later. He thanked her for cutting the take, too. But then both these incidents were pretty typical of the "making-a-film-together" approach used in Europe where the director acknowledges that any crew member knows his field well. Not so in Hollywood, where most companies distrust the knowledge of the very people they hire.

Somewhere near Lyon, I sat in a screening room next to John McEnery, watching the dailies that had been flown to us from the Paris lab. We'd been on the road for a few days. Litvak was sitting in front of me. The scene on the screen was between Sam and McEnery. A few moments into the scene and John suddenly rose and left. I thought he was going to the men's room. Later, when the lights went on, Litvak turned to me and asked, "Where's John?" I told him I didn't know. He'd never returned. "It was good work," Litvak said. "I wanted to tell him."

I rushed outside and started looking for McEnery. By chance, I ran across him alone on one of the streets, just wandering around. He seemed dazed. "John!" I called and caught up to him. "What happened? Why didn't you stay?"

"I couldn't stand it," he replied. "I was awful."

"No, John, you were not. You were quite good. Litvak will probably tell you that tomorrow."

"I just couldn't stand looking at myself."

"Then don't come to dailies. Peter O'Toole never does. He doesn't want to be influenced in his performance by what he sees. Did you go to dailies when you shot *Romeo and Juliet?*"

"I never did. This was the first time."

"It's always a shock to see yourself on the screen. It's always a shock to hear your own voice. If this is how you're going to react, don't come to dailies." Then I told him to have enough confidence in Litvak the next day when he would tell him the work was good. "You're in no position to judge," I said.

John never came to dailies again. That episode showed me how fragile McEnery was, perhaps how fragile all actors are.

Some days later, the crew all settled into a waterfront hotel in Sainte-Maxime, a Riviera town just east of Saint-Tropez. Even in 1969 Saint-Tropez itself had become a crowded and expensive hangout, a far cry from the sleepy fishing village it was when Brigitte Bardot first vacationed there in the late '50s. Oliver Reed and his entourage took a villa in Saint-Tropez. Across from the villa were some metal road signs. Armed with bags of potatoes and aided by drink, he and his companions would hold nightly contests to see who could hit the signs with the potatoes.

I asked John McEnery if he wanted to go to the island of Porquerolles on Sunday. It was known to have a great restaurant and a good beach. He said he'd love to do that. Accordingly, on Sunday, I drove the two of us to the coastal town of Hyères, where we caught a ferryboat to the little island. We weren't able to get into the restaurant I wanted as it was all booked up, but we did find a small, unpretentious spot on the port and ate a thick *pistou* soup and fresh fish. Then after lunch we went to the beach. John made it clear that he really didn't want to be in a crowded area, so we sought out a spot that was fairly isolated. We spread our towels at the edge of the beach in a grove of trees. Heliotropic child that I was, I immediately grabbed the one spot that was open to the sun and undressed to my under shorts, a common occurrence on European beaches. I'd been lying there several minutes impaled to the sand, when I realized that John was sitting on his towel fully clothed. "Why don't you strip down to your shorts?" I asked.

"I'm too thin," he answered.

"John, that's nonsense. Nobody cares."

"I just don't feel comfortable. My legs are too thin."

"Your legs? Your legs are just fine." I sat up and made eye contact with him. "You were running around in Elizabethan tights in *Romeo and Juliet*. Everyone saw your legs."

"I had on three pairs."

"What?"

"I had to wear three pairs of tights, because my legs are so thin."

"And that was your idea?" I asked. "Not Zeffirelli's?" He nodded. "Well, do as you please," I said and lay back down on the towel. "At least take your shirt off and get some of the sun. It's wonderful."

There was a long, long moment of silence, so long that when his response came it seemed disconnected to my last statement. "I'm too white," he muttered.

I bolted up. "John, it doesn't matter!" I gestured to all the brown bodies a few dozen meters away. "They were all white once!" He didn't answer. He just stared off at the shimmering water. "Do whatever you want, but I assure you, no one cares." Then I lay back down again and embraced the sun, thinking how ironic it was that the strongest, most riveting actor of *Romeo and Juliet,* portraying the charismatic, swaggering, self-assured Mercutio, had absolutely no confidence in himself.

About fifteen minutes went by and I heard a rustling sound. I opened my eyes and saw John at last removing his shirt and lying down on his back. He remained half-hidden behind the trees and the trousers covering his thin legs stayed on. Progress is made in baby steps, I told myself.

Fresson, Bozzuffi, and Stéphane Audran had all completed their work by the time we arrived in Sainte-Maxime, and I was dining frequently with Anatole Litvak and Ann Selepegno. Ann had been his personal secretary for so many years that she'd become a permanent fixture in his life. Though she was typically American and spoke pidgin French with a caricatural accent, Litvak was a wonderful *mélange* of several cultures. His generosity was American, his manners French, his anxiety Russian. He was in the middle of eating his favorite hors d'oeuvre of sardines and butter, when she started a subject that the two of them had obviously discussed many times before.

"I still think the picture has problems," Ann remarked, as if continuing some previous conversation.

"The cutting will help," he answered.

"You said that about the actors," she volleyed. "When I said I thought the script was weak, you said the actors would make it better."

"Don't you like the actors?" he challenged.

"I think Oliver's overacting. The others are okay. Anyway, they can't compensate for the problems with the script. And I don't think the editing will either."

Later, back in Paris, when Litvak had a rough cut assembled and Ann still had reservations about the film, he told her, "The music will help." Ann reminded him then that he'd used that logic before. The fact was that in that outdoor restaurant in Sainte-Maxime I was listening to a basic essential about moviemaking, one I've carried with me ever since: the script must be strong to begin with. That was also the dinner at which Litvak told me that he wanted me to start writing a story treatment when we returned to Paris. I was delighted and honored. The story had to do with a brief affair he'd had as an adolescent with an older woman he'd met on a train, so as a genre the picture would obviously be a coming-of-age story. Over the following few months I spent considerable time in Tola's apartment, working with him on the idea. We would sit at his desk or on his elegant black leather sofa, directly under an original Bernard Buffet, and discuss story line. I entered directly into Litvak's personal life at that point, and I felt a strong bond of friendship with this man who was many years my senior and whom I respected. It was also the first time I would actually be paid for writing something. Adding Litvak to Ray and Hepburn, I saw that my list of supporters was growing.

Except for one small scene, we completed shooting *The Lady in the Car* on the Riviera. The one scene left was on a train with Samantha. The next day, a portion of the crew needed for the remaining shot caught the train at Saint-Raphaël going back to Paris. The crew was packed into one coach car, and the grips had removed a seat in one of the compartments to make room for the camera. But the scene could only be shot after the train left Marseille and turned north; then the sun would be in the right position, with light coming through the window on Sam. The train pulled into the Marseille station for a ten minute stop. A few crew members got off to stretch their legs or buy drinks from the refreshment carts on the platform. Litvak and I descended and walked along the platform, discussing the scene we were about to shoot. He thought the dialogue needed tweaking, and as I had the script under my arm, we began to refer to it. A moment later we sat down on a baggage cart on the platform, and I made a few suggestions to him about the dialogue.

We'd been sitting there, totally engrossed in the scene and oblivious to everything else, when suddenly we heard great shouts coming from the train. We looked up to see it moving. The crew members were all yelling at us from the open windows and from the train's gangway platforms. Tola and I immediately began to run for the train, arriving in panic at the end of the car where the outstretched arms of the grips pulled him up with them onto the gangway. A split-second later, with the train going slightly faster, they yanked me aboard. We all stood there a moment, breathless and frightened, as the train began to gather speed. Then Tola and I burst out laughing simultaneously, and he grabbed me and hugged me for dear life, and I hugged him back. The crew were all making comments like, *"Mais vous êtes fous, tous les deux!"* ("You're crazy, both of you!") in total disregard for deference to the director. Still we laughed until there were tears in our eyes; tears, I'm sure, of relief.

The film over, I continued to work closely with Litvak for several more weeks. In the dubbing studio, of course, but also, for the first time, in the editing room. It is one of the best places to learn how a film is made as you see, shot by shot, how a story can be laid out, how a moment can be emphasized by favoring one actor instead of another.

Though Litvak had taken many precautions with Oliver Reed, making sure that every scene had coverage of another actor to whom he could cut if Reed's performance weren't good, one scene somehow slipped by him. It was a two-shot with Reed and Stéphane Audran, and Reed's facial expressions were way over the top. Unfortunately, Litvak only made that one shot for the scene, so he didn't have anything to cut away to, which would have allowed him to play Reed's lines off camera. "I should have done a close-up of Stéphane," he said several times. He ran the scene over and over, studying it, looking for a way to save it. But the truth remained that he had only one shot to work from. Finally he said, "There's just one thing I can do."

"Cut the scene?" I asked.

"I can't. There's a plot point made here. Come back Thursday and you'll see. And you'll learn how to make movies."

Two days later, he showed me the scene on the monitor. When Reed was about to say the line with his exaggerated expressions, there was suddenly a close-up of Stéphane Audran and his voice played over her. "Where did that come from?" I asked.

"Look closely," he said. I did, and then I saw it. He'd made a print of the two-shot of both actors and blown it up enormously. Then he framed only Audran, creating the close-up of her he was missing, and cut it into the two-shot.

"It's a little grainy," he said, "but I'd rather have that than Oliver's expression. My God, he was bad! I should have seen that when I shot it!"

I stayed in contact with the French actors long after the movie ended. Through Bozzuffi, I met one of Europe's leading clairvoyants, a Middle-Eastern woman by the name of Belly Sirakian, in whom both Bozzuffi and his lover, actress Françoise Fabian, absolutely swore. Belly (pronounced Bell-*lee*) was one of only four clairvoyants on the entire continent eulogized in a book on the subject. After dinner, she would tell my fortune over Turkish coffee silt in my cup. We soon became good friends and often dined together in her third-floor apartment near Notre-Dame-de-Lorette. She came up with some predictions that turned out to be frighteningly true. I still don't understand how clairvoyants manage this, or even if one *should* believe that clairvoyants manage this, but most of what she said came to pass. Just before I moved away from Paris to the United States in 1972, I had dinner with her. As I left, she stood on her landing, waving and watching me go down the winding staircase. "I'll see you again!" I called up to her optimistically.

"I know," she replied with a Cheshire smile. Eight months later, I was back in Paris to help dub Jean-Louis Trintignant for a film we'd worked on in Los Angeles, and had dinner with Belly again. I reminded her of my farewell to her at our previous meeting. She remembered and smiled, but said nothing.

That night when I left and she again stood on her landing watching me spiral down to the ground floor, I called back, "*À bientôt!*" ("See you soon!") This time she said nothing. She simply smiled and waved good-bye. I never saw her again.

When I'd officially moved to Los Angeles, I called Samantha Eggar. It was less than a year since I'd lunched at her house. Her divorce from Tom Stern had been granted (so had Gould's and Streisand's) and she was going to attend a play later in the week, with one of Hollywood's A people whom she was seeing. In the early '70s there was much talk about the A List people and their A List parties, the B List people and their parties, and so on through an alphabet of diminishing returns. Joanna Pettet and her date would be accompanying the couple, and Samantha was sure an extra ticket could be arranged for me to join the foursome. I told her I'd worked with Joanna on *The Night of the Generals*, and that I would be delighted to go with them. When I called Samantha the next day to confirm, she told me she was sorry but they hadn't succeeded in getting an extra ticket after all. "But I'll call you in a week or so, and we'll get together." Three weeks went by without hearing from her, so I called again. Her "hello" told me she'd picked up the phone.

"Sam?" I said.

"No," came the reply. "This is the maid. Miss Eggar is not home right now." I swore it was her voice.

"Do you know when she'll be back?"

"No. She didn't say."

"Would you let her know Frawley Becker telephoned?"

"I shall tell her. Goodbye."

I looked at the phone as if it were a lightning rod. *I shall tell her?* Who else but an English person would use the correct first person future tense? Any American would have said, "I'll tell her" or "I'll be sure to tell her." Americans never use the correct "shall" with "I" or "we." And what maid in Los Angeles would have an English accent and not an Hispanic one? And what maid wouldn't ask me to spell the name Frawley, which every office secretary in Hollywood stumbled over? But more to the point, every intonation of the voice had been Sam's! The inflections were exactly like those on any line from the movie. If there's one person in Hollywood with whom you must never try to pretend your voice isn't yours, it's your dialogue coach. Of course, the mistress of the house, the known Samantha Eggar, never called back, thereby confirming my thoughts.

Trying to analyze this charming episode would be like trying to analyze Hollywood itself. If it is true that you are only as important as your
last picture, then it follows that your friendship is only as strong as the
last time you were needed. I'd carried Sam through tumultuous times,
shared many a dinner with her, offered my shoulder for her heart, but
all that was yesterday. Had she even tried to get me a ticket to the theater? Could an actress in vogue and a Hollywood mover and shaker, A
List people by their own designation, entertain an unknown dialogue
coach? Columnist Joyce Haber in the *Los Angeles Times* once referred
to Sam as "the second bitchiest actress" in the film business. To this
Sam replied, "I don't have time for little fly-by-night performers, or
anybody, for that matter."

Most friendship is feigning, says Amiens sadly in *As You Like It*, for
nothing stings so sharply "as friend remember'd not."

And lilies that fester smell far worse than weeds.

~

CHAPTER TWELVE

Pure Imagination

In his *New York Times* article of October 22, 2000, "Dark Chocolate: '70s Movie Is an Unlikely Cult Hit," Allen Salkin mentions that *Willy Wonka and the Chocolate Factory* had just completed a six-month run at TriBeCa's screening room in New York. Jeff Kurtti devotes an entire chapter to the film in his book, *The Great Movie Musical Trivia Book*, where only ten musicals receive attention, two of them animated. How did *Willy Wonka* take its place with *Singin' in the Rain* (often considered the best movie musical ever made), *The Wizard of Oz*, and *My Fair Lady*? Why have there been several well-publicized, abundantly photographed reunions of the picture's children, now in their forties? Why has this flawed movie of 1971 endured? One theory is that those who saw it as children think it was better than it actually is. Those children, grown up, have passed it on to the next generation, and that one to the next, and so on. My explanation is that the continued excitement over this film is due to its dark side (actually even darker in Roald Dahl's book, *Charlie and the Chocolate Factory*, on which the movie is based). The dark side seems to appeal to modern tastes. Just as Sondheim's bittersweet, ironic lyrics replaced the bright golden haze of Rogers and Hammerstein's meadow, so the skeptical post-Vietnam and post-Nixon generations find that a musical that does away with bad kids one by one is pretty cool.

Since hindsight is the best available vision, none of us who worked on *Willy Wonka* ever thought we were working on a cult classic, any more than those who worked on *It's a Wonderful Life*, *Casablanca*, or *Miracle on 34th Street* had any inkling their pictures would go down in the annals of filmdom.

Once again, I received a phone call from Stan Margulies of Wolper Pictures, who told me about their intention to film Dahl's *Charlie and the Chocolate Factory*. The director would again be the screamer, Mel Stuart, and we'd be shooting in Munich, Germany. The film was to star Gene Wilder, who had attracted so much attention in a small role in *Bonnie and Clyde* and two years later would receive an Oscar nomination for his hilarious supporting work in *The Producers*, another film destined for art-house revivals. Wilder's costar in *Willy Wonka* would be Jack Albertson, later one of the rare recipients of all three top acting honors: the Oscar, the Tony, and the Emmy.

The air was clear and cool when I left Paris with Calvados in his basket on the seat next to me. After a night in the Alsatian city of Strasbourg, I pulled into the courtyard of the Schloss Hotel in Grün-wald, a suburb of Munich, the following day. *Schloss* is the German word for castle, and the walls of some ancient one still stood next to my nineteenth-century hotel, where Wolper Pictures had made a reservation for me.

As I descended from the car, I saw a magnificent child, perhaps the epitome of all children everywhere. A boy of twelve with abundant light blond hair was walking around the grounds. He stopped to stare at this strange auburn-haired man who had just made the most marvelous entrance of his life for a child, pulling up in a convertible green car, removing a wicker basket with a cat inside, and walking in his ultrahip maxicoat toward the hotel. We exchanged a momentary and mutually wordless stare, but in that second we both saw something in the other that would seize us for a lifetime. We were man and child, tutor and pupil, older brother and younger brother, mountebank and spectator, friend and friend. The look lasted but a second, but both of us would state later we felt something that marked each of us as being unique to the other. The boy was Peter Ostrum, who had been cast to play Charlie Bucket, and we were destined to become close friends for decades to come.

Stan Margulies would later tell me how Wolper Pictures had done a nationwide search for the boy who would play the leading role. In the hands of legendary casting director Marion Dougherty, child actors on both coasts were seen. Because almost all of them had TV backgrounds, they naturally singsonged their way through auditions, which is what badly trained child actors do. Then, out of the legitimate theater, the Cleveland Playhouse, came young Peter Ostrum, who had performed the role of young Rufus in *All the Way Home*, a beautiful and sensitive play based on James Agee's *A Death in the Family*.

"His audition knocked everyone else out of the running," Margulies told me when I caught up to him the day after my arrival. And still later, in the midst of filming, he commented on the dailies he'd just seen. "There are times when Peter has a very mature expression on his face, where he not only looks older, but plays older. Then it's gone and he's a child again." Margulies said that they never would have gotten that from anyone else.

The Schloss Hotel was a marvel. It was small, family-owned, and operated by the matriarch of the family, Frau Edel. The floors were uneven and there were antiques everywhere. A wonderful eighteenth-century, hand-painted Bavarian armoire sat in my bedroom, adjacent to a small sitting room with a Victorian sofa just inside the door. There was a large ground-floor terrace with parasols that overlooked a valley and a bridge, which was ideal for Sunday lunches. The night of my arrival, I ate in the dining room and I saw the same young blond boy at a table with three adults. At that point, I thought that the boy might be the lead of the film. Once more, our looks connected in curiosity.

The next day, I drove to the movie studio at Bavaria Filmplatz. Pia Arnold, the production manager, took me on a tour of the sets, whimsically designed by Harper Goff. I thought they were wonderful, a child's fantasy, everyone's fantasy. I caught up with Stan Margulies and together we went onto one of the stages where Mel Stuart was rehearsing. He was actually allowing the choreographer, Howard Jeffrey, to put Peter Ostrum and Jack Albertson through their steps for "I've Got a Golden Ticket." When they took a break, I said hello to Mel and congenially he told me how glad he was to have me on the picture. Though I would soon discover that his screaming hadn't abated in two years, he was, nevertheless, warm and apparently sincere. He introduced me to Alberston and to the blond boy I'd seen twice the day before.

"Hello, Peter," I said, extending my hand.

He was all smiles. "Hi. You're on the movie?"

"Yes. I'm the dialogue coach."

"That's great!" (I was glad he hadn't used "groovy," very much in vogue then) "Did you bring your cat?"

"Yes, I did."

"I thought so!" His eyes were dancing with excitement. Clearly I was still making points.

"His name's Calvados. You'll have to meet him."

"We brought our cat, too." That was Albertson chiming in. "Is Calvados male or female?"

"Male."

"Ours is female. We'll have to introduce them. Maybe they can make beautiful music together. Why'd you bring your cat?"

"He goes everywhere with me. Why'd you bring yours?"

"My wife's idea. It's a long story. And a dirty one." It was a vaudeville line and he delivered it, like so many others over the next few months, with impeccable burlesque timing. He'd come from Broadway by way of vaudeville and the Borscht Circuit and had worked with Milton Berle, Bert Lahr, Phil Silvers—only the greatest masters of comic timing. And the soft-shoe routine he was doing in the song with young Peter, who for all his great looks couldn't hoof worth a dime, was right off the Palace stage. Of all the Americans on the film, only Albertson and his family were interested in learning German. He hired a young German student to give them all lessons, and the young man was often seen dining with the Albertson family. Like Jacqueline Bisset, Jack Albertson treated everyone with exactly the same civility and warm interest, reaching out to the crew to find out who they were.

That night, I introduced myself to the Ostrum family at the hotel. Peter's father, Dean, was an executive in telephone communications and left Munich before we began filming to return to the States. His mother, Sari, remained there throughout the film, and as my friendship with young Peter grew, so did my relationship with the family, although there were a few of Peter's brothers and sisters that I wouldn't get to meet until his marriage in 1987. The third adult I'd seen at their table the night before was a young *au pair* Norwegian girl who would soon return home.

Over the next few days, I met the other actors. Julie Dawn Cole and Roy Kinnear, playing the spoiled Veruca Salt and her dad, were English. Michael Bollner and Ursula Reitt, playing the overweight Augustus Gloop and his heavy-set mom, were German. All the other actors were American. Gene Wilder would arrive later. Though everyone was easy to get along with, it was Peter Ostrum and the Albertson family I saw the most off the set.

As promised, Albertson brought the family cat to the Schloss Hotel one night to meet my cat. His wife, Wallace, and daughter, Maura Dhu, Peter and Sari Ostrum all sat around and watched when I led Calvados down the stairs into the hotel lounge. His entrance was almost as good as mine had been with Peter, for Calvados strutted on a leash and collar like a dog, and immediately headed for this exotic Siamese creature that his Frenchman's eye spotted immediately. Nose-to-nose contact was made and Calvados started chattering away voluminously in a voice I'd never heard before. It was obvious they were instantly head over paws in love.

"I think Minou is drawn to Calvados' cosmopolitan side," Wally Albertson suggested.

"You know that *minou* means kitty in French?"

"Yes, of course," she replied.

"But it's the masculine form of the word. *Minette* would have been more appropriate."

"Maybe it would have," Jack retorted, "But I'd hate to confuse the cat now. She's confused enough, trying to learn German."

After a few minutes, Peter and Maura Dhu took the two cats up to my room and left them together. Then we all sat down for a hearty dinner. It was the fall of the year so there was game, goose, and the usual pork and veal dishes on the menu, all of it accompanied by red cabbage, sauerkraut, and tiny dumplings called *spaetzle*. An hour later, the Albertsons took Minou home and Calvados spent most of the night trying to sniff her down in my hotel suite. Though there would be several trysts between the two cats over the following months, either they coupled but their act produced no issue, or they enjoyed a purely platonic love. Whatever it was, there was never a hiss between them.

I was standing next to Jack Albertson on the set a few days later when Stan Margulies approached us. "Jack, I've just seen yesterday's dailies!" he exclaimed. "You were wonderful! The whole scene is great! In fact, all the dailies have been great!"

"Good, good!" Albertson replied. "I was afraid I'd have to go back to hoofing for a living." And he broke out into a few buck-and-wing steps, ending with a ta-dah gesture with his arms outspread.

"I don't think you have to worry," said Margulies. "The dailies are great! Just great!" And he walked away.

Albertson turned to me. "Don't believe it. They always tell you, 'The dailies are great! The dailies are great!' Then the movie comes out and it's a piece of shit."

Willy Wonka and the Chocolate Factory is basically divided into two parts. The first part deals with Charlie's humble background, the hard work he and his mother have to do to support four grandparents, all of whom sleep in the same four-poster bed, and Charlie's eventually winning the last golden ticket. It is fantasy on top of reality. The second half deals with the holders of the winning tickets touring the chocolate factory and meeting Willy Wonka, the eccentric owner. Then the audience is caught up in a pure fantasy world of chocolate rivers and edible teacups, gobstoppers and fizzy-lifting rooms. Stan Margulies would say to me that they had a hard time keeping Charlie and Grandpa Joe alive in the second half.

We shot much of the first half before Gene Wilder arrived. His first scene would be his exit from the factory, as he limped to greet the children. He would move slowly toward them, leaning on his cane and dragging a foot, then suddenly fall into a somersault and spring up limberly in front of their eyes. The children, relieved, would then laugh, although I'm not sure how handicapped persons would respond to that gag today. I was told later that the entire piece of business was Wilder's idea, that he wanted to show that Wonka couldn't be trusted.

I usually rehearsed with Wilder in his dressing room, and then brushed up his memory on the set. I had to monitor his singing of "Pure Imagination" very closely, since, as with almost all musicals, the actor had to mime the song, while his own voice, previously recorded, would sound over the playback while we filmed. Having worked a great deal in the Paris sound studios, where actors had to re-record their lines, I was familiar with the process of making soundtracks and lip movements fit. It was essential to match labial sounds b, m, and p, when the lips closed, and labiodentals f and v when they were half-closed. I explained this to Mel Stuart, and shortly after we started shooting Wilder's song, Mel gave me permission to cut a take if it were not good. As it turned out, Wilder's lip synchronization was better than most actors' so there were only a couple of takes where I actually had to call, "Cut!" But call it I did, adding myself to the continuity girl and the key grip as European technicians who had cut takes.

"Where are the damned oompa-loompas?" Mel screamed one day with his usual ear-shattering decibel power. The Oompa-Loompas, of course, as everyone who ever saw *Willy Wonka and the Chocolate Factory* knows, were "the little people." One of the dwarfs had told me that that was the term they all preferred, both dwarfs and midgets: "the little people." I also learned that midgets were proportioned exactly as normal people were, only all their body parts, including their heads, were smaller. Dwarfs, on the other hand, generally had fully developed, even largish heads and fairly well-developed torsos, but foreshortened limbs. Because the torsos of dwarfs are close to normal size, a female dwarf can produce children, usually by a caesarean; a female midget with a small torso is sexually immature, and cannot. Dwarfs were often seen in the Renaissance Spanish courts. Michael Dunn, nominated as best supporting actor in 1965 for his work in *Ship of Fools*, was a dwarf. The Munchkins in *The Wizard of Oz* were mostly midgets. In *Willy Wonka and the Chocolate Factory*, one Oompa-Loompa was a female midget disguised as a man; all the others were male dwarfs. For some reason, dwarfs seem to have more fun in life than midgets.

Mel was screaming because not all the Oompa-Loompas were ready, and he was getting dangerously close to shooting with them. Like the other actors, the little people all had to lip-synch their songs, so I'd been rehearsing them and getting along very well with them. "My lips are absolutely in synch with the playback!" Rusty Goffe, the youngest of the little people, would exclaim proudly in his London accent. Most of our Oompa-Loopas were English, but one, Rudi, was German and a little wild. They occasionally held drinking parties to which big people were not invited, and Rudi was reputed to be a heavy drinker and a heavy sexual performer, or so the others said. Malcolm, the oldest and most settled of the lot, had no use for him.

"Where the hell is Rudi?" Mel was screaming. "That damned pervert!"

"Why pervert?" I asked him.

"All dwarfs are perverts! They're all queer! They've always got their faces in your crotch!" I almost burst out laughing, but Mel Stuart was actually serious. "I can't stand dwarfs!" he continued. "I wouldn't use them if I didn't have to! Go tell Pia Rudi's missing!"

"She already knows," I said, "But I'll see if they've located him."

A few moments later, Wolfgang Glattes, the German 1st assistant director, told me the production office had located Rudi in some lady's apartment in Schwabing, the artistic quarter of Munich. He had just been transported to the studio and had been placed in the hands of the makeup department. "He was with a woman," Wolfgang said with a grin. "A big woman. I gather she was very satisfied with him," he added, instantly clarifying any further questions about the torsos of male dwarfs. It also told me why dwarfs had more fun than midgets.

One Sunday morning, Peter and Sari Ostrum and I went to visit the nearby town of Dachau. Despite my very decent German, the local townspeople there didn't seem to understand me when I asked for directions to the former Nazi concentration camp. It was denial, of course, the same denial by those same townspeople who never smelled burning flesh twenty-six years earlier. Eventually, the three of us found our way to the former camp and soberly and silently stared at the brick ovens with their semicircular black metal doors, which had consumed so many bodies. I told Peter there had been many such death camps, that six million Jews and many others had perished in these camps during World War II. The boy's brow was knit with pain and concern, and once again he was not a child but an adult trying to assimilate such a dark chapter of human nature. Outside, he walked with his head down, his eyes on the pebble-strewn path that took us back to the car. He stooped and picked up two beautiful ivory- and rose-colored stones. "Amazing," he contemplated. "Look how beautiful these are. In this place." Then he put the two pebbles in his pocket and we returned to the car.

And there were many times when Peter and I spent time alone, cementing a solid friendship. When Oktoberfest arrived, we went out to the carnival attractions on a Sunday evening, the last night of the festival. We barreled through the funhouse, rode a Ferris wheel that was probably the tallest I'd seen in my life, and ended up in an enormous cavern of a beer hall, miles long it seemed, with long wooden tables and benches and an oom-pa-pa band in one corner. Was that really World War II's "Beer Barrel Polka" they were playing? Or had "Beer Barrel Polka" been based on a German tavern song? The place was packed with men and boys in traditional lederhosen and women in lacy blouses. Everyone wore Bavarian felt hats with feathers sticking up.

A waitress appeared in colorful folk dress. "*Guten Abend. Was trinken Sie?*" she asked.

"*Ein Bier, bitte!*" Peter promptly answered with a decent German accent.

"*Für mich auch,*" I added.

The waitress disappeared to get us our beers. Peter had now turned thirteen and had been given permission by both his parents to drink wine or beer with meals if he wanted. He never abused the privilege, knowing exactly how much he could handle.

It wasn't two beers that came; it was two bathtubs. Each enormous glass stein contained a liter of beer. "Do not even attempt to drink more than a normal glassful!" I told him. We looked around to see the local citizens ballooning up over their colossal steins of beer.

"I'll bet there's a long line at the men's room!" Peter remarked. We laughed ourselves silly.

The next evening, Peter burst into my room. "Sit down," he said, "I want to talk to you." We sat down on the Victorian sofa. "If anything happened to my parents, would you adopt me?"

"Peter, nothing's going to happen to your parents."

"But if it did, would you adopt me? I need to know."

I didn't flinch. "Yes, of course I would."

His face relaxed. "That's what I thought. I just wanted to be sure." Then, almost as suddenly, he opened the door, ready to leave, as if he didn't want to handle any questions on the matter. "Are we eating downstairs or out?"

"Let's go out. I know a place that serves ice cream with a flaming cherry sauce for desert."

"What makes it flame?"

"Kirsch. You can get a little drunk on it."

"Perfect! That'll make up for the beer I didn't drink!" He laughed and closed the door.

I walked around the room, assimilating what had just happened. The boy had *selected* the person he wanted to be his parent. I was honored and immensely moved. It was obvious that through our many conversations, our working together, our numerous dinners, our "bachelor nights" on the town, he had been scoping me out. I guessed that the Oktoberfest celebration had clinched it. Strangely, I thought of my own father, thought that I hadn't selected him, and wondered for a moment if there had ever been anyone in my life I might have chosen for a parent instead, as Peter just had. There wasn't.

I told this story a few years ago to Peter's wife, Loretta, when I went to New York for the christening of their son, Leif. Just weeks earlier, Peter had called to tell me he wanted me to be the child's godfather. "One way or another," Loretta laughed, "Peter was determined to make you part of his family."

On the set, we were about to lose another bad kid, rich and nasty Veruca Salt. Julie Dawn Cole threw herself into her big number, "I Want It Now," with wicked glee, running all over the stage, and finishing by going down an egg shoot where all the bad eggs were. Two months earlier, she had interviewed with musical director Walter Scharf at the Park Lane Hotel in London, where she sang for him. Scharf had been doing dramatic and musical scoring since the early '40s and had been nominated many times for Academy Awards. He might well have received one for 1968's *Funny Girl* had it not been for *Oliver!* The veteran music maker was impressed with Cole's voice, and almost immediately after that she prerecorded her song in London. Then, two months later, she lip-synched her own voice before the cameras in Munich, each labial sound matching perfectly.

"I have nothing to say," I told Stan Margulies on the stage, after a take with young Cole. "Her synch is perfect."

"And what a voice!" Margulies chimed. "She's like a young Judy Garland."

"She's a belter, that's why. There aren't many belters around." We both agreed that she probably had a singing career ahead of her, and, in fact, Julie Dawn Cole would be the only one of the five children who would become a professional performer. As an adult, she would act in soap operas and costume dramas and do stage singing as well. She is settled in Surrey, England, now, a mother of two, but her amazing voice in *Willy Wonka* still resonates in your ear long after the picture ends.

Gene Wilder had a big scene coming up and asked if I could come to his hotel and rehearse with him, and then have dinner. I went to the Vier Jahreszeiten in downtown Munich, where he was staying, and we began to work on the scene. It was a scene near the end of the picture where Wonka informs Grandpa Joe (Alberston) and Charlie (Peter) that they haven't really won anything, because they broke rules during the tour of the factory. The moment is a test that Charlie, the only honest child of the group, passes with flying colors. At that point, Wonka tells him he's just inherited the factory. The scene was admittedly not easy because Wilder had to go from berating Charlie to embracing him. Wilder felt very insecure about the scene. How should he play it? Was he being a father figure? After all, he did refer to him as "my boy." We spent over an hour rehearsing, with Gene rendering a dozen different readings. The longer we worked on the scene, the more he seemed not to know what he wanted. Over and over I'd hear him say, "Maybe that's not what I should do." Or, "I don't think that's right."

Finally, I felt the only way I could guide him was to take little clues from the direction in which he himself was leaning: the father–son relationship. I suggested he play the father role internally, and become a warm friend by the end of the scene. Wilder worked with that and soon was pulling the scene together. But I saw that he was starting to get a little too strong in the part where he reprimanded Charlie, which then made the shift too great.

"Thank you for telling me," he said. "I'll keep it under control."

The next day, I informed Mel Stuart about the work with Wilder. Mel never seemed to mind whenever I entered the domain of character interpretation with an actor. It hearkened back to our first conversation two years earlier in London, when he'd asked me how you talk to actors. He agreed to the interpretation completely, but I warned him that Wilder might go too far with it, make it too strong and too obvious. And later that was exactly what happened. Between camera rehearsals and the shooting, I approached Mel again to tell him I thought the performance was getting too hard-edged, too big.

"I don't agree," he said. "I think it's fine. It's an emotional moment."

There was nothing I could do. Unlike the incident with Jean Gabin where I was the only one on the set who could evaluate the performance in English, this time I was not justified in pursuing the point.

Filming that scene, Wilder went through the roof as assuredly as Wonka's elevator would later go through the roof of the factory. He was so nasty to Charlie in the first part of the scene that he appeared to be insane when, like a screaming harpie, he yelled, "You lose!" Then the turnaround went too far in the opposite direction a few seconds later. His overly unctuous "My boy!" became false, almost frightening. To this day, I shudder whenever I see the end of the picture. I don't believe Wilder for a second. If his idea at the beginning of the picture was to present Wonka as an infirm man with a cane in order to make him untrustworthy to the children and to the audience, he alas succeeded in doing that in the final moments of the picture as well.

Where Wilder did his best work was everywhere in between his first and last scenes. He handled the poetry of the movie deftly, combining philosophy, which appealed to adults, and whimsy, which appealed to children, on such gentle lines as O'Shaughnessy's "We are the music-makers, we are the dreamers of dreams." Tersely, that line is the summation of the entire picture, and Wilder's delivery there is perfect.

As we neared the end of filming, David L. Wolper offered Peter Ostrum a three-picture contract. His parents considered the matter, but when the impatient producer pressed them many times for an answer, they backed off, saying it was Peter's decision alone.

"What do you think I should do?" he asked me in my hotel room, the surrogate son seeking advice from the surrogate father. It was a moment I couldn't afford to screw up.

"Well, you'd have to go to Hollywood, at least some of the time. Maybe live there."

"Yeah, I know."

"And your background is theater," I replied. "Did you enjoy working on the movie?"

"Not entirely. I liked meeting Jack and Gene. And you, of course. And I liked working with the other kids. But I didn't like Mel screaming at us all the time. I hated that."

"Peter, if you go to Hollywood, somewhere out of a crew of fifty people, there are always going to be a few you don't like to work with. Some of those people will be directors and producers or other actors. There'll always be somebody."

He sat still for a moment, thinking, and then replied quite calmly, "I don't think that's what I want to do with my life."

Today, Roald Dahl's "Charlie" is Dr. Peter Ostrum, a big animal veterinarian in upstate New York, trouncing heavy snows into chilly barns to deliver foals and calves.

It was late fall, but early winter for northern Europe, when the picture ended. As the sets were being taken down, Bob Fosse's designer arrived to begin construction at the Bavaria Film Studio on *Cabaret*. Dean Ostrum returned from the States with one of Peter's brothers, sixteen-year-old Danny, and with Sari and Peter, went on a family skiing trip to the southern German Alps. Jack Albertson, his wife, and his daughter would travel a bit in Germany in the new BMW he had bought before returning to the States. There was a farewell scene at the Schloss Hotel between Minou and Calvados with both cats touching noses once more, and Calvados talking in that special voice of his. When they were parted, I swear there was a wistful look in both cats' eyes. The Albertsons drove off in their new car, as Calvados watched the only love of his life leave forever. I fully expected to hear Dooley Wilson at the piano, singing "As Time Goes By," but then I've been told my sense of reality has been deformed by my profession.

Throughout the filming, both Margulies and Stuart had kept referring to *Willy Wonka and the Chocolate Factory* as "another *Wizard of Oz*." This, of course, it never was, and I imagine both men were a little disappointed when the film was released to tepid reviews. Pauline Kael called it "stilted and frenetic." In time, both men have certainly been rewarded by the film's latter-day popularity. For me the film is a musical manqué. A few more numbers and I'd have a category for it. I miss a song from young Charlie early on to tell us what he'd like to have in life, the equivalent of Oliver's poignant "Where Is Love?" or Dorothy's "Over the Rainbow" or Louise's "Little Lamb" in *Gypsy*. A waif's plaint is always irresistible. I miss a second rousting comedy number from Jack Albertson, whose dancing and singing would have lit up the second half of the film, where there is only Julie Dawn Cole's song,

"I Want It Now" and variations of the oompa-loompas' song. The perfect time would have been when Grandpa Joe and Charlie go airborne in the Fizzy-Lifting Room. Why didn't Albertson sing something like, "I'm Dancing on Bubbles!" which would have predated "I'm Walking on Sunshine" by almost twenty years. Finally, I miss a production number. Wouldn't it have been wonderful to see all the townspeople closing up their shops and singing and dancing their way to the gates of the chocolate factory, instead of our just "finding" the citizens there, crammed in behind the children who have won the golden tickets? A high crane shot would have been needed for that, à la "Consider Yourself" from *Oliver!* with shopkeepers galore filling the streets. And if it's the dark quality of the film you like, maybe Wonka might have sung something like "One Kid Less." One could go on, ad infinitum. In truth, it wasn't simply Stuart and Margulies who carved the shape of the movie; nor was it just the budget. I have to put some of the responsibility on the creators of the music and lyrics, too. Anthony Newley and Leslie Bricusse did a most pleasant score but, like their *Stop the World, I Want to Get Off* and *The Roar of the Greasepaint, the Smell of the Crowd* before it, the scope is intimate, designed for a small theater, not a big screen. Had it not been for Sammy Davis Jr.'s version of "The Candy Man" (which some say was a euphemism for a dope dealer, anyway), the entire score might have remained unnoticed. As a musical, *Willy Wonka* simply lacks sweep. For those who swear by it, and they are legion, I say, "Welcome to the cult!" But is it a great musical? Pure imagination.

A week after I left Munich, the Ostrum family, off the snowy slopes of Garmisch, arrived in Paris for a few days, and I took them sightseeing. We visited the monuments and museums and frequented my favorite restaurants, none of which was on a tourist list. One night after dinner, we dropped Sari back at the hotel where the family was staying and then headed for one of the strip shows at Place Pigalle. The barker-doorman of the club we chose hesitated for a second on seeing Peter, but once assured that his father was with him (in fact, two fathers!) we were waved inside. We sat at a ringside table and drank the worst champagne in France and watched rosy ladies strip down and cavort around the stage. It was a show the Ostrum family couldn't get in Shaker Heights. Danny was ecstatic, Dean nonchalant, and on the way out I asked Peter if he'd enjoyed the show. His reply was, "I'm glad I saw it. But I think it's sad they have to take their clothes off to earn a living."

In the mid-'70s, I ran across Gene Wilder in the parking lot at 20th Century Fox. "Gene!" I called as I rushed toward him.

He put his hand to his head and cried out dramatically, "The name! The name!"

"What?" I asked. I didn't know what he meant.

"Don't tell me! The name! What is the name?"

"Frawley Becker," I answered. I would subsequently learn that unless you are a class A person, you must always announce your name when you see someone you know (or think you know).

"Yes! Yes! Yes!" Wilder exalted in that triple yes of Rex Harrison's. We chatted for a moment, and I told him I'd stayed in contact with both the Albertson family and Peter since we'd worked on the movie. "I should call Jack," Wilder said at one point, which was about as definite as, "We must do lunch someday."

Not long after that, in 1977, Peter came to visit me in Los Angeles during spring break. He was nineteen and had already done a year and a half in college. His acting career was behind him. He'd had one final audition in New York almost two years earlier. It was for the Broadway production of *Equus*, and he narrowly missed getting the principal role of Alan Strang opposite Richard Burton. He felt the producers were looking for someone more frail looking. "Where'd you get those shoulders?" they'd asked him.

"Shoveling snow, I guess," was his Midwest answer.

I placed a call to the studio and asked for Gene Wilder, since Peter wanted to say hello. I left a message with a secretary. The call was not returned. Nor was a second. The third time around, I asked for his assistant and soon was speaking to a young lady who was obviously part of the army of persons hired to form an impenetrable wall around an actor. "Oh, Mr. Wilder is very busy right now. He's shooting a new movie." (I think it was *Silver Streak* with Richard Pryor.)

"I'm calling for Peter Ostrum. He's in town and they worked together on *Willy Wonka and the Chocolate Factory*. He wanted to say hello."

"I don't know Peter Ostrum."

"He was the star of the film."

"I thought Gene Wilder was."

"Gene and Jack Albertson both were. And so was Peter Ostrum, who played the little boy. There were three leads. Look, just give Mr. Wilder Peter's name and the phone number, would you?"

"I'll see what I can do."

I said goodbye and hung up. Then I had to explain to Peter how the whole striated class system in Hollywood worked and how it was possible that Gene might not return the call. Peter uttered a little laugh of incredulity, shrugged, and said nothing.

The following evening the telephone rang. "Is Peter Ostrum there?" a very familiar and very depressed voice asked. I knew it was Wilder. I wondered if he'd worked on that delivery as neurotically as he had the final scene of the picture.

"Just a second," I said, not identifying myself. I called Peter to the phone. Though I could only hear Peter's portion of the short conversation that ensued, it was obvious that Wilder was not going to meet with him.

Peter hung up and said, "It's pretty much what you thought. He's too busy with the movie to see me. Do you know what he said when I picked up the phone?"

"Tell me."

"When I said, 'Hello,' he answered in a very low voice, 'I don't know if you remember me, but my name is Gene Wilder.'"

"Was his voice full of suffering?"

"Yes!" yelled Peter, and we started laughing hysterically.

Peter's telephone call to the Albertson family had the opposite results. Both Jack and Wally were delighted to hear from him. We were invited to attend one of the live segments of *Chico and the Man*, a sitcom that Albertson was doing at the time. We went and thoroughly enjoyed the show. Afterward, Albertson introduced Peter to the director and producers, always identifying the boy as the star of *Willy Wonka and the Chocolate Factory*. The film hadn't achieved its cult status then, so no one appeared terribly impressed. Then Jack, Wally, Peter, and I all went out to dinner. On the way home, Peter commented to me that like Gene Wilder, Jack Albertson had also been busy working, but that he'd made time to see him. I never really knew how hurt Peter was by Wilder's snub. And though he didn't mention it, I'm sure Peter was thinking that he'd made a wise decision turning down Wolper's three-picture deal.

CHAPTER THIRTEEN

~

For Richer, for Poorer,
in Sickness and in Health

Sebastien Japrisot, the author of the novel *The Lady in the Car with Glasses and a Gun*, phoned me. This time, he'd written a screenplay adaptation of *Black Friday*, by David Goodis. He wanted me to do the English translation of his script, which once more was to be shot in two languages. The producing company would be Greenwich Films. It was to have a combined French and American cast, the exterior locations would be done in Montreal, and the sets would be in Paris. I subsequently went to Greenwich's offices on the Champs-Élysées to make my deal with production manager Ully Pickard. There I met producer Serge Silberman, who threw his arm around me and gushed, "Welcome to Greenwich Films!" A year and a half later, he would win an Oscar for producing *The Discreet Charm of the Bourgeoisie*, the best foreign language film of 1972. He had several favorite people he liked to work with, Luis Bunuel, René Clément, and Sebastien Japrisot among them. He had collaborated with these last two on *Rider on the Rain*, a popular French thriller that pushed Charles Bronson into European stardom.

The title to Japrisot's script was unwieldy and puzzling. *La Course du lièvre à travers les champs* was barely translatable as *The Path of the Hare As It Crosses the Fields*. I told both Silberman and Japrisot that such a title didn't mean anything in English. (I never really understood what it meant in French, either.) Eventually, I would spend days during the filming in Montreal with Japrisot trying to find an appropriate title in English. He wanted something a child might say while playing. The writer finally settled on my suggestion of *And Hope to Die*, which is the title on the video today.

There were several exciting reasons to be involved with *La Course du lièvre*. First and foremost, it gave me the chance to work with French director René Clément. Clément had helmed a host of first-class films that included *Is Paris Burning? Purple Noon* (both with Alain Delon), *Rider on the Rain*, and most importantly, *Forbidden Games* immediately after World War II. Like de Sica's *Bicycle Thief*, *Forbidden Games* has appeared on most critics' lists of the world's ten best pictures. A second reason was the star of *La Course du lièvre*, Jean-Louis Trintignant, who achieved immediate fame with Claude Lelouche's *A Man and a Woman* and held a principal role in *Z*. Trintignant was also a theater actor, having tackled nothing less than *Hamlet* in French. The third reason was the Hollywood portion of the film: American actors Robert Ryan and Aldo Ray. Ryan came into prominence in 1947 with *Crossfire*, for which he received a best supporting actor nomination, although he'd been acting for almost a decade before that. And Ray burst on the scene as the gravel-voiced dim jock in 1952's *Pat and Mike*. Though *La Course du lièvre* was a French-produced and French-financed film that had a decent success in France, it is amazing to me that despite so many "big" elements, it apparently had little or no release in the United States.

Besides Trintignant, there was young French character actor Jean Gaven, Italian actress Lea Massari, Tisa Farrow (Mia's younger sister), and Carol Kane. Along with Ryan and Ray, this made the casting very international. Kane, totally unknown at the time, would come into her own five years later and receive a best actress nomination for *Hester Street*.

The key crew members were from Paris, and we all flew together to Montreal at the rag end of August. By now, almost every French film technician had made a movie with Calvados, *le chat du cinéma*, so he was dubbed the official mascot of the picture. We settled into a high-rise hotel in downtown Montreal, and when we all convened later in the lobby to go out for dinner, every one of us had the same cry. "It was so cold in my room! I had to turn off the air-conditioning!" None of us had air conditioning in our Paris apartments in 1971, nor in our automobiles, nor in the restaurants we frequented. Welcome to the New World. A local crew of French Canadian grips, electricians, and drivers were added to the mix, and all the Parisians thought the locals had the strangest accent in French. They did. It was Québécois French mixed with some words translated directly from American speech.

"What time is it?" one Parisian technician asked Auguste the grip in French one day.

"I don't know," he replied, pointing to his bare wrist, *"Ma montre est sur le boom."* This was a literal translation of "My watch is on the bum!" But if you didn't know both American jargon and French, there was no way to understand his response.

"Speak to me in English!" the technician from Paris said, annoyed. "I'll understand you better!"

Like Philippe Noiret and Jacques Perrin before him, Jean-Louis Trintignant had a good ear, and so quickly had no problem acting in English. But getting Robert Ryan and Aldo Ray to perform in French was a different matter. Neither Hollywood actor had anything but the most rudimentary knowledge of the Gallic tongue. Aldo could follow some French from his knowledge of Italian, which had been his first language until he was eight. I wrote out all their French text in phonetic English, so they could pronounce the French properly. And they knew what they were saying because of the English version. Still, the first time Ryan had some French to deliver, it didn't meet with René Clément's academic approval. He started to correct Ryan's French, which had been understandable in every way, but for the exacting director it was not precise enough. Several times, he corrected him and the actor repeated the words patiently, but unhappily.

"Good!" Clément said, and moved away to attend to something else.

Ryan looked at me. "This isn't going to work," he said. "I can't act if I have to be an elocutionist at the same time. I don't know French that well but I thought I was doing fine."

"You were," I said. "Let me talk to him."

And I did. I knew Clément liked me a lot. Of all the crew members, I seemed to hold a special place for him. I had already dined with him and his wife, Bella, several times and later, when she returned to Paris, the director and I would dine together many more times. "*Maître*," I addressed him, which always made him smile. It meant "master" and "teacher" both. I learned later that Alain Delon had sometimes used the term with him, too. "About Ryan's French, you know he's playing a gangster. And he's supposed to be American or Canadian. So does his French have to be so precise?"

He put his arm around me. "Ah, I see he's hired a very good lawyer! But you are right, I shouldn't have given him a French lesson. Bronson was far worse."

Unfortunately, Ryan now wouldn't retreat from his position. "I just don't want to have to think about the French," he said. I went to Serge Silberman to discuss the problem.

"What can we do?" he asked. "Even if we dub him later, he has to say the French words or it won't match."

"I have a suggestion. I can write a phony text in English for him to say where his lip movements will match the French. Then the French can be dubbed in easily."

"That's a lot of work," he said. "Do you want to do that?"

"I think it's the only thing we *can* do."

I went back to Ryan and told him the plan. He said he thought that would work fine and thanked me for making the suggestion. Subsequently, I wrote a special text for him and Aldo Ray in English where all the lip movements would match the French text they were supposed to be speaking, but weren't. Once or twice, Ryan mumbled that the phony text was too similar to the real text, so he had a tendency to confuse the two. But whenever he raised the point, I reminded him what the alternative would be, and he'd buckle down and work on the phony text until he got it right.

There was something else that threw Ryan. Clément had a unique way of shooting that often combined a master shot with a medium shot and a close-up, all together at one time. The actors would walk through the rehearsal of a scene and move to various spots during the action. Clément would follow them with his lens finder, all the while changing the lens, making the actors bigger at moments. Then the actors would be dismissed, the stand-ins would replace them, the grips would lay down dolly track, and there would be several camera rehearsals that often started the scene at a distance, dollied into a medium shot, and finally dollied in further to a close-up at the end. Each camera set-up thus became three set-ups in one. The problem was for the actors. In normal filming, movement and action are captured in long shots, while close-ups tend to be static. With Clément's method, the actors had to hit taped ground marks exactly on the spot in the master shot, or their faces would not be correctly framed in the close-up moments later. Ryan cursed a few times during this process where just centimeters would misplace him and bring a "Cut!" from Clément. Serge Silberman totally supported Clément's method, because the director was saving time doing three set-ups in one. But since the actors frequently moved out of frame in the close-ups, I don't think the time saved was as much as the producer thought.

In the long run, Ryan seemed to admire Clément for his work on characterization but was annoyed with him for his overmeticulous camera work. "It's a strange way of shooting," he said to me one day, seated in his chair while the electricians readied the next shot. "But I guess I shouldn't complain. I had a dry spell for a long while where I didn't work. There was a story going around Hollywood that I had heart problems, that I was a risk."

"It wasn't true?"

"Not at all. My heart's as sound as a drum. I wish the rest of me was as strong as my heart." I knew he was telling me something with that statement, but it was too early for me to know what it was. Later I learned he had cancer.

On the set one day, I asked Aldo about his famous voice, which was rasping and gravely. It had been used to comic effect in *The Marrying Kind* with Judy Holiday and in *We're No Angels* with Humphrey Bogart in a rare comedy performance. And, of course, in *Pat and Mike*, which started it all. "Do you know that after *Pat and Mike*, M-G-M hired a voice coach for me, so I could work on keeping my voice rough, like sandpaper. This wasn't my natural voice. I've forgotten what my original voice was!" he said, laughing good-naturedly. "The studio really ran your lives then! At least they kept me working!"

But Ryan added another dimension to this. He said that Ray had no money. He'd had three marriages and three divorces. And there had been too much drinking and too many women, Ryan said critically. Of course, this would be an index of instability to Robert Ryan, who married once and remained married for thirty-three years. "He doesn't even have his house anymore," Ryan continued. Apparently, he'd had some serious conversations with Aldo while on the film, but it was evident that Ray's life was in tatters. "I really like the guy. I wish I could help."

Who couldn't like Aldo? A big guy, he was like an oversized Saint Bernard. He'd gained considerable weight since his days as a leading man, relegating him to character parts. His is the best performance in *And Hope to Die*, where he is alternately dim, petulant, childish, and menacing. Always professional and in good spirits, he didn't have a mean bone in his body. He spoke constantly of his two sons, Paul and Eric, disappointed that they weren't there in Montreal with him. Whenever possible, Aldo negotiated a clause in his contracts that allowed for the children to be with him while filming. At one point during *La Course du lièvre* he received news that his younger son, Eric, had had a bicycle accident and had split his forehead open. Aldo was instantly on a plane to Los Angeles to be at the boy's side. I told Aldo I would certainly look him up in Los Angeles, because I was planning to move there early the following year. He gave me his agent's phone number, since he wasn't sure where he'd be living by then.

Besides Calvados, we had another mascot on the movie: the French Canadian grip and clapper, Auguste. His nickname was Gus (pronounced in French as "goose") and often the affectionate Gugusse ("goo-goose"). He was one of the youngest in the crew, probably not more than twenty, had blond hair and good looks despite a slightly long nose. He was always in good spirits, laughing and working hard at the same time, and addressed all the actors as if they were lifelong friends. One evening, Lea Massari decided to make a pasta dinner in her hotel suite and invited only those few people she absolutely adored on the film. Aldo Ray, Jean-Louis Trintignant, Jean Gaven, and I were invited. And Gugusse. Again, this was something you would never see in Hollywood: a star inviting a grip for dinner.

So there we were, Lea, Gugusse, and I, three self-appointed chefs, shopping together one evening after wrapping the day's shoot. We had finished at five o'clock. French filming hours on location, usually 8 A.M. to 5 P.M. with an hour's break for lunch, were far more civilized than American ones, so there was always time to relax in the evenings. The three of us ran to several downtown shops where signs all bore

French and English (both languages were still official back in 1971), buying up pasta, ripe tomatoes, black olives, salad greens, and tons of fresh fruit. It was the first time Lea and I saw this strange New Zealand fruit, the kiwi, although Gugusse told us he thought it had been on the Canadian market for about a year.

In the hotel suite, Gugusse and I did most of the vegetable washing, while my eyes never left Lea as she prepared an absolutely authentic Italian sauce for fettuccine. The ripe tomatoes, onions, garlic, parsley, basil, tomato paste, and red wine all simmered together. Then small pieces of anchovy were dropped in that disintegrated in the sauce. Finally, to my astonishment, a small amount of sugar was added.

"To balance the anchovy," she said.

"Won't the sugar make it too sweet?" I asked.

"You'll never taste it," she answered. "This is the way we cook it in the country."

And she was right: the blend of anchovy and sugar simply made the sauce very rich. Aldo arrived with several bottles of wine and Jean-Louis and Jean arrived with a bottle each, so soon we were all drinking and cooking at the same time. Gugusse produced several joints of marijuana that everyone shared, and it wasn't long before we were all laughing our asses off. But despite the buzz, the dinner was in itself memorable, once again by its simplicity. Lea's fettuccine was, of course, *al dente*, and there was freshly grated *parmigiano* to go with it, green leafy lettuce alone with olive oil and lemon, and then the array of fruit. Lea put some of her favorite records on the portable record player she'd brought from Rome, and the voice of Bill Withers and "Ain' No Sunshine When She's Gone" wailed through the hotel suite. Gugusse accompanied him on Lea's guitar, which she'd also brought with her. (Did anyone under forty *not* own a record player and a guitar in 1971?) Lea and I sat on the floor, while Aldo and Jean-Louis talked of their wives and their children. Aldo said how he was fighting his ex-wife to see his boys, and Jean-Louis talked about the death of his child and how his wife, Nadine, decided to make a film, *Ça n'arrive qu'aux autres* (*It Only Happens to Others*) so that both of them could deal with their loss. We drank, we talked, we laughed, we bared bruises, four different cultures within six people, and we all loved each other more than a little before the night was over.

The camaraderie was contagious among the entire cast and crew throughout the filming, although there was certainly a special affection among those of us who had been at Lea's dinner. A few days later, just before I got into a car with Lea, I accidentally spilled some coffee on my shirt. Sitting in the back seat, I whined like a child. "I just bought this shirt before I left Paris!" I cried. "My father sent me some money for my birthday. And I can't afford another shirt!"

Lea turned to me, all compassion, and said, "Let me buy you a new one. It's my pleasure."

I looked at her sheepishly and simmered down. "Thanks, Lea, but I don't want you to do that," I said. "In fact, I don't know why I became excited. It's just a shirt."

"I understand," she replied. "It was a gift from your father. You probably didn't want to take money from him. I have the same problem with my father."

I sat there, stunned. With a few words she'd distilled the matter. A year had expired from the time I'd worked on *Willy Wonka and the Chocolate Factory*, and in that time the only work I'd had prior to coaching *La Course du lièvre* was doing the English translation of the script and, for two weeks, coaching Alain Delon's wife, Nathalie, in her apartment on rue François 1er for a role she was to perform in English in another film.

My father somehow knew when I wasn't working and would look for an excuse to send me a small check. Like bound Prometheus, I would scream to be free, then end up accepting the check and hating myself, and him, for it. Additionally, I'd had to swallow my pride the year before, when I'd sent him a collection of old French stamps that I'd unearthed at the flea market at Porte de Clignancourt. I asked him to sell them to a philatelist in Rochester, hoping to receive a better price outside France. "They should bring about five hundred dollars," I'd written him. A couple of weeks later I received a letter back saying he'd been successful in selling the stamps, and he enclosed a check for that amount. Still, it bothered me enormously that I had to let my father know that the movie profession itself was unreliable, or despite the many celebrities I worked with, that I was occasionally pinched to make ends meet. The coffee stain on my shirt suddenly spread into the frustration of trying to achieve emotional and financial independence from my father. What had Lea said? "I have the same problem with my father"? Yet she took it all calmly, as part of her life.

Why had my father become such an issue for me?

To my knowledge, Lea was seen only once in a film that was distributed in the United States. She played the young mother in Louis Malle's *Murmur of the Heart* in 1972 having a sexual relationship one night with her fifteen-year-old son when they both have had too much to drink. The daring of the topic was matched by the tenderness and beauty with which Malle and the actors handled the subject. He would say later that he'd shot the movie very rapidly before anyone could reflect on the matter or do anything but act instinctively. This prevented the film from becoming heavy. Performing the lead role, Lea Massari was beautiful, warm, touching, incandescent. As she was when I worked with her that autumn in Montreal.

As my friendship developed with Clément, little by little he divulged more about his life to me. He spoke about his wife, Bella, whom he cared for very much, but I sensed theirs had been a marriage for business reasons, a marriage of art and money. And he spoke openly of his fondness for Alain Delon. Then, out of nowhere, the director stated he was an accomplished sailor, and invited me to Menton on the French Riviera, where his boat was moored.

"Do you like sailing?" he asked.

"I've never done it. But I know from coming over from New York on the *Île-de-France*, I don't get seasick. So I think I must have sea legs."

"Good! You can come down after we finish the picture. I have a house down there, at Monte-Carlo." That would be in addition to the apartment he and Bella had on Avenue Henri Martin in the elegant 16th quarter of Paris.

"You'll be cutting the picture then, René. And I'll be leaving soon for the United States."

"When you return, then. And you will return, often. There is too much of France in you." He smiled knowingly and raised his glass to me. I was flattered by the invitation, flattered that one of the great directors of French cinema had taken such a personal liking to me. I wondered for a brief moment if the feeling was anything like the one Alain Delon might have had when he worked so closely with him on *Plein Soleil*.

Suddenly, we were nearing the end of the shoot in Canada. It was the first week of October, and the trees were on fire. The red maple of the Canadian flag was everywhere, and our last locations were in a blaze of color in the woods. Tisa Farrow's boyfriend arrived from Toronto one weekend, and Tisa told everyone that he was a Mafia member, which no one had any reason to doubt. Ryan's wife, Jessica, joined us a few days before our departure and was going to spend the rest of the shoot in Paris. Ryan told me that she was not in good health, and they were both looking forward to spending time in the City of Light.

Gugusse actually came to the airport to see us all leave. He handed me a photo that he'd taken on the set, signed on the back, "From your favorite clapman, Monsieur Gus." His infectious laugh seemed to board the plane with us. And then we were off! Flying back to Paris for studio work, with only a day of down time. The moment I arrived, I sent a simple bouquet of marguerite daisies and anemones to Ryan's hotel for Jessica, and the following night I picked the Ryans up to take them to my favorite restaurant, Chez Laurent, for dinner. When I walked into their suite, the first thing I saw was an enormous bouquet of white lilacs and velvety Baccarat roses towering on the mantelpiece. It was classic, elegant, and expensive. Ryan told me Serge Silberman had sent it for Jessica. With my modest means, I felt eclipsed. But then he led me to their bedroom, where my simple bouquet sat on a night table.

Jessica smiled and said, "How did you know I love garden flowers? Much more than—." She made a dismissive gesture toward the living room, "—that thing Serge sent!" I told her I didn't think "that thing" quite summed up white lilacs and Baccarat roses, but she would not be assuaged. I found out that evening that Jessica was a sometime writer of children's books, so I guess the garden flowers appealed to her simplicity.

I apparently could do no wrong that evening, for Bob and Jessica loved Chez Laurent as well. They both ordered the *dorade à l'estragon*, a white fish indigenous to European Atlantic waters that was grilled and served with a fresh tarragon sauce. In California, I have now found the New Zealand fish John Dory to be the closest equivalent of the *dorade*. Ryan told me this was the first fish he'd eaten that he enjoyed as much as swordfish, his favorite. He also talked to me about his performance on the stage in O'Neill's *Long Day's Journey into Night*, which he'd performed with Geraldine Fitzgerald in New York, just before starting *And Hope to Die*. "I like to think our performances had a lot of truth in them," he said. "What with both Gerry and I being Irish." Then Madame Laurent sent over her *livre d'or* for Ryan to sign, and I showed him all the signatures of the actors I'd worked with in 1964: Broderick Crawford, Red Buttons, and Cliff Robertson, and Robertson's comment about his not winning an Oscar as the other two actors had. By now he'd gotten one for his work in *Charly*.

"I should write something similar," Ryan said. "Then maybe I'll get one, too." But Robert Ryan never won an Oscar. He performed in over seventy-five films, and in most of them he played a second lead, often the "bad guy." *Bad Day at Black Rock* opposite Spencer Tracy, *Billy Budd* opposite Terence Stamp, *The Set-up*, his favorite film, with Audrey Totter, and Peckinpah's *The Wild Bunch* opposite a stellar cast, were just a few. There were never fireworks in his performances, but always carefully sketched inner torment or anguish, the dark side of our natures, and sometimes, as in *Billy Budd*, pure evil. As ironic as Robertson's comment in Madame Laurent's book was, so was the fact that the real Robert Ryan was an intelligent and reflective man, something he was almost never asked to portray on screen. A few days later, he told me Jessica had taken ill again, and their beautiful autumn in Paris was shadowed by her uneven and fragile health. He made no allusion to his own condition.

The final portion of the filming went without incident. A few days before we completed the picture, Trintignant came to me on the stage and said that an Italian director friend of his was at the studio and starting to prepare a film that would be shot in Paris in a few months. Trintignant wanted to present me to him, because the director was going to shoot the entire film in English.

"Thanks for thinking of me, Jean-Louis, but I'm going to move back to the States in a couple of months. I was actually planning to leave before this film, but Japrisot called me and I decided to stay on a little longer."

"I really think you'd enjoy working with this director. He's very good. And the principal actor will be American."

"I've already moved out of my apartment, I've put my furniture in storage, and I'm staying with a friend in Saint Maur. I don't want to abuse her generosity. I really can't do another picture."

"Wouldn't you like to meet him? I've told him about you. He's right down the hall."

"No, Jean-Louis, that's very nice of you, but I need to go back. I want to start writing."

He shrugged. "*Comme tu veux,*" he said. As you wish. And he walked off.

Blockhead! Lummox! Idiot! This is what I call myself every time I think back to this moment when Trintignant tried to get me to stop in the Italian director's office and I refused. The director was Bernardo Bertolucci, the American actor was Marlon Brando, the film was *Last Tango in Paris.* Over the years friends have asked me again and again, "What's the greatest film you've worked on?"

And I've always replied, "I never worked on anything that I'd consider "great." But probably the best picture was *The Night of the Generals.*" *Last Tango in Paris* was a great film. And Frawley Becker was a great fool.

It would be almost nine years before I would finally go sailing with René Clément, but nine years during which we corresponded often. On a return visit to Paris in 1981, I called him at his house in Monte-Carlo. He was delighted. "And you will get to meet my crew!" he exclaimed. I could feel the old devil in him, even over the phone.

"Do they all look like Delon, René?"

He roared with laughter. "You are wicked! That's why I love you! But you will see!" he replied and offered no further information at that moment.

I drove down to Monte-Carlo, then east to Menton, the last city before the Italian border. I followed René's directions to the Menton-Garavan port, and from there the nautical control tower reached him by radio. It was midafternoon and the port was still and drenched in white-hot sunlight. A few minutes later, Clément came striding into the building, his smile beaming at me, his hair a little more silvery, his face very suntanned. We embraced, then walked out toward his boat, the *Sally Mara.*

"Well, so now you will get to meet the crew!" he said.

"Do you have a big crew?" I had no idea how large his boat was, or how many hands there would be aboard.

"No, not really." A few moments later, we came up to the *Sally Mara,* moored at the dock. On deck, in white pedal pushers, was a very pretty, dark-haired young lady who seemed to be in her midthirties. "This is the crew," he announced, grinning from ear to ear. We shook hands.

"I'm pleased to meet you," Johanna Harwood said in British English. René has told me so much about you."

"*Je t'ai eu, là!*" Clément said, laughing. ("I got you on that one!") Then Clément took me by the arm and we all walked to a nearby café for coffee. On the way, he said to me, "You know, I have my life in Paris with Bella. And I have my life here with Johanna. I don't tell everyone, but you are one of the exceptions." As it turned out, Johanna would become the next Madame Clément.

René and Johanna slept on the boat that night and I slept in a small bachelor's quarters reserved for boat owners and their guests, right on the port. The next day, the three of us went sailing. We sunbathed and swam and ate tuna from a can and drank white wine. Clément's silvery hair glistened under the noonday sun and he hummed when he was at the helm or when he made the boat "come about." Almost seventy, he was still a very young man.

Because I had left France when *La Course du lièvre à travers les champs* was released, and because *And Hope to Die* was not released in the States, I would have to wait thirty years before I would see the film on video. I am proud of the work I did with Jean-Louis Trintignant's English, which is completely understandable. The scene with Carol Kane was cut from the picture, and she is not listed in the credits. Nor, to my astonishment, am I, despite the fact that I gave the film its title, its English version, a special version for Ryan and Ray, and three months of coaching. Thanks, Serge Silberman, for the welcome to Greenwich Films.

I would see both Ryan and Ray again in Los Angeles in 1972. I located Aldo at the Carleton Lodge, a modest motel on Highland Avenue near the Hollywood Freeway, a space now occupied by a Great Western. Ryan would say when I met him for lunch that he wished Aldo would get out of "that damned cheap motel" and find a decent place to live, but I knew that he didn't have the money to do that. Ray's joy was still his two boys. His tragedy was that since he was no longer a leading man, he no longer earned a high salary, and had to direct most of what he was paid to his ex-wife for the support of his children. And he had heavy drinking sprees that were devastating to both his wallet and his body. Generous to a fault, Ray often scattered what little money he had on those he considered even less fortunate than he, hangers-on in cheap bars, hotels, and pool rooms near Hollywood Boulevard. The down-at-heels, the no-fixed-domicile's; these people tore at his heart. Bearing heavy costs to support his family and throwing money and caution to the wind meant he had to live in an inexpensive motel in a dubious area. He didn't seem to care. Besides, he had a protector. Aldo's younger son, Eric, at eight and nine, would run away from his mother's home and take the bus into Hollywood to find his father. The boy knew all the dingy haunts where he could locate him: the Powerhouse Bar and the St. Moritz Hotel bar on Sunset Boulevard, sometimes just huddled in the alcove of some store front, lost in a drunken sleep. Aldo's impecunious lot was not unique. Oliver Hardy and Veronica Lake, to name but two, found times hard when they fell from Hollywood grace and were quickly forgotten. Unlike the others, Aldo never stopped working. In his last years, he took any role in any film that came along so he could continue to support his family.

I invited Ray to come have dinner at my apartment with my brother and sister-in-law who were in Los Angeles for a few days. In a town that forgets as fast as it adulates, Ray's social calendar was wide open. He laughed his good-natured laugh when he said, "I'm free these days!" He arrived a few nights later at my tiny east Hollywood apartment, presenting me with a bottle of wine. I had set up a card table in the living room, since the kitchen oven made that room too hot, and the four of us ate off the card table. My surroundings, too, were modest, even poor by Beverly Hills standards, but poor was something Aldo Ray could relate to. Larger than life, he was, as always, in good spirits, laughing, joking, and enjoying the food and wine. As with E. E. Cummings's Olaf, Ray's heart was glad and big. He stayed late into the evening and didn't seem to mind the ratty, unfashionable surroundings that had made Ian McShane bolt out the door.

I met Ryan for lunch shortly after that. He came by himself, since Jessica was once more not well. He told me he'd just finished shooting *The Iceman Cometh* with Lee Marvin, Frederic March, and a new young actor named Jeff Bridges, who had attracted attention in *The Last Picture Show*. *The Iceman Cometh* was directed by John Frankenheimer and produced by Ely Landau. It was part of the American Film Theatre series that sold tickets for filmed plays for specific performances on specific nights.

Ryan said he thought that his work on the stage in *Long Day's Journey into Night* had helped him land the role of Larry in *The Iceman Cometh*, Eugene O'Neill's last play. It would also be one of Ryan's last films. In it, all semblance of meanness was gone from his character, as he seemed to reflect on his own ebbing life in the interpretation. Jessica died that year, and Ryan followed her the following year, both of them eaten up by cancer. It is curious that the role of Larry in *The Iceman Cometh* deals with unfulfilled dreams and imminent death, the "iceman" being the Grim Reaper. Shown in 1973, the film came out shortly after Ryan died. His nuanced performance showed great dignity and acceptance, even impatience while awaiting death. This exchange with one of the prostitutes in the play summed up the character:

MARGIE: *Hey! . . . Ain't you died yet?*
LARRY (Ryan): *Not yet, Margie. But I'm waiting impatiently for the end.*

Robert Ryan was at last playing himself.

CHAPTER FOURTEEN

~

You Can Take the Boy
Out of France, But . . .

"How long do you think you'll be staying in Los Angeles?"

My father had waited until the dessert to ask the burning question. We were sitting at a booth in a restaurant in the West Fifties in New York, seventeen years after I'd sailed from that city for Le Havre. The food was average, but my father seemed to be enjoying it. He'd met me earlier at the airport. I'd arrived wearing a faubourg du Saint-Honoré maxicoat and a handmade broad-brimmed leather hat, and held the cat basket with Calvados in my hand. I guess I'd picked up something from all the actors I'd worked with. It was called an entrance.

"I don't know, father," I said. "Six months, I hope. Maybe a year. It all depends on whether or not I sell this script. In any case, it's temporary."

"So you're gonna rent an apartment?"

"Yes."

"In Los Angeles."

Of course, in Los Angeles. Isn't that what we were talking about? My father wasn't dense. I think he felt that the black sheep of the family, the son who'd lived abroad for so long, was simply unpredictable. He was walking on eggs with me, so the "in Los Angeles" was an assertion. No need to get ruffled over that. There would be time enough, and readiness, too, for confrontation at the drop of the wrong word. I hadn't seen my father since my mother's funeral nine years earlier, when I'd had to rush from Paris to New York and from New York to Rochester, causing the funeral services to be delayed because the flight out of Paris had had an engine catch fire. The plane had turned around over the Atlantic and returned to Orly, and I had been put on another flight the following day. He hadn't changed much, my father. At eighty-one, his salt-and-pepper hair still had more pepper than salt.

A few months after *And Hope to Die* was completed, I finally did move from Paris. There had been bon voyage toasts and farewell dinners with friends, and I had once more obtained a health certificate and shot records for Calvados. I had decided to break up the trip to Los Angeles by stopping in New York for a few days. I told myself that this was for the cat's benefit, and oh, yes, I suppose my father could meet me in New York and spend some time with me, too. I'd asked him to reserve rooms at the Algonquin Hotel, the hangout of Alexander Woolcott, Franklin P. Adams, Heywood Broun, Dorothy Parker, and other critics and wits almost five decades earlier. I had missed that part of literary history and had hoped that some of their ghostly pixie dust would fall on my shoulders. As it turned out, the Rose Room off the lobby, where the Round Table group met, was very ordinary and my hotel room was overpriced, across from the elevator shaft, and absolutely miniscule. I had rented better rooms in the transient, trysting hotels that surrounded Gare Saint-Lazare. My father's room was only slightly larger, and though he had every reason to complain about his son's choice in a city of countless hotels, he never uttered a word.

Across from me, he finished his cheesecake and lit up a cigar. "Optimo Blunt?" I asked, remembering his favorite from childhood days when the apartments we lived in were constantly perfumed with cigar smoke.

He laughed. "You remember? No, I can't hardly find them no more. Besides, there are a lot of good ones on the market now. Cheap, too."

My gaze swept over the room. Two or three tables were occupied by African Americans. I commented on it. I said that when I'd left the States in 1955 you rarely saw black people in restaurants. It had been a racial issue, of course, but also an economic one. Few black people earned decent livings in 1955, even in northern cities.

"Yes," my father said, "things have changed. And I, for one, am very pleased to see it. They've been held back far too long." While I didn't make the connection yet, my father, a self-made man who'd left school in the tenth grade, was a great supporter of the underprivileged. I was pleasantly surprised by his remark.

"You know, when I was a kid I spent a lot of time drawing," I suddenly found myself saying.

"And you were good," my father was quick to reply.

"I just wondered why you never sent me to art school. There was one in Philadelphia." He was silent. "I eventually attended art school in England, under the G.I. Bill, as you know. That led me to the theater, and the theater led me to the movies. They're all connected, the arts. I just wondered why you never sent me to art school."

There it was. I'd finally said it. The burr under the saddle in my ride through life. My father switched his cigar from one side of his mouth to the other. With thin lips, he really did look like Darryl F. Zanuck. Or a monkey. "We didn't know anyone whose son was an artist," he finally replied. "People of my generation raised their sons to be doctors or lawyers. We probably thought artists all starved. We just didn't know anyone."

I considered his answer. Can a man be blamed for what he doesn't know? Oh, certainly, I could tell myself that if I had a son, wouldn't I try to *find out* about his calling? But what was the point of that? He and I were two different people. I searched for answers, he accepted the status quo. Did that make him a bad person? He'd probably tried the best he knew.

Then my father reached into his suit jacket pocket and brought out a weathered beige envelope, unmistakably French, that bore my handwriting and two blue *par avion* stickers. "This is yours," he said. I slid out the contents. The old stamps I'd sent two years earlier were all there, carefully arranged in cardboard pockets as I'd originally prepared them. He'd never taken them to a philately store to sell them as I had requested when my funds were low, and instead he sent me the five-hundred dollar check that they were worth from his own account. I think he saw me about to object and added. "It's okay, you can pay me back some day. Besides, I was snowed in when I got them."

I looked at the postmark on the envelope. "The 20th of July," I said.

My father grinned. "Well, whadya know? I musta gotten it mixed up. I'm just a dumb bunny."

I sat there bewildered, trying to put together disparate elements. On the one hand, I held a seventeen-year image of an insensitive man who had no comprehension of the arts, and whom I frequently decried as never understanding me. I could battle that man at Agincourt. On the other hand, across from me sat a man who had accepted a small hotel room, a traveling cat, a downtrodden race (and felt compelled to comment on it), and a long-haired son who was loathe to admit he'd had a few hard times in his vainglorious career. A very ordinary man whose son simply went beyond him. What was there to confront? I remembered then Walt Kelly's comment in one of his *Pogo* cartoon strips that when we met the enemy, they were us.

I said nothing more and took the stamps.

When I arrived in Los Angeles, I stayed at the apartment of some friends for the first few days. But before the week was out, I'd found my own place, the one with the Murphy bed in it, opened a checking account, and met with an agent who'd read a script I had sent ahead from Paris. And before the second week was out, I owned a car and found myself seated at a small desk in my two-room apartment, writing every morning.

I have since learned that just about anyone in America has a culture shock coming to Los Angeles. Perhaps more accurately, a lack-of-culture shock. Though I had a U.S. passport, I had European eyes. I looked everywhere for a style, an architecture to the city. But Los Angeles was all stucco, a pastel pastiche of structures so one-dimensional in appearance that, like a movie set, they might be taken down the next day. Buildings with no history, hostile and void of appeal. There were drug dealers and Jesus freaks on Hollywood Boulevard, muscled hustlers on Selma Avenue, often selling their charms from the steps of the First Baptist Church, X-rated films on Western Avenue, sex ads in vending machine newspapers, and zealous cult followers of something called Synanon in a building on the Santa Monica beach. There were bronzed bodies everywhere, usually with a volleyball or beer bottle in hand. The city's two newspapers gave very little world coverage, and I struggled to find out what was going on in Europe until Sari Ostrum supplied me with a year's subscription to the *Christian Science Monitor*. The downtown Music Center had only opened the last of its three legitimate theaters five years earlier. There was no resident opera company, no ballet company, and no one to talk about either. There were no truck drivers whistling *Rigoletto*, and as I would soon learn, no one who had read Proust, Molière, or Zola. In sad fact, no one who had read much of anything. It was a movie town; like Chauncey Gardner, they liked to watch.

I took assiduous notes on the new language. I picked up hitchhikers so I could jot down their words as soon as they left the car. *Rinky-dink hotel. Bad-ass dude. Cat's got a gig. We rapped all night. A trip and a half.* Words that had made their way through beatniks and jazz musicians and shoeless flower children in the years I was gone. Words that never flew over the Atlantic and landed in a Paris dialogue coach's dictionary. Words a writer needed to know.

I had been diligently writing for several months when I received a call from French producer Jacques Bar, who was in town with director Jacques Deray and Jean-Louis Trintignant. They were about to begin filming *The Outside Man* in Los Angeles, and after Bar made the initial overture of asking me to do the film, he put Jean-Louis on the phone.

"I cannot do this picture without you," he said in French.

I laughed. *"Arrête ton baratin!"* It was a slang expression, roughly the equivalent of "Stop the vaudeville act!" "I already told Jacques Bar I would do it!"

Later that day, I drove to Beverly Hills to meet them all for a five-o'clock drink in Bar's hotel suite. Jean-Louis and I embraced at the reunion and Bar presented me to Deray, who in France was a well-known and highly respected director. It was he who had been directing Alain Delon and Romy Schneider in *La Piscine* when news of the Marković Affair had broken. Apart from my working with Jean-Louis on his English, Deray told me he would want me pretty much at his side.

"My English is not so good," he said in English with a Chevalier accent as he snuffed out one cigarette and lit another. "I speak just a little." I told him there was no problem whatsoever, that I would enjoy being his sidekick. Deray and Bar had heard about me through Clément and Verneuil as well as Jean-Louis, so with the highest recommendations I slid easily into coaching my last feature film.

"We're shooting this entirely in English," Bar said. The few short years of shooting French pictures in two languages were over. (I had done three such films.) "Besides, the entire picture takes place here in Los Angeles. We have Ann-Margret, Roy Scheider, and Angie Dickin-

son." I thought that that was a terrific supporting cast to back up a
French star.

In the days that followed, I accompanied Deray everywhere. Together, we went to Ann-Margret's house in Benedict Canyon so that
Deray could discuss wardrobe and hair with her. In her open garage sat
two motorcycles that I rightly guessed belonged to her and her husband, Roger Smith. Greeting us first was plump Allan Carr, wearing a
sweatshirt with the word "Manager" across the front. Some years later,
he would produce the Broadway musical, *La Cage Aux Folles*. He was
fun and funny, and there was obviously a real friendship with Ann-
Margret when she appeared, greeting us with a broad smile and the perfect, even teeth one finds only in Hollywood. Ann-Margret's career had
been jump-started ten years earlier, when she sang one of the nominated best songs at the Thirty-Fourth Academy Awards. She subsequently made her reputation as a "sex kitten" (whatever that meant) in
films like *Bye, Bye, Birdie* and *Viva Las Vegas*, and then surprised the
film industry with two razor-sharp dramatic performances, one in *Car-
nal Knowledge*, for which she received a best supporting actress nomination, and one for *Tommy*, where she was nominated in the best actress category. In the '80s, she tackled the role of Blanche Dubois con
brio in a TV movie of Tennessee Williams's *A Streetcar Named Desire*.

The meeting went well, I made an appointment to come back and
work with Ann-Margret, and we left. As soon as we were outside, Deray turned to me and said in complete deadpan, "Do you think I should
get a shirt that says 'Director' on it?"

"How about a shirt that says 'Shirt' on it?"

"Why not?" We laughed, but it was obvious that his French eye, acute
to cultural differences, would spot things that the average American
might not think about. This would eventually give *The Outside Man* a
unique flavor. Apart from the fact that the story dealt with a French hit
man, Deray's vision would give the viewer glimpses of an uncustomary
Los Angeles. The downtown 6th Street Greyhound bus station (now in-
operative), the downtown Hotel Clark, a dubious Venice apartment, a
modest motel on Ventura Boulevard, and for the finale of the film, a
desolate lot under the old 4th Street bridge, just east of downtown, were
all part of an unpretty picture. But the mood Deray painted was correct.
Only the Beverly Hills estate of Albert Broccoli, the producer of many

James Bond films, which played as the house owned by Angie Dickinson, would give an upscale breathing space to an otherwise dark look at the City of Angels. Walking around the area underneath the 4th Street bridge, Deray said to me, "This is the perfect place for him to die." He was referring to Trintignant's character, Lucien. "It's the opposite of Beverly Hills, the opposite of what we think of as Los Angeles. The opposite of a dream." And it was here in solitude that Trintignant's character met his fate, dying at the wheel of a rented car, and bringing the movie's total body count of principal characters to equal *Hamlet's*.

Years later, I would come to realize that even many Los Angelenos knew nothing about this image of the city. Somewhere in the early '80s, I scouted locations for *Quicksilver*, a film that starred Kevin Bacon as a bicycle messenger boy. While it would eventually be shot in San Francisco, there was a moment when producer Dan Melnick thought they might film Los Angeles for New York, and I photographed many locations in the freeway city that didn't look like Los Angeles. "Here are some shots of the mid-Wilshire district," I told Melnick.

"Amazing. It looks just like New York," he said, then added, "And where—exactly—is the mid-Wilshire district?"

The atmosphere set by Deray was one of relaxation, of détente, and often of loving moments where the director teased the actors with a totally serious expression on his face, so that they didn't always realize that he was having fun with them. "*Je blague à froid*," Deray would say. Literally, I joke coldly. The actors were all easy to work with. Scheider spoke of investing in a restaurant in Paris and Ann-Margret taught me how to greet someone in her native Swedish (*Hur mår du idag?*). Jean-Louis invited me to his rented Beverly Hills house, where he baked corn on the cob in the oven. (Corn was not a vegetable used for human consumption in France then, so it had an exotic appeal to him.) Deray took me out to dinner with his visiting girlfriend, actress Claudine Auger, and practically chain-smoked through the evening. The only slightly jarring notes to the halcyon atmosphere of the movie were the union practices. Deray would be irritated when his 1st assistant director, Bob Rosenbaum, would tell him that he needed to break the scene for lunch or incur meal-penalty costs. Though this was certainly part of Rosenbaum's job, it was adverse to French filmmaking and the director's artistic interest to complete a shot.

"Look at that!" Deray cried to an American reporter who had come to the Broccoli estate to interview him. Deray's arm made a sweeping gesture toward the street and the endless line of huge trucks parked there. As always, he had called me over to be his interpreter with the reporter, who had just asked him what the difference was between filming in France and filming in America. "Why are all those trucks here?" asked Deray. "I know every shot I'm going to make today. I know every piece of equipment I'll need. You could put it all in one truck! But, no, here you must bring the whole studio along!"

About three-quarters of the way through the film, Deray focused on casting the role of a cosmetician working in a mortuary. Francesca Hilton, the blond and fleshy daughter of Zsa Zsa Gabor and Conrad Hilton, had constantly and devotedly been part of Jacques Bar's entourage, and she sometimes worked for the production. She soon let everyone know that she wanted to audition for the part.

"She could do it," Deray confided in me, after he'd auditioned her. "But you know, we already have so many blondes in the movie! Ann-Margret, Angie, the girl who played the prostitute."

"And Georgia," I added, referring to Georgia Engel, who supplied the only humor to the film as a media-conscious housewife.

"And Georgia, yes. So I'd rather have someone dark."

Enter Talia Shire, who had just been seen in a small but noticeable role in *The Godfather*. (Can anyone forget the plate-throwing scene?) Pretty, mousey, puckish, funny, and complex, Talia had dark eyes that stared out from under dark strands of hair, and looked like a child seeking approval. She was the sister of Francis Ford Coppola, and her name was short for *Italia*, the country of their heritage. She made a point of telling me that she never called on her brother to help her career, and that is probably true. Her husband was composer David Shire, who would later win in the best song category for *Norma Rae*. Talia was quickly Jacques Deray's choice for the role, in a scene between her and Jean-Louis. Deray's decision about wanting a dark-haired actress was also a lesson to me on how a chance element could determine the selection of an actor. Francesca Hilton could have done the role; she just had the wrong color hair.

Talia told me the story about what happened with her when *The Godfather* was released. She said she stood in one of the many long lines that always formed for that movie. But when she arrived at the box office, she returned to the end of the line instead of buying a ticket. "Why did you do that?" I asked.

"I thought I didn't deserve it," she said. Then she shrugged and added, "Catholic guilt, I suppose." Yep, complex.

She later appeared in an equity-waiver production of Herb Gardner's A Thousand Clowns at the tiny Callboard Theatre, now gone, on Melrose Place, just east of the then-fashionable Le Restaurant. The production was dull; her performance was not. "What are you doing in this show?" I asked her afterward. "The direction, the cast, the entire production—none of it is up to your work. You'd do better just working on scenes at home or in class with another actor!" My castigation probably appealed to her sense of guilt. I never saw her in another play. Four years later, she was nominated as best actress for Rocky.

When shooting ended, Deray and Bar told me they wanted me to handle the dubbing for them, as they were returning to Paris. There were some scenes with exterior noise (at the Los Angeles airport, for one). Additionally, Italian actor Umberto Orsini, playing the villain of the piece, needed to be revoiced to sound American. Some time later, Jacques Bar sent over the loops from Paris, and I found myself in a dubbing studio with an actor named Richard Davalos. I knew instantly who he was. James Dean's brother and rival for Julie Harris's love in East Of Eden. The brother that Dean physically combats in a house yard, the brother he forces to look at his mother in the brothel. In the years that had passed, the blond god had grown stout and lost his matinee-idol looks, but he was warm and personable and his voice work turned out to be totally professional. He said that most of his jobs at that time were in television or dubbing and revoicing characters, that he was only occasionally called for a big feature film.

"I always wanted to work with Angie Dickinson!" Davalos joked when the first loop to be dubbed popped up on the screen of her and Orsini together. Years later, Davalos would tell me that during East of Eden Dean and he took an apartment together over a drugstore that was across the street from Warner Bros. The two actors had wanted the reality of living together so they could relate to the two rivaling brothers living in the same house in the movie. And, not without humor, he related how a scream of his that was originally part of his performance in *The Sea Chase* had been lifted and placed in the sound track of *Rebel without a Cause* when the car went over the cliff.

When it came time to loop Ann-Margret, there was sudden disaster. Appearing in Lake Tahoe, she had fallen twenty-two feet off a platform and fractured her jaw. The doctors there were ready to operate, but to do so they would have had to make an incision through her skin, which would have left scars on her face. She told me afterward that her husband, Roger Smith, insisted that the doctors in Nevada not even touch her. He immediately flew her back to Los Angeles, where she was placed in the hands of specialists, I believe at the UCLA hospital. "They operated from the inside of the mouth," she told me when I visited her at her house. Her jaw was wired shut, so she spoke between clenched teeth, and there were dark circles under her eyes. But her chamois-like skin was unmarred. "I can't chew, I have to drink through a straw. We put everything in the blender. Even pizza!"

Obviously, the looping of her lines would have to wait. I called Jacques Bar in Paris to let him know. He had planned to fly me to the City of Light to take charge of Trintignant's looping there. With the news about Ann-Margret, he decided to put that off for a few weeks, and I was simply to wait until the wiring of her jaw would be removed. Some weeks later, our delayed date in the dubbing studio was kept. Effervescent and full of life, Ann-Margret appeared in her usual state of joyousness, talking and laughing at the same time, her mouth with the beautiful teeth intact. She was serious only for a second when she said, "I owe so much to Roger."

It was near the end of the year when I finally flew to Paris with all the celluloid loops. I thought that Jacques Bar was truly a considerate producer to go to the expense of hiring me for one more week, paying my air fare, hotel room, and living expenses in Paris, all as a courtesy to Trintignant. I would later learn of another courtesy, this one directed to me. Bar gave me a screen credit not as a dialogue coach, but as a dialogue director. Consecration on my last big picture.

Jacques Deray was with me and Trintignant in the dubbing studio, but as usual, in deference to my English, the director let me be in charge of the session. Deray even left the room a couple of times to attend to other matters, or to have a coffee, while Jean-Louis and I worked on. Years later on a vacation in Paris, I would meet Deray again in Le Paris, one of my favorite cafés. He would still be smoking like a chimney. At that time, I was working as a Hollywood location manager and had just finished my first feature for Paramount. I told him of the sixteen- to eighteen-hour days the job required. *"Mais c'est inhumain!"* was his outraged response. ("But that's inhuman!") Every time I would relate the job demands to an American, the reply was almost always, "But think of the money you're making!"

Jean-Louis' looping went smoothly. As with *And Hope to Die*, his voice in English remains in the sound track and he is completely un-derstandable. My only criticism to his performance as an outside hit man is that I found him a little too phlegmatic and passive. It had been an actor's choice, and obviously Deray had agreed with him. Following this final session in the sound studio, Jean-Louis and I lunched together in a little café–restaurant near the Studios de Billancourt. After three courses of hors d'oeuvre, main dish, and salad were completed, he or-dered the cheese board brought to the table. And a half-bottle of red wine to replace the carafe of house wine we'd been drinking. In minutes I was again succumbing to the sensuality of a familiar French culinary experience. "I haven't had cheese like this in almost a year!" I extolled. "They don't ripen cheese in America, they manufacture it."

"I remember," he said. "It was plastic."

"I am with the angels," I replied, using a common French expression, as I savored the pungent cheese in my mouth and followed it with the wine. Then a thought hit me. "Jean-Louis, you ordered this on purpose, didn't you?"

"Why on purpose?"

"To remind me of what I'm missing. So I will come back and do your next movie. You're seducing me!"

He smiled. "Not really. I just thought this would give you pleasure, that's all."

God, I missed the French.

CHAPTER FIFTEEN

~

At Long Last Literature

Early the following year, I received a telephone call from a French television producer in Paris. Michèle Arnaud, with a charming accent, asked for me. I quickly answered in French. "I am making a documentary," she said, "on Henry Miller. I expect to be in Los Angeles in two weeks. Do you think you could put together a very small crew for me?"

"What do you need?" I asked.

"A sound man, a grip, an electrician, a continuity person to take notes for the editor here in Paris. That's all. And you would be the production manager."

"I'm sure I can do that. Where would we be filming?"

"In Miller's house."

"In Big Sur?"

"No, he's living in Pacific Palisades now." It was an affluent section of Los Angeles not far from the coast. Michèle gave me his address and telephone number, so I could start to make the arrangements. She also wanted me to reserve some hotel rooms, one for her and her husband, one for the director, and one for writer Lawrence Durrell. Durrell and Miller together? I was impressed.

"They are old friends, you know," Michèle said. "And Durrell lives in France, so I thought it would be a good idea to get them in conversation."

While the documentary would be mostly about Miller, part of it was to include a dialogue between these two literary giants.

I made a few phone calls to crew members with whom I had worked on *The Outside Man* and shortly had lined up the people Michèle needed. I discussed their rates and made the deals. Then I went out to Pacific Palisades to visit Henry Miller.

His house was a classic two-story stucco with a wrought-iron balcony on Ocampo Drive. Miller's young and beautiful Japanese wife let me in, escorted me into a sort of large sun room just off the living room, and presented me to the revolutionary writer who had once said, "Instead of talking about God, I talked about sex." Then, all discretion, his wife disappeared and I never saw her again during that visit. Miller rose to meet me and we shook hands. He was tall, lanky, mostly bald with a band of snow-white hair connecting two very large ears. He had a laugh in his eyes, which I would think later was his way of laughing at all of life, and he immediately addressed me by my first name. He was eighty-two years old. We sat down in the room that I would continue to think of as a sun room but in latter American terms is more often described as a family room.

We almost instantly began to speak of Paris. Of the Shakespeare and Company bookstore and Sylvia Beach and Alfred Perlès and Anaïs Nin and Gertrude Stein, all Miller's contemporaries in pre–World War II Paris. I had read only portions of his two "tropics," as they were sometimes called, *Tropic of Cancer* and *Tropic of Capricorn*.

"Don't you miss Paris?" I asked.

"Certainly," he replied. "You always miss Paris once you've lived there, doancha know? But it's very pleasant here. It's very comfortable."

"I've been back in the States about a year now and I'm still amazed by some of the things I see."

"Like what?"

"Well, the head shops on Hollywood Boulevard, for one thing. Have you seen them?"

"No."

I pointed to the ceiling of the room we were in. It was covered with psychedelic-type posters: intricate and wildly colored floral patterns, Maxwell Parrish, Gustav Klimt, Jimi Hendrix. "All those are in the shops. Where'd you get them?"

"My son, Tony, put them up."

"Well, that's one of the things that earmarks a head shop. But mostly it's about marijuana. They pretend all the paraphernalia they sell is for tobacco, so that's how they stay legal."

"Whatdya know! Isn't that wonderful!"

"They're selling glass water pipes and joint papers and chellums in these stores. Have you ever seen a chellum?"

He said he hadn't, and I explained they were used in North Africa. That they were small ceramic stemless pipes you held vertically in your hands as you clasped them tightly, created a stem, and drew breath and marijuana fumes through your hands. Chellums may now have disappeared from the market.

"There's no end to man's resourcefulness when it comes to pleasure, doancha know?" marveled the libertine of all libertines.

"You should go visit some of these head shops, Mr. Miller," I said.

"I will! I will!" he answered enthusiastically. "And please call me Henry."

So began my relationship with Henry Miller, a relationship that went beyond the little French television shoot we were about to do. For a couple of years afterward, I would on occasion make him homemade soups, and then take him a quart jar, usually containing a purée of vegetables, like the soups we'd both had in a million Paris restaurants. Once, I surprised him with *osso buco*, which he'd told me was a favorite dish of his. Each time, we'd sit and talk for about a half-hour. In return for soup, he'd entertain me with stories. How, while in Paris and when he was quite young, he began to keep a big copybook of words he hadn't heard of before. He wrote them down, along with their definitions. Then when he started to write, he'd open up his copybook and place as many of the new words as he could into what he was writing. "That's how I thought you became a writer!" he said, chuckling over the memory. "By using big words! After a while, I threw the book away!" A lesson for me, I thought. Keep the writing simple.

Another time, he told the story of how ashamed his mother had been of him when he was growing up in Brooklyn. Even as a young child Henry wanted to write, and said so to everyone. That embarrassed his mother, for whom writers were disreputable. When guests came to the house, she would enclose him in a closet, where he would sit on the floor and, with the light on, write. He wouldn't be allowed out until the guests left. Stories like this turned Henry Miller into an instant entertainer, a raconteur, and every anecdote he told was a veritable short story. And in his own earthbound way, he was a sage. The one immortal line I retain to this day was when he said, "No man becomes a man until the death of his father." That one chilled me to the bone.

Michèle Arnaud and her husband, Patrick Lehideux, the director, Jacques Boumendil, and English writer Lawrence Durrell all arrived as planned in early February 1973 and checked into their rooms at the Sunset Marquis Hotel. Durrell immediately asked me about California wines and in no time the two of us were walking into a liquor store on Sunset Boulevard to purchase a few cabernets, one of which he immediately opened in his room as we all sat around and enjoyed the "little local wine" that the Englishman was lauding. Durrell, of course, was a literary colossus equal to Miller. He had written, among other things, *The Black Book*, which I'd read, *Bitter Lemons*, which I had not but possessed, and one of the grandest opuses of literature ever, *The Alexandria Quartet*. Of those four books, I had read all of *Justine* and portions of *Mountolive*, but that was it. I'd also read some of the letters that passed between Miller and Durrell, published as *Henry Miller–Lawrence Durrell, a Private Correspondence*.

I would soon learn that Durrell had a strong leaning toward all wines, and though he was perfectly mannered most of the time, every once in a while an unannounced outburst would shatter the air and remind us that we had a great artist and great drinker on our hands.

"Les singes ont assez joué!" he cried on the third day of shooting, and slammed down the ping-pong paddle he had in his hand. The monkeys have played enough! He stalked off into the living room and sat down. It had been Michèle Arnaud's idea, not the director's, to have Miller and Durrell play ping-pong in Miller's sun room while the two men conversed about life and literature. Durrell had been annoyed from the start. He would gladly sit in a chair and talk to his old friend, Henry, about any subject French television wanted. He could also play ping-pong. But doing it all at the same time with cameras rolling mercilessly many times over on the aging writers was more than he could endure. I saw in a lightning flash that French television mentality wasn't much better than American television mentality. The ping-pong had been a dumb idea.

Michèle and Boumendil went into a football huddle and probably decided it was fourth down, but not time to kick. They chose instead to break the set-up at the ping-pong table and start one in Miller's living room. The grip and the electrician began moving furniture. I asked Miller if he thought Durrell would continue to do the filming.

"Oh, sure," he said. "Larry's always been a little like that. Flying off the handle. It doesn't mean anything, doancha know?" After almost three days of filming with Miller, I realized he used "doancha know?" as an equivalent of *n'est-ce pas?* It was simply a rhetorical confirmation on his own statement.

I moved over to Durrell. "Are you all right?" I risked asking.

"Of course. It's all stuff and nonsense, isn't it?" Then he added, "And it'll all be over today anyway."

"Let's have dinner tonight," I said, "so we can get back to those little California wines you like so much."

"Now *that's* intelligent!" he answered with a laugh.

Larry Durrell and I did go to dinner that night, to an excellent Chinese restaurant on the Strip, one that Miller had recommended. I'm sure Durrell was glad the shoot was over, and he seemed even more relaxed that there were just the two of us. He didn't have to be filmed, he didn't have to perform. Later, I would get a letter from Sommières in the south of France, where he lived, that read:

> Here is a brief line to tell you how grateful I am for the wise and considerate way you looked after me in Hollywood. It roused not only my gratitude but also my professional envy as an ex-press-attaché.

That thank-you note would begin a correspondence between Durrell and me that lasted five years. I don't think it involved literary genius like the one between Miller and Durrell did, but over the years, the difficult Hollywood years when I wasn't writing the car chases that agents wanted, Larry's encouragement and advice would keep me following the North Star.

Two months later, Michèle telephoned from Paris to state she was having a hard time editing her film. She needed more shots on Miller and wanted to do two more days of filming with him. Would I again line up a crew for her? I said I would. The French contingency arrived at the end of April, this time without Lawrence Durrell, and at Michèle's request again checked into the Sunset Marquis. Once more, we would invade the house on Ocampo Drive. Henry took it all with good-natured nonchalance, even when his desk had been pushed into a corner of his living room by the grip and electrician as they prepared a set-up. Miller simply threaded his way into the corner, sat down behind his desk, and unperturbed, began to while away the time writing. He suddenly seemed as boxed in as I'd imagined him to be in the family closet as a child. I went over and stood alongside of him, watching the literary giant amuse himself with a brown felt pen on a yellow legal-sized tablet.

"Just as there is no end to knowledge, so there is no end to stupidity," it began. It was a great line. I watched as he wrote to the end of his thought, about three-quarters of the way down on the page. Then he stopped, looked at me, and smiled.

"What are you going to do with that, Henry?" I asked.

"Do you want it?" he asked in return.

"If you're not going to use it for something."

"It's yours," he said. He wrote "For Frawley" at the bottom, signed the page, and dated it with the brown felt pen. Then he tore off the page and handed it to me. I had it framed and it has since traveled from abode to abode in the three decades I've lived in Los Angeles. One time, in my first Hollywood apartment, there was a break-in in the middle of the afternoon, probably by two youths looking for something to steal in order to buy drugs. It was then that I lost the two sets of cuff links that Audrey Hepburn and Peter O'Toole each had given me at the end of filming *How to Steal a Million*. When the police came to take a report, they walked around the apartment, asking questions.

"Did they take anything else?" one of the officers wanted to know.

"Not that I'm aware of," I replied. I had no television or stereo set, items young hoods snatched for fast turnovers. I pointed to the signed Henry Miller letter on the wall. "This is probably the item of the greatest value," I stated. "It's signed by Henry Miller."

The second officer came up to the framed letter and stared at it. "Henry Miller. Isn't that the guy who writes those dirty books?"

At least he recognized the name.

Of all the famous people I had met and worked with over the years, perhaps the greatest legend was still to come my way. I'd missed working with her twice, on *The Lion in Winter* and *The Madwoman of Chaillot*, but *La Forza del Destino*, as my opera-buff friends would say, would be kind to me one more time. I would get to meet the only actress to have received four Academy Awards, all for best actress: Katharine Hepburn.

Sometime after the second filming of the Henry Miller documentary, I began to work as an assistant to Dr. Jessie Marmorston and, to a lesser degree, her husband, producer Lawrence Weingarten. Their two fields could not have been more different, his being film, hers cardiac research. Weingarten had been for many years one of the most stalwart producers at M-G-M. His credits read like a roll call of Hollywood films in their heyday: among others, *A Day at the Races*, *Libeled Lady*, *I'll Cry Tomorrow*, *Cat on a Hot Tin Roof*, *The Unsinkable Mollie Brown*, and three Hepburn–Tracy films—*Without Love*, *Pat and Mike*, and *Adam's Rib*. Though he was semiretired when I met him, there were still a few odds and ends he wanted me to take care of in his office on Sunset Boulevard, and he seemed relieved that I was helping organize his wife, whose professional work was brilliant and whose personal organization was scattered. They lived on a quiet street above Sunset Boulevard, next door to director George Cukor. Behind them was Katharine Hepburn's house, so all three celebrities who had often worked together, found themselves also to be neighbors. Hepburn had no pool at her house, and she frequently came to the Weingarten residence through the back way to use their pool. It was after one of these swims that Jessie Marmorston introduced me to her. In a terry cloth robe at the side of the pool, she reminded me of how she looked in her night swim scene in *The Philadelphia Story*, the robe not unlike the one she wore when James Stewart carried her, quite drunk, back to the house. Though that had been thirty years earlier, the face was much the same. The high cheekbones were still her trademark. Regal, patrician, elegant without make-up, here was a real match to the French aristocracy I'd known. And there were the freckles and the unruly hair, the American side of her. We shook hands and spoke very briefly, Jessie mentioning my work in Europe in the film industry.

"Yes, I'm very fond of France," she said, in her brittle Eleanor of Aquitaine voice.

"A country of infinite variety," I answered. It wasn't brilliant, but how do you sum up seventeen years with a bon mot for a legend?

"Yes," she reiterated. With nothing more to add, I excused myself and went inside to Jessie's desk and the papers awaiting me there. I kicked myself for not being more scintillating.

A few days later, Larry Weingarten approached me about a script I'd written and that he'd most kindly read. We sat in Jessie's office in their home and he told me that he thought the script was good. It was a medical thriller, to use the jargon label of Hollywood. "With your permission, I'd like to give it to Kate to read," he said. "There's no role there for her, but I'd like to get her opinion. She's always been good at that."

A week later, Hepburn came over to the house while I was in Jessie's office and sat and talked to me about the script for about twenty minutes. Like Larry, she thought the script was well-written and probably commercial as well.

"Do you know Ibsen's *An Enemy of the People?*" she asked me.

"I read it a long, long time ago."

"It has a similar theme. What I liked about yours is that you gave some justification to the mayor's position. He does have valid reasons for doing what he did. So the argument isn't completely one-sided. I liked that."

The mayor to whom she was referring was essentially the antagonist of the screenplay, locking horns with the idealistic doctor who was trying to bring the truth about an epidemic to the people. "Thank you," I said.

"The only thing I don't agree with is that the wife leaves the doctor when things get tough. If she really loved him, she wouldn't have left him."

"It's for the safety of the children. The son's been run over. It's the only thing she can do."

"Yes, that is a hard decision. But I wouldn't have left him."

Of course, she wouldn't have. She was Katharine Hepburn, a Trojan woman, queen of the Scots, Babe Dietrickson Zaharias, Tracy Lord, Jo March. She was iron will itself. She had faithfully stayed by Spencer Tracy through all his drinking, supported him on the set of *Guess Who's Coming to Dinner?* when his health was failing, and finally who remained with him at home until his death, two weeks after they'd completed their ninth film together. I didn't say any of that to her. "You may have a point," I answered. "I'll consider it."

When she told Larry how much she liked the script, he went into action and sent it to Lew Wasserman, the former head of Universal Studios, who must have sent it down to the head of the feature story department there. In less than a week—record time for anyone to read a script in Hollywood—Larry got a call from that department. They thought my screenplay was well-written, but it wasn't what they were looking for. "Wasn't what they were looking for" became a common phrase, and it's still used today to the point of predictable tedium whenever a studio or an agency really doesn't know what to say when they are rejecting a script, and they don't know why they are rejecting it. They also don't know what it is they *are* looking for.

Larry told me later that he flew off the handle. "Well, you see he can write! Give him a writing assignment then! That's what we did at Metro when we liked someone's work!" He was livid even as he recounted the episode to me. A few days later, I received a call from a Universal TV story editor, who set up a meeting with me. I was given a paid assignment to write a story for the *Columbo* television series. After I turned in some twenty pages, I was given a second assignment to do another, and I was paid for that, too. Neither story was ever developed into teleplay, at least not by me, either because I missed something they wanted, or because they were doing an act of obeisance to Lew Wasserman, or as I theorized, because the story editor himself was a *Columbo* writer, so the more teleplays he himself wrote, the more money he received. Much later, the screenplay Larry liked was optioned by 20th Century Fox for a movie-of-the-week, but it was dropped when a new man was put at the helm of NBC and wiped the development slate clean. Who could keep up with the tangled web of Hollywood's goings and comings?

The next time I saw Katharine Hepburn was quite by accident in Dave's, a very small produce market on Hillhurst Avenue run by a Japanese man, in the unfashionable east end of Hollywood. This was the area I was living in when Ian McShane hastily ran off from dinner at my studio apartment. Obviously, what had been unfashionable to him didn't mean tuppence to Kate.

"Oh, hello!" she said, immediately recognizing me. She was with her secretary and frequent companion, Phyllis Wilbourn.

"How are you?" I asked, not knowing how to address her. I was beyond Miss Hepburn and not near enough for Kate.

"You remember Phyllis, don't you?" Of course, I did. I'd met her during one of Hepburn's visits to the Weingartens. "Is this where you go marketing?" she asked after Phyllis and I had shaken hands.

"Much of the time," I said. "I live in this area."

"How fortunate for you! I come all the way across town to buy fresh vegetables!" This was 1973; gourmet produce stores hadn't been born yet.

"I followed the owner when he opened this store. He used to be on Prospect Avenue, in a tiny store right around the corner from my apartment. It was the only place in L.A. I ever found that had ripe persimmons."

"Do you buy things for Larry and Jessie here?"

"I haven't, but I should."

"Yes, you must."

"Good seeing you both again," I said, acknowledging them together with a head nod. I started to move on.

"Oh, uh . . ." she called after me. Since she was quite aware of my name, I figured she didn't know how to address me either.

I turned around. "Yes?"

"Whatever happened to your script? The one I liked so much?"

"Larry is working on it. He wants to get it to one or two other people."

"Good!" she said. "It should be made." We nodded to each other once more and I moved on.

After the second *Columbo* treatment, all was quiet again on my professional front. Then, with another script of mine, Jessie Marmorston arranged a meeting with a friend who was an agent at William Morris, then regretted it, because she realized he would not understand the material. Larry made a few phone calls and I had more meetings with agents who were either too big to be interested in someone without a track record or too small to do me any good. Before the end of the year, I'd seen a dozen literary agents. I was baffled by the title. Why not "screenplay agents?" I asked myself. "Or teleplay agents?" Why literary agents when they seemed to know so little about literature? Two of them stared blankly when I mentioned my correspondence with writer Lawrence Durrell. "What's he done?" asked one of them. "What's he done recently?" asked the other. A third agent had been the former secretary of a fourth and had stolen his files when she left, then called up all the writers that had been interviewed by her former boss. Every agent I met seemed about as honorable as Brutus and as knowledgeable as Tony Lumpkin.

Early in 1974, Larry Weingarten announced that he'd been honored by the Academy of Motion Picture Arts and Sciences with the Irving Thalberg Award, which he would receive at the Oscar ceremonies in April. It is one of the few awards for which the winner is announced ahead of time. The Irving Thalberg Award is given to a producer for the ensemble of his achievements and overall contribution to the film industry. The award is not presented every year. Larry had a few invitations for the Oscar ceremony and he wanted me to have one. I felt honored and touched; all the other invitations were for family members.

"And Kate's going to present the award to me!" Larry told me. "It's a complete secret. She's going to be a surprise presenter." I was flabbergasted. I knew the entire movie world would be as well. Katharine Hepburn, the ultimate private person, had shunned the Academy Award ceremonies, including every one in which she'd gotten a nomination. (At that point she'd received three Oscars; her fourth, for *On Golden Pond*, was yet to come.) I don't think she harbored a disdain for the awards. She just shied away from public appearances.

But then, just a couple of weeks before the ceremony, Kate went into UCLA Medical Center for hip surgery. That itself was hard to fathom because, her sixty-seven years be damned, she was often seen vigorously bicycling around the neighborhood. The operation also occurred with the utmost secrecy, and I don't even recall any press on the matter at the time. She came home and was creeping around her house with a cane. It was days before the Academy Awards.

"She told me she'll make the presentation if she can put down the cane," Larry said. "She won't come on stage with a cane, and I don't blame her. If she can't do it, Liz will." He was referring to Elizabeth Taylor, not a bad backup.

The day before the Oscars, I arrived at the Weingarten house with a bottle of Dom Pérignon, an extravagant gift for someone whose earnings were modest. I gave it to Larry along with my personal congratulations. I knew this had to be one of the most exciting moments of his life. He opened the gift and smiled. "Wonderful!" he said. Then, turning from the room with the champagne, added, "I'll put it away for a special occasion."

Eleven o'clock, the morning of the ceremony. It wasn't a workday for me; I just wanted to be at the house to make sure that Larry and Jessie had everything they needed. The phone in the house rang and Larry answered it. A moment later, he came into Jessie's office. "She just put down the cane. She's going to do it."

It was late afternoon when we all arrived at the Dorothy Chandler Pavilion. Besides Larry and Jessie, there were their three daughters and a son-in-law, everyone in formal attire. I was in a rented tuxedo, as I'm sure many others were that night. The immediate family all sat in the orchestra section, while my seat was in the balcony. Larry, of course, apologized for that, but it was of no importance to me. I was delighted just to be there, the only Academy Award ceremony I've ever attended. I looked at the oversized program in my lap. There were three masters of ceremony and one "Ms" and forty-three award presenters, some of them the biggest names in Hollywood: Warren Beatty, Susan Hayward, Bob Hope, Alfred Hitchcock, Liza Minnelli, Gregory Peck, Charlton Heston, Elizabeth Taylor. Katharine Hepburn's name was nowhere to be seen.

And it truly was a surprise for everyone there when, in a simple and elegant black pant-suit and with no limp whatsoever, she walked out on the stage to present Larry with the award. There was an audible gasp from the audience, which turned into a whooping cheer, and everyone immediately jumped up for a resounding standing ovation for that most private of stars who had never before graced the awards ceremony with her presence. "I'm the living proof someone can wait forty-seven years to be unselfish," she said, and brought the house down. Later, she referred to Larry as, "this most productive producer."

The 46th Annual Academy Awards presentation had another surprise that evening, one that *no one* knew would happen. Just before David Niven introduced Elizabeth Taylor, a "streaker" ran across the stage in all his natural glory, holding his hand up in a V-for-peace sign. British calm at its zenith, Niven simply commented that the man had probably gotten the only laugh of his life by "stripping off and showing his shortcomings."

All in all, it was one of the most memorable evenings of my life. I felt proud and happy for Larry and the family in his crowning achievement.

There was, however, a shadow over the momentous occasion. Shortly afterward, Jessie learned from some blood tests that Larry had contracted leukemia. As a doctor and as a wife, she decided to keep the news from him. "Why?" I asked. "Shouldn't he know?" My own family had played the denial game with my mother and an aunt. I said that perhaps Larry might want to do something or say something if he knew, and that that opportunity was being denied him. "If I had a fatal illness, I'd want to know!"

"You're the kind of person we'd tell! Larry isn't!" she exclaimed in no uncertain terms. I said nothing more. It was her decision. During the months that followed, Jessie Marmorston set into motion an elaborate plan. Whenever Larry felt extremely tired and weak, she would feign fatigue herself and suggest they both go into the hospital for blood transfusions. "It'll pep us both up!" she would say and Larry would agree. And she'd check them both into the Good Samaritan Hospital, as if there had been no specific reason.

During one of these stays, Kate came over to the house and gave me a bowl of chicken salad that she'd made herself and asked me to take to Larry. Correction: she *told* me to take it to him. "Make sure he gets it!" she said, just before she left. I watched her head toward her house, disappearing through the back gate. I realized that with her decision to appear at the Academy Awards, my being given an invitation to that event by Larry, Jessie's medical cover-up, and now even Kate's homemade chicken salad, there was a lot of love going around in that corner of Los Angeles.

I went to the hospital to see Larry and to deliver Kate's thoughtful dish. But Larry was clearly disturbed and showed it. Weeks earlier, he'd spoken to Steve McQueen about my script, which Larry never ceased championing. Larry thought the lead role of the doctor could interest McQueen, and he told him. Since the actor had his own company, the entire affair could be put together there. I then took the script out to McQueen's house in Malibu, where I handed it to the house staff person who answered the door. A week after that, Larry called McQueen, who said that he didn't know where the script was, that he hadn't seen it. He suggested a second copy be dropped off at his in-town office. I then delivered a second copy, placing it directly in the hands of McQueen's assistant. But when several weeks went by without a word, Larry began to call McQueen again, both at his home and his office. McQueen did not return the call. Nor the next. Nor the one after that.

For well-mannered Larry Weingarten, it was a slap in the face. No wonder he was upset.

"I don't understand it," Larry said. "I helped him get his start in the business. Now he's not returning my calls." What could I say to Larry? That the times were changing in Hollywood in the mid-'70s? That the producers who were once the grist of the studio mills were being replaced by ambitious agents who had no finesse and no allegiances? That art dealers had conceded to souk carpet sellers? That actresses pretended to be maids on the phone? That literary agents didn't read literature? That good manners were dying as surely as he was? As if in answer to these questions, Larry took my hand and held it. "I've called him three times, Frawley. Forgive me, but I just can't call him any more." I told him he shouldn't and thanked him for everything he'd tried to do to help me. Then I went to see the nurse to get a plate and fork, so Larry could focus his attention on Kate's chicken salad, which at that moment was infinitely more important.

At Larry's funeral at Hillside Memorial Park, most of the family sat in a screened side section. I sat on the front row near it. Behind me was a large crowd of mourners, Esther Williams, Fernando Lamas, and Johnny Green among the many familiar faces. Kate and Phyllis were there, also on the front row, close to the side exit. As soon as the ceremony was over, they made a fast eclipse out the side door, and I imagine Kate probably paid her personal respects to Jessie later by telephone or simply stopped in to see her. Despite the moment, there had probably still been too much of a ring of a public appearance for Hepburn to hang around the chapel.

My path would cross hers one last time, almost twenty years later, when I was the location manager for *Love Affair* in 1993. It was the second remake of the original *Love Affair* done in 1939 with Irene Dunne and Charles Boyer, the first having been in 1957 as *An Affair to Remember* with Deborah Kerr and Cary Grant. This time around it was Warren Beatty and Annette Bening. Though in preproduction, we were getting dangerously close to the start date with the important role of Warren's Aunt Ginny still not cast. We were scouting the island of Moorea, just across from Tahiti, when Warren asked me what French actresses might be able to play the role. We were sitting across from each other at a wooden table in Le Bateau, a wonderfully informal restaurant on a boat that served the best fresh fish on the island. In answer to his question, I mentioned Michèle Morgan and Danielle Darrieux, both of whom he'd already considered.

"Who else?" he asked.

"Edwige Feuillère," I replied. She was doubtless still the reigning queen of the lively arts in France.

"Good idea. How old is she now?" Of course, Warren Beatty, a veritable *homme du cinéma*, would be the one person in Hollywood who would even know who Edwige Feuillère was.

"Very possibly too old. In her eighties, at least."

"That may be okay."

"I'm not sure she speaks any English."

"Who else?"

"Suzanne Flon. A wonderful actress. She was in *Moulin Rouge*. I've seen her many times on stage. And she speaks excellent English."

"How old?"

"I don't know. In her early seventies."

"What do you think of Katharine Hepburn?" Warren was always doing that. Throwing questions that were little tests to people. I knew he'd probably already made up his mind.

"The best. Can you get her?"

"I can try," was his succinct answer.

Some weeks later, we started shooting in Los Angeles, with the role of the aunt still not cast. There were rumors that Warren had talked to Kate on the phone. One of the producers said she'd apparently asked Beatty, "Why should I do this?" Then we shot on the island of Moorea, and came back to Los Angeles. Warren had the production coordinator, Nan Morales, send Hepburn flowers or chocolates every day to her New York apartment or her Connecticut home. Mike Nichols supplied Morales with the names of the finest chocolate makers in New York. Then the Thanksgiving holiday arrived. In addition to the days off, an extra week off for the entire crew was added. Warren needed time to go to the East Coast to see Kate personally, probably to her home in Connecticut. It was a smart move, an homage to her. But for him to stop a film and hold a major studio like Warner Bros. at bay while he courted her was the flair of the producer one no longer sees in Hollywood, the producer who simply wanted the best. *Love Affair* credits him as actor, writer, and producer, but his unofficial hat also included behind-the-scenes director. I have no idea what Warner Bros. would have said to him if he hadn't succeeded in getting Hepburn and the costs of production had gone up during the sudden hiatus in filming. But Warren is a charmer, an absolute charmer. And he's intelligent and a gentleman. A Renaissance man with whom I'd work again in a minute. So of course he succeeded in bagging the legend that was Katharine Hepburn for *Love Affair*.

Subsequently, I was called into the producer's office and told I needed to find a house for Hepburn to live in that the production would rent for a month. The house needed to be one-story, so there would be no stairs to climb. I was immediately in the car heading for the old neighborhood above Sunset Boulevard where the Weingartens, Cukor, and Kate had all once lived. Kate was the only survivor now, but I knew the area of the city would please her. With incredible luck, I found a house high above the boulevard that was a sort of Connecticut farmhouse, a one-story affair with a pool and a view over Century City. The sign said "For Sale," but I contacted the realtor anyway. When I told him whom the house was for, he, in turn, contacted the owner, who accepted a one-month rental before putting the house back on the selling market. I stipulated that there be no visits from prospective buyers during that month. Accordingly, the house soon came to be Kate Hepburn's house during her filming in Los Angeles.

A few weeks later, when my location manager work ended, I visited the stage where a brilliant set, designed by Oscar winner Ferdinando Scarfiotti, had been built. It was the interior of a house the exterior of which we had shot two months earlier with Warren and Annette in Moorea. Their entrances and exits to the house had been filmed there, and now the dialogue portion of the scene between the two of them and Hepburn was to be done. I asked the assistant director if Hepburn was on the set, as I wanted to say hello to her. I was convinced she'd remember me from the days with Larry and Jessie. The A.D. told me she was on the set, in the next room, adjacent to the room they were lighting and readying.

I walked around the set and found her completely alone, but asleep. She was curled up on a sofa, with a woolen shawl thrown over her. I looked down at her, at her now very silvery hair, still as unkempt as ever, and thought that I'd probably want to take naps, too, at eighty-six. I also thought of what she was reported to have said to Laurence Olivier when they met on the set of *Love among the Ruins* in 1989: "We're the best of what's left."

So I just turned around and walked off. It was the last time I saw her. I never got to tell her I was the one who'd found her house, but then I'd never told her how I'd almost worked with her on *The Lion in Winter* and *The Madwoman of Chaillot*. I never told her I'd seen her in 1950 as Rosalind in *As You Like It* on Broadway, where she startled everyone by wearing tights and revealing a pair of legs that were comparable to Dietrich's. I never told her all those things, because over the years, working with the biggest stars in the film business and often socializing with them, I learned not to fawn over them. The biggest compliment you could pay them was simply to treat them like anyone else. It is, after all, the common man in the artist that makes him the artist.

For a while I believed that one of my screenplays might sell. Then, I thought, I could return to France and write there. But a whole series of unpleasant episodes, probably not unlike anyone else's unpleasant episodes in Hollywood, would turn me away from screenwriting. Unbeknownst to me, my agent had been presenting himself as the producer and sole owner of my material, a practice that is totally illegal. A telephone call from Motown to me brought the matter to light. My agent had presented my script to them, the same script that had intrigued Weingarten and Hepburn, and Motown, ascertaining that I was the lawful owner of the material, wanted to make a deal directly with me. Honorable fellow that I was, I referred them to my agent, the very person they were trying to circumnavigate! Hollywood waters were deep and dark and teeming with stinging rays. Did I really want to swim there?

I turned to other avenues. I wrote my first short stories in 1975, and sent copies to Lawrence Durrell and to the first film director I'd worked with, Bob Parrish. Their responses were enthusiastic. Durrell wrote back, "We have both [he and his wife] read the stories and find them excellent. It really is a mystery if you can't place them." And Parrish wrote, "One thing is clear. You must write. You must not waste your time teaching Disney characters to speak English or Cliff Robertson to speak French." Eventually, the stories would be published, one in *The*

Hudson Review, another in *Short Story International*, which had been home to Joyce Carol Oates, Arthur Miller, John Cheever, and Isaac Bashevis Singer. Other stories were published, each piece giving me new confidence. Later, plays of mine would be mounted and published, and prizes won. None of this would bring substantial income until, in 1996, twenty-four years after I'd arrived in Los Angeles, CAA sold a screenplay of mine to Columbia Pictures. Not an option, mind you, an outright sale. I said goodbye to the child I knew they would cripple and took the money and ran.

But back in 1975, a year before my first short story would be published, when I could have papered the walls of my apartment with rejection slips, when there seemed no light ahead in that endless tunnel, something happened. My father came to visit me. I'd moved to a larger, two-bedroom flat in West Los Angeles, just ten minutes from the beach. The winters of upstate New York were notoriously severe, especially for the elderly, and so my father arrived to warm his brittle bones. With him was a wonderful and glad-hearted companion appropriately named Pearl, with whom he'd been living for several years. She had, in fact, already attained some importance in his life when I'd met him in New York three years earlier, but she remained a hidden secret to both me and my brother for an inordinate amount of time. While I'd been busy trying to gain my father's approval with a glittering career, he'd been equally busy trying to gain mine by pretending he still mourned my mother. And I'm certain he did miss her. But *l'un n'empêche pas l'autre*, as the French with their superior logic would say. One thing doesn't prevent the other. And so, several appropriate years after my mother's death, my aged father once more invited love into his life.

Pearl, of course, turned out to have a character that was similar to my mother's. My mother had been outward-going, social-minded, articulate, warm, and manifestly loving. Pearl's traits echoed hers. Both women were all the things my father wasn't. And it had been what my father wasn't that had consumed me for years, never what he was.

I welcomed him and Pearl with open heart, and together the three of us visited the tourist spots of Los Angeles. My father had the same naiveté about the city he was visiting as I had had about the film industry in Hollywood. On the boulevards, he brushed up against hookers, hawkers, and hustlers and never knew what they were. Innocence stuck to his skin like the Mormon garment, never to leave his person. He enjoyed the mild weather, the fact that his younger son had an apartment that was larger than his own in Rochester, and probably most of all the fact that that son was spending all his time taking him around. At one point, irritated for some unknown reason, he answered Pearl hastily and sharply and she grew unusually quiet. Later, I would draw his attention to the incident.

"I don't think you should be talking to Pearl like that," I said, playing father to my father. "She's a very loving woman." We were outside my apartment building, walking Calvados on his leash.

My father chewed on his cigar a moment. "You're right, son," he said. "If it wasn't for Pearl, I'd be in an old-age home right now." There was a pause while he chewed on his cigar again and considered the matter further. "I can change. If I put my mind to it, I can change," said the eighty-four-year-old man.

That night, he was on the telephone with one of his two brothers who also lived in Los Angeles. The phone was adjacent to the kitchen where I was preparing dinner, so I couldn't avoid hearing the parts of the conversation my father spoke. I heard him say that he was visiting me in a very spacious apartment, and was happy to be there. Then his brother must have asked him what kind of work I was doing. "What's he doing now?" my father repeated the question. Then in a tone that was both authoritative and proud, he answered like a shot, "He's a *writer!*"

I stopped stirring my *sauce Béchamel* and stared at a man I didn't know. Never knew. Somehow I'd missed seeing the biggest star of all.

Index

20th Century Fox, 1, 2, 35, 37, 50, 61, 86, 146, 185, 221; dubbing *The Blue Max* for, 29–31; European offices of, 26; producing *Secret World*, 132, 136

46th Annual Academy awards, 223–24

Academy Awards. *See* 46th Annual Academy Awards

Actors Studio, 8, 13

Aimez-vous Brahms?. *See Goodbye Again*

Albee, Edward, 2, 8, 9, 47

Albertson, Jack, 172, 173, 174, 175, 176, 181, 182, 183, 184, 186

Albertson, Maura Dhu, 175

Albertson, Wallace, 175, 186

The Alexandria Quartet, 216

Algonquin Hotel, 203

Allégret, Catherine, 106, 109; daughter of Simone Signoret, 105; screen test for John Huston, 107–8

Allégret, Yves, 105, 142

American Film Theatre, 200

And Hope to Die, 199, 203, 212; filming of, 187–98

Ann-Margret, 206, 207, 208, 209, 211

Arles, 133, 137

Arnaud, Michèle, 213, 216, 217

Attal, Philippe, 81, 82

Audran, Stéphane, 160, 162, 165, 167–68

Auteuil, 27

Avignon, 133, 138

Bacon, Kevin, 1, 208

Baker, Josephine, 7

The Bald-Headed Soprano, 4

Bar, Jacques, 206, 209, 210, 211

Baron, Sandy, 118, 123, 124

Barr, George, 12

barricades, 110, 111

Baumanière. *See* Oustaù de Baumanière

Bavaria Film Studio, 183

Bayeux tapestry, 11

Beach, Sylvia, 4, 214

Beatty, Warren, 1, 89, 224, 226–28

Becker, Arthur A., 3, 6–7, 10, 25, 30, 60–61, 63, 90, 194–95, 230–31; at dinner in New York with, 202–5; phoning during illness, 155–56

Becker, Donald, Dr., 7, 155–56, 230

Becker, Mildred, 202, 230

Becket, 43

Belmondo, Jean-Paul, 105, 146

Bening, Annette, 226, 228

Benzi, Roberto, 90

Bergman, Ingrid, 65, 66
Bernhardt, Sarah, 122
Bertolucci, Bernardo, 198
The Bicycle Thief, 126, 188
Bisset, Jacqueline, 132, 134–40, 174
The Black Book (following French
    Revolution of 1968). *See Le Livre noir*
The Black Book (Lawrence Durrell), 216
blackmail, 144
Blair, Isla, 87, 92
The Blue Max, 29–31, 68
Bois de Boulogne, 95, 143
Boumendil, Jacques, 216, 217
Bourvil, 111
Boyer, Charles, 51–52, 58, 104, 226
Bozzuffi, Marcel, 160, 165, 168
Brach, Gérard, 136, 139
Brachet, Marguerite, 61
The Brain, 111, 112, 116, 133
Brando, Marlon, 198
Brandt, Lou, 38
Bristol Old Vic, 81
Britton, Pamela, 118, 122
Broccoli, Albert, 207, 209
Brooks, Mel, 38
brothel, Paris' famous. *See* Madame
    Claude
brother. *See* Becker, Donald, Dr.
Browne, Coral, 67, 75
Brynner, Yul, 28, 104
Bunuel, Luis, 160, 187
Burton, Richard, 45, 73, 76, 185
Buttons, Red, 2, 12, 14–15, 20, 23–25,
    197

C. R. S., 111, 113, 115
Café des Arts, 137, 138, 139–40
Café Les Deux Magots, 4
calvados, the brandy, 11–12
Calvados, the cat, 20–21, 59, 119, 188,
    192, 202, 203, 231; visa for Poland
    for, 67; during *Willy Wonka and the
    Chocolate Factory*, 172, 174, 175, 183
Canovas, Francine. *See* Delon, Nathalie
Capelier, Margot, 64, 65, 87, 104–5, 108,
    109, 157
Carmen, 91
Caron, Leslie, 89–90, 109
Carr, Allan, 207
Carter, Jody, 9
Cass, Peggy, 118, 119, 120, 123

Cassavetes, John, 119, 123
Chabrol, Claude, 160
Chandon de Briailles, Francesca, 9
Chandon de Briailles, Frédéric, 9
chantage. See blackmail
Chaplin, Geraldine, 35, 38
Charlie and the Chocolate Factory, 171,
    172
Charly, 25, 197
Charon, Jacques, 87, 93, 96, 97
Château de Roussan, 135
chellum, 215
Chez Castel, 44, 78–79, 143
Chez Laurent: with the cast of *Up from
    the Beach* at, 24–25; with Peter
    O'Toole at, 76–78; with Robert Ryan
    at, 196–97
Chico and the Man, 186
Circle in the Square, 46
Clément, Bella, 189, 195
Clément, Johanna, 198–99
Clément, René, 142, 187, 188, 195, 206;
    method of filming of, 189–91; sailing
    with, 198–99
Cocteau, Jean, 4, 9
Cohn-Bendit, Daniel, 110–13
Cole, Julie Dawn, 175, 180, 181, 183
Colette, 7
Collins, Gary, 9
Columbia Pictures, 66, 67, 230
Columbo, 221, 222
Comédie Française. *See* La Comédie
    Française
Communist Party, 113, 114
Corsica, 88–91
Costa-Gavras, Constantin, 105, 158
Countess Paola de Rohan-Chabot. *See*
    Rohan-Chabot, Paola (de), Countess
Courtenay, Tom, 61, 67, 68, 75, 81, 84
Crawford, Broderick, 12, 15–17, 24–25,
    32, 151, 159, 197
Crowe, Cameron, 18
Cukor, George, 219, 230

Dachau, 178
Dahl, Roald, 171, 172, 183
DaRe, Eric, 192, 200
DaRe, Paul, 192
Davalos, Richard, 210
Dave's Market, 223–24
Davis, Pamela, 131

de Gaulle, Charles, 120, 143, 145; during the French Revolution of 1968, 111–15; protects Madame Claude, 28
de Havilland, Olivia, 155
de Rossi, Alberto, 40, 51
de Rossi, Grazia, 51
de Sica, Vittorio, 126–29, 188
The Death of Bessie Smith, 8
Deauville, 59
Dean, James, 33, 36, 210
Deering, Olive, 8
Delon, Alain, 105, 188, 190, 194, 195, 198, 206; early films of, 142; filming *The Sicilian Clan*, 146, 147, 148; impressions of, 149–50; and the Marković Affair, 141–46
Delon, Nathalie, 194; and the Marković Affair, 141–42, 144–45
Demick, Irina, 27, 29; filming *The Sicilian Clan*, 146, 150, 155; filming *Up from the Beach*, 12–13, 15, 20, 21–23; Deray, Jacques, 206, 207, 208, 209, 210, 211, 212
Descrières, Georges, 87, 88, 96; in Corsica with, 88–91
Desire under the Elms, 46
Dewhurst, Colleen, 46
dialogue coach: definition of, 1–2; playing a love scene off camera as, 23
Dickinson, Angie, 206, 208, 209, 210
Dietrich, Marlene, 73–74
The Discreet Charm of the Bourgeoisie, 160, 187
The Doctor and the Devils, 34–36, 38
Donovan, 123
Donen, Stanley, 61–62
Dorothy Chandler Pavilion, 104, 105, 224
Dotti, Andrea, 62, 63
Dougherty, Marion, 173
Douglas, Kirk, 137
Dreyfuss, Richard, 49
Dunn, Michael, 177
Durrell, Lawrence, 37, 213, 216, 217, 218, 222, 229; annoyed at playing ping-pong, 216–17

East of Eden, 210
Eckardt, Steve, 146, 148, 149, 153, 155
Eggar, Samantha, 158, 159, 162, 163, 166; dining in Paris with, 160–61; pretending to be her maid, 169–70

Engel, Georgia, 209
Epitaph for an Enemy, 12

Farrow, Tisa, 188, 196
father. *See* Becker, Arthur A.
Fellini, Federico, 104, 151
Ferrer, Mel, 53, 61–62
Ferrer, Sean, 53, 62–63
Ferry, Christian, 26–27, 30, 31
Feuillère, Edwige, 142, 227
Feyder, Paul: assistant director on *How to Steal a Million*, 40, 41, 47, 51, 56–57; assistant director on *Secret World*, 133, 137; working on a screen test for John Huston, 105, 109
Finney, Albert, 61–62, 86, 87
A Flea in Her Ear, filming of, 86–99
Forbes, Bryan, 109
Forbidden Games, 188
Ford, John, 2
fraise des bois, 25
Franchet, Alain, 137
Frankenheimer, John, 200
Freeman, Robert, 132, 135
French cinema, golden age of, 4
French filming hours, 40–42
French Mafia, 144, 145
French revolution of 1968, 110–15
Fresson, Bernard, 158, 165

Gabin, Jean, 5, 40, 162; filming *The Sicilian Clan*, 146–49, 150, 151–54, 155; requesting another take of, 152–54
Garland, Judy, 65–66, 180
Gaven, Jean, 188, 192–93
Gazzara, Ben, 119, 123
Giraudoux, Jean, 104, 109, 110
Giscard d'Estaing, Valéry, 28, 145
Glattes, Wolfgang, 178
The Godfather, 209
Goffe, Rusty, 177
Goldman, James, 98
Gomez, Michel, 111
Gonzales, Michel, 36, 38
Goodbye Again, 65–66
Goring, Marius, 19–20
Gösta Berling, 99–102
Gould, Elliott, 161, 169
Grace of Monaco, Princess, 9–10
Grahame, Gloria, 33

Grant, Cary, 19, 71, 226
Gray, Charles, 67, 68, 75
Gréco, Juliette, 4
Greenwich Films, 187, 199
Griffith, Hugh, 32, 47, 48, 49–50, 160;
    dubbing with, 54–55
Gromoff, Marina, 19
the Group Theatre, 37
Guérini, Mémé, 144, 145
Gugusse, 189, 192, 193, 196
Guinness, Alec, 44, 160

Hamilton, Murray, 118, 119, 120, 121,
    123, 125, 160; acting with Vittorio de
    Sica, 126–29
Hansberry, Lorraine, 7
Hardwicke, Edward, 87, 92
The Harlequin Guild, 7
Harris, Julie, 210
Harris, Rosemary, 87, 92, 93, 95, 96, 97;
    quoting The Lion in Winter, 98
Harrison, Rex, 1, 87, 88, 91, 92, 93, 95,
    158, 159, 185; black silk socks
    incident with, 96–97; rehearsing
    with, 93–94; singing I've Grown
    Accustomed to Her Face, 98–99
Harvey, Laurence, 35, 38
Harwood, Johanna. See Clément, Johanna
Hepburn, Audrey, 1, 26, 31, 37, 42,
    43–44, 46, 47, 48, 50–54, 60, 73, 117,
    119, 132, 140, 156, 166, 218; called
    back from Switzerland, 57; dubbing
    with, 61–63; first meeting with,
    39–40; receiving cuff links from,
    58–59; William Wyler directing,
    55–56
Hepburn, Katharine, 43, 60, 98, 219, 220;
    at the Academy Awards, 223–24; at
    Dave's Market, 221–22; delivering
    chicken salad for, 225–26; filming Love
    Affair, 227–29; in The Madwoman of
    Chaillot, 104, 105, 109, 110
herbes de Provence, 133–34
Herlihy, James Leo, 8
Hilton, Francesca, 209
Holloway, Stanley, 44
Honfleur, 60
Horton, Percy, 5–6
Hôtel des Antiques, 133, 137
Hotel Europejski, 69, 71
Hôtel George V, 31

Hôtel La Trémoille, 1, 10
Hôtel Prince de Galles, 36
How to Steal a Million, 34, 37, 38, 64, 76,
    84, 119, 218; interview with William
    Wyler for, 31–32; filming of, 39–63
Huston, John, 104, 105, 109; meeting
    with, 106–7; screen test with, 107–8
Hutto, Jack, 8

"I Want It Now," 180, 183–84
The Iceman Cometh, 200–201
If It's Tuesday, This Must Be Belgium,
    filming of, 116–30
Île-de-France, 3, 195
Île Saint-Louis, 33–34, 100
Ingels, Marty, 118, 119, 123
Ionesco, Eugene 4
Irving Thalberg Award, 223
Is Paris Burning?, 141, 188
Isherwood, Christopher, 95

Japrisot, Sebastien, 157, 187, 197
Jerry Maguire, 18
jewelers in Paris, 58
Joly, Paul, 41–42
Jones, James, 9, 33
Jourdan, Louis, 87, 92, 93, 95, 96, 97
Jouvenel, Colette (de), 7–9, 47, 143
Jules and Jim, 12, 17, 18
Justice, James Robertson, 12, 15, 32, 159

Kane, Carol, 188, 199
Kaplan, William, 41
Kaye, Danny, 104, 110
Kazan, Elia, 37
Kelly, Grace. See Grace of Monaco,
    Princess
Kelly, Jack, Jr., 10
Kelly, Martine, 160
Kennedy, John F., 29
Kessel, Joseph, 9, 68
Kinnear, Roy, 175
Kissinger, Henry, 29
Kohlmar, Fred, 31–32; producing A Flea
    in Her Ear, 87, 91, 92, 96; producing
    How to Steal a Million, 41, 46–47, 58
Kurnitz, Harry, 34, 57

La Comédie Française, 12, 87
La Course du lièvre à travers les champs.
    See And Hope to Die

La Fureur de vivre. See Rebel without a Cause

La Piscine, 144, 206

La Promesse. See Secret World

La Résidence d'Auteuil, 26–29

The Lady in the Car. See The Lady in the Car with Glasses and a Gun

The Lady in the Car with Glasses and a Gun, 187; filming of, 157–68

L'affaire Markovíc. See The Markovíc Affair

Lagerlöf, Selma, 99

Lair, Georges, 65

Landau, Ely, 109, 200

Landes, Marie-Gisèle, 33–34, 35, 99, 102, 103

Lang, Charles, 40, 42, 48, 56

Last Tango in Paris, 198

The Lavender Hill Mob, 44

Lawrence of Arabia, 43, 44, 67, 76, 79–80

Le Livre noir, 115

le tout-Paris, 9

Lean, David, 79–80, 160

L'Échelle Blanche. See Secret World

Left Bank, 34, 44, 75, 77; during French Revolution of 1968, 110, 111, 112

Leggewie, Edward, 27, 30

Leighton, Margaret, 104, 105

Les Baux-de-Provence, 137

Les Cahiers du cinema, 33

Les Films du Siècle. *See* 2Oth Century Fox

les Halles, 5

The Lion in Winter, 85, 87, 98, 219, 229

Litvak, Anatole, 63, 157, 160, 161, 162, 163, 164, 165, 166; in the editing room, 167–68; and friction with Samantha Eggar, 158–59; in the Marseille train station, 166–67; meeting with 64–66; recalling Judy Garland, 65–66; shooting *The Night of the Generals*, 67, 68–69, 85; shooting around Peter O'Toole, 81–84

Lodge, Bill, 69

Long Day's Journey into Night, 196, 201

The Longest Day, 2, 12, 25

Lord Jim, 70, 77

Loren, Sophia, 117, 126

Los Angeles, 1972 description of, 205–6

Love Affair, 226–29

MacLaine, Shirley, 1, 141

Madame Claude, 28–29

Madame Laurent, 24–25, 76, 197. *See also* Chez laurent

The Madwoman of Chaillot, 104–10, 219, 229

Mai 68, au jour le jour, 111

Marais, Jean, 4, 8

Marcantoni, François, 145, 146

The Markovíc Affair, 141–46, 150, 206

Markovíc, Stefan, 141–46

Marello, Henriette, 19

Margulies, Stan: producing *If It's Tuesday, This Must Be Belgium*, 116, 120, 130; producing *Willy Wonka and the Chocolate Factory*, 172, 173, 176, 180, 183, 184

Marmorston, Jessie, Dr., 219, 220, 222, 224, 225

Masina, Giulietta, 104, 105

Massari, Lea, 188, 194, 195; cooking dinner in her hotel suite, 192–93

Maurin, Jean-François, 134, 135, 138

Maxim's, 81

McEnery, John, 160, 163–65

McShane, Ian, 117, 119, 120, 123, 126, 129, 200, 221; dinner at home with, 130–31

McQueen, Steve, 132, 225–26

Melnick, Dan, 208

ménage à trois, 143

Mendès-France, Pierre, 114

Merrill, Dina, 25

Miller, Henry, 2, 213, 216, 217, 218, 219; anecdotes told by, 215–16; first visit to, 214–15

Minou, 175, 183

Minouche, 162–63

Mitterand, François, 112, 113

Monsieur Silvio, 137, 139

Montand, Yves, 65, 108

Monte-Carlo, 195, 198

Moorea, 226, 228

Morgan, Michèle, 5

mother. *See* Becker, Mildred

Mrozek, Slawomir, 37, 72, 73

Munich, 172, 178–79, 181

My Fair Lady, 43, 44, 60, 72, 171

Natwick, Mildred, 118, 122, 126

Nazzari, Amedeo, 150, 151

New Wave French directors, 56
The Night of the Generals, 43, 97, 106, 116, 163, 169, 198; filming of, 64–85
Niven, David, 111, 224
Noiret, Philippe, 67, 75, 84, 106, 189

O'Brien, Patrick, 118, 121, 125, 130
Oktoberfest, 178–79, 180
the Old Vic, 86, 87
Oliver! 160, 180, 184
Olivier, Laurence, 229
O'Neill, Eugene, 47, 196, 201
Oompa-Loompas, 177–78, 184
Orsini, Umberto, 210
Ostrum, Danny, 183, 184
Ostrum, Dean, 174, 183, 184
Ostrum, Leif, 180
Ostrum, Loretta, 180
Ostrum, Peter, 172, 173, 174, 175, 178, 180, 181, 184–85; attending Oktoberfest, 178–79; selecting a parent, 179–80; snubbed by Gene Wilder, 185–86; three-picture deal offered to, 182–83
Ostrum, Sari, 174, 175, 178, 183, 184, 205
O'Toole, Peter, 1, 31, 32, 92, 97, 98, 119, 164, 218; filming *How to Steal a Million*, 44, 46, 48, 51, 55–59; filming *The Night of the Generals*, 64, 65, 67, 69, 80, 85; first meeting with, 42–43; night out in Paris with, 75–79; night out in Warsaw with, 72–74; Oscar nominations of, 45; Peter Perkins' assessment of, 45; quoting *Macbeth* to, 69–71; receiving cuff links from, 58–59; returning from Bristol Old Vic party, 81–84; shooting at Maxim's, 80–81; using rhyming slang, 70–71
Oury, Gérard, 111, 112, 116, 133
Oustaù de Baumanière, 137–38
The Outside Man, 214; filming of, 206–12
"Over the Rainbow," 66, 183

Paris, 1955 description of, 3–4
Paris Match, 9, 113, 155
Paris Playhouse, 8–10, 143
Parker, Charlie, 4
Parrish, Kathie, 17, 24
Parrish, Robert, 5, 9, 10, 27, 31, 32, 46, 151, 229; dinner at Chez Laurent with, 24–25; filming *Up from the Beach*, 12–13, 14–17, 19, 21; meeting with, 1–3
Pascal, Giselle, 134, 137
Pat and Mike, 188, 191, 219
Patachou, 4
The Path of the Hare As It Crosses the Fields. See And Hope to Die
Patton, 47
Pearl. *See* Ware, Pearl
Perkins, Anthony, 65, 66
Perkins, Peter, 42, 58, 73–74; assessing Peter O'Toole, 45; night out in Paris with Peter O'Toole and, 76–78; returning from Bristol Old Vic party, 81–83
Perrin, Jacques, 105, 106, 109, 189; and his screen test for John Huston, 107–8
Pettet, Joanna, 67, 169
Pevsner, Tom, 81, 82; as production manager for *If It's Tuesday, This Must Be Belgium*, 116, 120, 125, 129–30
Piaf, Edith, 2, 4, 66
Pickens, Slim, 12, 15
Piwowski, Marek, 72
Pleasence, Donald, 67, 68
Plein Soleil, 141, 142, 188, 195
Pleshette, Suzanne, 117, 120, 121, 122, 123, 125, 126, 129
Plummer, Christopher, 67
Polish vodkas, 71–72
Pompidou, Claude, and the Marković Affair, 143–46
Pompidou, Georges, 28; during French revolution of 1968, 113, 114; and the Marković Affair, 143–46
Porel, Marc, 134, 136, 137, 138
Pré Catalan, 95
Price, Vincent, 75
Princess Grace. *See* Grace of Monaco, Princess
"Pure Imagination," 176
Purple Noon. See Plein Soleil

Quicksilver, 208
Quinn, Anthony, 80, 137
Quintero, José, 46

Radziwill, Lee, Princess, 8
A Raisin in the Sun, 7

Ray, Aldo, 188, 189, 190, 191, 192–93, 199; hard times for, 199–200; having dinner in my apartment, 200
Ray, Nicholas, 52, 72, 103, 156, 166; meetings on Île Saint-Louis with, 33–35; preparing *The Doctor and the Devils*, 35–38; working on *Gösta Berling* with, 99–102
Rebel without a Cause, 33
Reed, Oliver, 2, 158, 159, 160, 162, 164, 166, 167–68
Revolution of 1968. *See* French revolution of 1968
Rhodes, Jane, 90–91
rhyming slang, 70–71
Roberts, Rachel, 87, 92, 93, 96, 99, 159; and barbs with Rex Harrison, 91, 94; at a Hollywood party, 94–95
Robertson, Cliff, 2, 32, 197, 229; dinner at Chez Laurent with, 24–25; filming *Up from the Beach*, 12–16, 20, 21–23
Rohan-Chabot, Paola (de), Countess, 7–9, 10, 47, 143
Roman Holiday, 40, 60
Romeo and Juliet, 160, 164, 165, 168
Rosay, Françoise, 12, 13, 20, 40
Rosenbaum, Robert, 208
Rossi, Jean-Baptiste. *See* Japrisot, Sebastien
the Round Table, 203
Royal Monceau Hotel, 140
Ruark, Robert, 15
rue des Belles Feuilles, 100
Ruskin School of Fine Arts, 5
Ryan, Jessica, 196, 197, 200
Ryan, Robert, 188, 189, 190, 191, 192, 199, 200–201; at Chez Laurent, 196–97; state of health of, 191, 197, 201

Sagan, Françoise, 8, 9, 65, 66
Saint-Tropez, 164
Sainte-Maxime, 164, 165–66
Sainte-Mère-Église, 11
Sarrazin, Michael, 138
Scharf, Walter, 180
Scheider, Roy, 206, 208
Schloss Hotel, 172, 173, 175, 183
Schmidt, Lars, 65, 102
Schneider, Romy, 142, 149, 206

Scott, George C., 32, 49, 51, 159; firing of, 47–48; meeting with, 45–47
Secret World, filming of, 132–40
Selepegno, Ann, 64, 65, 157, 165–66
Shakespeare and Company, 4, 214
Sharif, Omar, 1, 67, 68, 70, 71, 75, 81, 83, 84; getting cast in *Lawrence of Arabia*, 79–80; at the horse races with, 79; and screen test for *The Night of the Generals*, 66–67
Shaw, David, 118, 119, 120, 123
Shaw, Irwin, 68, 118
Shepard, Richard, 9
Ship of Fools, 19–20, 177
Shire, David, 209
Shire, Talia, 209
The Sicilian Clan, 27; filming of, 146–55
Signoret, Simone, 20, 65, 105, 108
Silberman, Serge, 187, 190, 191, 196, 199
Sinatra, Frank, 118, 132, 161
Sirakian, Belly, 168–69
Smith, Liz, 8
Smith, Roger, 207, 211
Spiegel, Sam, 66, 67, 68, 79, 80
St-Rémy-de-Provence, 133–34
A Star Is Born, 65, 66
Sterling, Edward, 7, 9
Stern, Tom, 161, 169
Strauss, Jacques, 146, 147
Streisand, Barbra, 161, 169
Stuart, Harriet, 118, 130
Stuart, Mel: directing *If It's Tuesday, This Must Be Belgium*, 117, 118, 120, 121, 125, 129, 130; directing Vittorio de Sica, 127–29; directing *Willy Wonka and the Chocolate Factory*, 172, 173, 181, 182, 183, 184; yelling for the Oompa-Loompas, 177–78
student revolution. *See* French revolution of 1968
Studio 128, 6
Studios de Billancourt, 104, 106, 212
Studios de Boulogne, 38, 39, 45, 61–62
Studios de Joinville, 142, 148
Sunset Marquis Hotel, 216, 218

The Taming of the Shrew, 7
Tango, 37, 72, 73
Taylor, Elizabeth, 223, 224
Thanksgiving dinner, 23–25
Thary, Claudie, 71, 92

Théâtre Charles-de-Rochefort, 9–10
Théâtre Montansier, 6
Thomas, Dylan, 34, 38, 55
Thompson, Walter, 87
Thulin, Ingrid, 99, 101–2
Todd, Olivier, 145–46
Torn, Rip, 46
Tracy, Spencer, 43, 219, 220
Trintignant, Jean-Louis, 140, 146, 168;
    dining in Lea Massari's hotel suite,
    192–93; filming And Hope to Die,
    188, 189, 197–98, 199; filming The
    Outside Man, 206, 208, 209, 211, 212;
    lunching with, 212
Trintignant, Nadine, 193
Trouville, 59–60
Turkish cabinet, 4
Twenty-Four Hours, 145
Two for the Road, 61, 62, 132

U.C.L.A. Medical Center, 223
Under Milk Wood, 55
Up from the Beach, 1, 26, 32, 46, 76;
    filming of, 11–25

Vallone, Raf, 38
Van Gogh, Vincent, 133, 134, 137
Vier Jahreszeiten Hotel, 181
Ventura, Lino, 146, 147, 148, 150
Verneuil, Henri, 146, 148, 149, 150, 151,
    152, 153, 206
Visconti, Luchino, 142
Volpone, 75, 77, 78

Wait until Dark, 62
Wallach, Eli, 47, 49, 51, 54; blocking a
    scene, 48–49
Ware, Pearl, 230–31
Warner Bros., 227, 228
Warsaw, 67–70, 73, 74; 1966 description
    of, 71–72
Weingarten, Lawrence, 219, 220, 221,
    222, 228, 229; attempting to contact

Steve McQueen, 225–26; funeral of,
    226; receiving the Irving Thalberg
    Award, 223–24
Weinstein, Henry, 109
Werner, Oskar, 12, 17–20, 25, 27, 46,
    48
Wheeler, David, 8
The White Ladder. See Secret World
Whitehouse, Denis, 121–22, 125
Who's Afraid of Virginia Woolf?, 89
Wilbourn, Phyllis, 221, 222, 228
Wilder, Gene, 172, 175, 176–77; anxiety
    over final scene of Willy Wonka and
    the Chocolate Factory, 181–82;
    snubbing his costar, 185–86
Williams, Tennessee, 49, 72, 101, 207
Willy Wonka and the Chocolate Factory,
    filming of, 171–84, 185, 186, 194
Winchell, Walter, 15
Wolper, David L. 117, 123; producing
    Willy Wonka and the Chocolate
    Factory, 182, 186
Wolper Pictures, 116, 172, 173
Wottitz, Walter, 21
Wyler, William, 33, 35, 38, 46, 47, 49,
    52, 60, 61, 64, 158; directing How to
    Steal a Million, 44, 48, 50, 54, 55–56,
    57, 58; discontent with French
    filming hours, 41–42; introduced to
    Audrey Hepburn by, 39–40; meeting
    with, 31–32

Z, 105, 158, 160, 188
Zanuck, Darryl F., 2, 18, 19, 22, 25, 68,
    117, 132, 204; dubbing The Blue Max
    for, 29–31; housing a girlfriend in La
    Résidence d'Auteuil, 26–29; and Irina
    Demick, 12–13; meeting with, 30
Zay, Jean, 88
Zeffirelli, Franco, 160, 165
Ziller, Alice, 160, 163
Zimmer, Pierre, 134
The Zoo Story, 8

~

About the Author

Of his seventeen years living in Europe, **Frawley Becker** spent almost all of it in Paris, working first in theater and later in films. Arriving in Paris in 1955, he had a chance to glimpse the last images of the post-war City of Light before living through the tumultuous '60s. First hired as a civilian for the Department of the Army, he formed several theater companies on military bases around Paris, including *The Harlequin Guild*, probably the first African American theater company within the U.S. military. Later, as managing director, he was the driving force in establishing a professional English-speaking theater in Paris in 1963 and produced the first Edward Albee plays in France.

The following year he began working as a bilingual movie dialogue coach, and over the next nine years coached such luminaries as Audrey Hepburn, Peter O'Toole, Rex Harrison, Omar Sharif, Jacqueline Bisset, Gene Wilder, Jean Gabin, and Jean-Louis Trintignant and worked under directors William Wyler, Nicholas Ray, John Huston, Anatole Litvak, and René Clément.

Mr. Becker returned to the United States in 1972 and shortly began working as a film location manager, and now has many big feature films to his credit, including *Footloose*, *Summer Rental*, *Steel Magnolias*, *Love Affair*, and *Jerry Magure*. In between jobs, he wrote. His published short stories have appeared in *The Hudson Review* and *Short*

Story International, several of his plays have been produced throughout the country, and one play, *411 Joseph*, received first prize in a national playwriting contest and was subsequently published. A screenplay of his was sold by CAA to Columbia Pictures in 1996, and he is presently listed in the Marquis *Who's Who in America*.